Elites

A General Model

Murray Milner, Jr.

polity

First published in 2015 by Polity Press

Polity Press
65 Bridge Street
Cambridge CB2 1UR, UK

Polity Press
350 Main Street
Malden, MA 02148, USA

ISBN-13: 978-0-7456-7182-6
ISBN-13: 978-0-7456-7183-3 (pb)

A catalogue record for this book is available from the British Library.

Library of Congress Cataloging-in-Publication Data

Milner, Murray.
  Elites : a general model / Murray Milner, Jr.
    pages cm
  Includes bibliographical references.
    ISBN 978-0-7456-7182-6 (hardback : alk. paper) – ISBN 978-0-7456-7183-3 (pbk. : alk. paper) 1. Elite (Social sciences) 2. Power (Social sciences) 3. Elite (Social sciences)–United States. 4. Power (Social sciences)–United States. 5. Elite (Social sciences)–India. 6. Power (Social sciences)–India. I. Title.
  HM1263.M554 2014
  305.5′20973–dc23
                              2014015223

Typeset in 10/12 Sabon
by Toppan Best-set Premedia Limited
Printed and bound in the Great Britain by Clays Ltd, St Ives PLC

For further information on Polity, visit our website:
politybooks.com

Elites

For the non-elites

Contents

Preface

I am always a bit suspicious of authors' descriptions of why they write what they do, including my own accounts. There is a tendency for most of us to underestimate the effects of social context, contingency, luck, and providence in what has happened – at least when it is linked to the completion of a project for which we can and must take credit. With this reservation and warning, I want to state what I now see as the influences that led to this book. While I was never a scholar who specialized in studying sociology's intellectual ancestors, for a number of years I taught courses in classical social theory. I was always struck by the differences in how Marx, Pareto, and Weber understood the link between social inequality, social conflict, and social change. Each one was extremely insightful, but I sensed that they told only part of the story. It was a number of years, however, before I considered trying to create a more complete picture. The second stimulus to this book came out of my study of the Indian caste system. The idealized indigenous description of castes – at least by those from privileged castes – draws on what is usually referred to as the varna system that suggests that there are four social categories of people and each one is called upon to carry out a particular social function. This scheme has been influential for several thousand years even though there is only the vaguest link between this idealized description and the actual organization of castes in village

India. It was the interactions between these two stimuli – my questions about classical theories and my puzzle about how something as inaccurate as the varna system could continue to be the standard description of the caste system – that led to this book.

I also frequently taught courses in social inequality and became reasonably familiar with the literature on contemporary "power elites" and "ruling classes." I often agreed with this literature – I think power in many contemporary societies is far too concentrated and unchecked – but the questions that I was asking seemed unaddressed. It seemed to me that the concentration of power, and many other important phenomena, derived, in part, from the patterns of conflict and cooperation between various types of elites and between elites and non-elites. Moreover, recurring patterns seemed to exist across a number of very different societies. That is a central focus of this book. There are three additional emphases. First, most treatments of elites and ruling classes do not give enough attention to non-elites. Second, elite theory tends to focus on economic and political elites – who are obviously important – but to ignore other important categories of elites. Third, class analysis can usefully be subsumed within a model of elites. To deal with these issues I am proposing a new model of elites and non-elites. The sources, content, and application of this model to three very different societies is the subject of this book.

I am indebted to many people: some because they encouraged me, some because they made me think harder about what I was doing, and some for a lifetime of personal support. To name all of these would both strain my memory and bore my readers, but some must be named. I learned much from the graduate students in a course I taught on several occasions called Elites and Non-elites. Paul Kingston, Simone Polillo, and Rae Blumberg provided useful critiques on earlier abbreviated versions of this work. Even though much of the year he lives in Italy, my good friend Gianfranco Poggi has phoned about once a month, in part to inquire about how the work is progressing, implicitly providing a much needed and much appreciated reminder that I needed to get the book finished. Jon D. Mikalson of my university's Classics Department provided invaluable advice and guidance, including reading several versions of the chapter on Classical Athens. He was the very model of a good colleague. Another longtime colleague James Davidson Hunter has provided me an office and encouragement at the Institute for Advanced Studies in Culture, an especially congenial and stimulating work setting. Mieke Thomeer and Megan Quetsch served as outstanding undergraduate research assistants and were of great help in finding sources and proofreading. I am also appreciative of the help and guidance provided by Jonathan Skerrett of Polity Press and the careful copyediting of Ian Tuttle. As always, I am indebted to Sylvia Milner for a lifetime of companionship.

1

Introduction

Introduction

Two of the recurring issues in social theory are (1) who has power and (2) how does the exercise of such power shape subsequent events? In an attempt to answer these questions, analysts have drawn on the concepts of class and elite. Sometimes these are made more specific by notions of ruling class and power elite. Often the analyses of classes and elites are linked to implicit or explicit arguments about what produces or limits social change. Some of the factors focused upon include production technology, weaponry, demography, and culture. The notions of class and elites have produced insights into the nature and direction of social life, but they seem increasingly inadequate to understand the complexity of contemporary social life. Moreover, they have been inadequate for understanding both the commonalities and the differences between societies, and between the past and the present.

The purpose of this book is to improve the analytical tools for addressing such problems by proposing a new model of elites and non-elites. The model suggests that it is important to look at the relationship between different types of elites *and* between elites and non-elites. The aim is to create a model that is general enough to usefully analyze a variety of societies and historical periods without lapsing into a philosophy of history, which already "knows" what the future will bring. While serious intellectual endeavors build upon the work of previous scholars, in my opinion this too often leads to a kind of scholasticism that makes new work more arcane and inaccessible than it needs to be.

Much if not most of the literature about elites focuses on how concentrated or dispersed power is in a particular society or community or how the actions of those with power have shaped the past or will shape the future. While I do not completely ignore the first question my primary focus is on the second question. My approach to answering the second question does not focus on studying the biographies of past elites to explain the past, or interviewing current elites to predict the future. Rather, I look at the relationship between different types of elites and non-elites in such a way that we can begin to see patterns that cut across multiple societies and how these patterns are related to key social changes. I am especially influenced by Max Weber's notion that there are three main types of power: political power, economic power, and status power. Elites typically specialize in one of these types of power and in different cultures and historical periods the type of power and the type of elite that is most prominent can vary. I want to avoid the tendency to assume that a particular category of elites is always the most powerful, or that the future is predetermined. This has been the tendency of both Marxism and the elite theory. Marx assumed that history was driven primarily by class conflict. In capitalist societies the proletariat would be the key mover of history by bringing about a revolution and the eventual establishment of communism, which would eliminate class and class conflict. Elite theorists tended to assume the opposite. Elites make history and for the most part others were primarily their pawns. Any apparent moves toward egalitarianism, such as electoral democracies, were largely illusory and eventually succumbed to what Robert Michels called the "iron law of oligarchy." Who made up the elite may change, but real power was always held by a relatively small group. In contrast, the approach I am proposing attempts to avoid notions of inevitability – whether they are "optimistic" or "pessimistic" ones. The future is shaped by the past, but not determined by it. To paraphrase Marx's famous epigram, people make their own history, but they do not make it just as they want.

I have found four theorists especially helpful in formulating a new model: (1) Karl Marx, (2) Vilfredo Pareto (and other elites theorists such as Gaetano Mosca, and Robert Michels), (3) Max Weber, and (4) Pierre Bourdieu. I will discuss each of these in turn as a way of identifying some of the key elements that should be incorporated in a new model.

The "Classical" Theories

Since the pattern of cooperation and conflict between various elites and non-elites is my primary concern, rather than the precise concentration of power in particular settings, several classical social theorists seem most relevant to this task. I focus on how their work is useful in suggesting the relevant elements of a new model, though I try to present enough of their theoretical perspective to show how their theorizing about elites is related to their broader body of work.

Marxian theory

After a brief prologue, the *Communist Manifesto* begins: "The history of all hitherto existing society is the history of class struggles." This pregnant sentence introduces three central concepts in Marx's thinking: history, class, and conflict. In Marx's vision, class differences, which were the basis of conflict, could and would be transcended following a Communist revolution. History, however, would not stop. Stated in another way, Marx's notion of class conflict was placed in the context of a broader theory of social change. The power of Marx's analysis is not in his systematic and detailed analysis of the notion of class – he never got around to that. Rather, it is in his ability to throw light on the changes that were occurring as Europe was transformed from agrarian feudalism to an industrialized bourgeois society with new forms of exploitation and conflict. This part of Marx's analysis is not particularly controversial. More debatable has been the Marxian view of the long-term economic, political, and cultural consequences of these changes.

The classical Marxist sketch of capitalism goes something like this: New technologies and the dynamics of capitalist market competition usher in an enormous increase in productive capacity. Because of the pressure of competition, capitalists need to keep costs low, including the costs of wages. To lower costs, forward-looking capitalists invest most of their profits in more efficient technologies that produce more products with less labor. The working class experiences increased economic insecurity and a decline in their share of the income. As consumers they cannot afford to buy the increasing supply of products. This reduces consumer demand and lowers prices and profits. Many businesses go broke or have to lay off workers. This leads to recessions and depressions. The longer-term result is that capitalist economies go through alternating periods of booms and busts with the downturns becoming increasingly severe. This leads to political unrest and protest. Such protest may be reduced by various forms of ideology that mislead workers into a false consciousness. The state is primarily an instrument of the capitalist class and the police and army are used to suppress working-class dissent, protests, and strikes and to protect private property, especially private capital. Increasingly repressive measures must be used to maintain order, intensifying working-class hostility. Eventually this leads to a proletarian revolution and the creation of a socialist state. The new state substitutes rational economic planning for the "anarchy of the market" and gradually morphs into fully developed Communism. This process is not limited to particular capitalist societies, but is an international process. Workers see that the key conflicts were not between different ethnic, religious, occupational, or national groups, but that this is a worldwide struggle between a capitalist ruling class and an increasingly internationalized proletariat. This is expressed through the effort to organize international associations of workers movements such as the "First International" (1864–1876) and the "Second International" (1889–1916).

In retrospect we know that the model was incorrect in predicting a series of proletarian revolutions and the disappearance of nationalism and religious affiliations. Most popular revolutions were supported by rural peasants rather than an urban proletariat. Following World War II, the Communist regimes of Eastern Europe were established under the military hegemony of the Soviet Union, which is not to say they had no popular support. These regimes not only failed to result in utopias, but were generally highly authoritarian and economically inefficient. The collapse of the Soviet Bloc and the economic liberalization of China (as well as Vietnam and Cambodia) are obvious indicators that these societies have not been economically sustainable.

The Marxian model has, however, been amazingly prescient with respect to pinpointing the economic dilemmas of market economies: The contradiction between keeping wage costs low and sustaining consumer demand continues. This tendency to boom and bust has been problematic for most capitalist economies. This was certainly true of the U.S. economic downturn of 2008.

What Marx did not anticipate is that the state could significantly soften and limit these instabilities by manipulating taxes, public expenditures, and the money supply. These possibilities are the great insight and contribution of first Keynesian economic theory and policies, and, a little later, monetary theory and policies. While capitalist societies have not "solved" the contradictions that Marx identified, they have been able to manage them sufficiently to avoid the degree of economic instability and revolution that Marx predicted.

Marxism has often attempted to take into account Keynesian and monetary efforts to manage the economy by seeing the state primarily as an instrument of the capitalist class (Miliband 1969). There are, however, two fundamental problems with this view of the world. First, the vast modern welfare state has interests and goals of its own such as adequate funding for its bureaucracies and their expansion. Moreover, in democratic states the ruling government must retain the popular support of at least a large proportion of the non-elite voting population. The most urgent concerns of non-elites cannot be ignored with impunity. Second, defining government economic policies as the state pursing the interests of the capitalist class assumes that this class has a high level of consensus, solidarity, and farsightedness. This is unlikely in large, complex, and diverse societies in which many of the key actors are global multinational corporations.

It is in this context that Fred Block's work is useful (Block 1987, esp. chap. 3). He characterizes modern capitalism as having a "ruling class that does not rule." The basic argument is that the managers of the state have a strong interest in maintaining a productive and expanding economy. First, this is the basis of taxes and other sources of government income. Second, a stagnant or declining economy tends to erode popular support for the government in power. Since productive economic activity is highly dependent upon the willingness of individual capitalists and corporations to invest private capital in business enterprises, it is in the state's interests to avoid policies that would discourage such investment. Political elites are, however, interested in the productivity of the economy as a whole, rather than simply the profits of a particular capitalist, corporation, or industry. Therefore they sometimes pursue policies that benefit the economy as a whole, even though they may reduce the profits of particular economic enterprises. In Block's terminology, a key role of the state is to maintain "business confidence."

The essence of Block's argument is that political elites have a strong vested interest in seeing that economic elites as a class prosper and in maintaining "business confidence," but this is not primarily because they are "instruments" of that class, but because they are pursuing their own long-term interests.

To summarize, some of the key limitations of Marxian theory are:

1. While class conflict often leads to social change, other types of power and conflict are also important sources of change and these tend to be ignored or attributed to economic interests.
2. The Marxian assumption that polarization will lead to essentially two classes has been largely inaccurate with respect to historical developments in modern societies. (This is not to say that this could

not happen in the future.) More specifically, the theory does not pay enough serious attention to the significance of either the middle classes or the excluded and outcast groups.

3. While more recent versions of Marxian theory do not reduce political elites and the state to mere flunkies of the economic elites, Marxian theory still does not provide adequate tools for considering the non-economic interests of elites.
4. Similarly, Marxism does not provide the tools for an adequate analysis of status and status elites, for it still assumes that various forms of ideological hegemony are primarily disguises for economic interests.

Yet Marxian theory is especially useful for our purposes in the following respects:

1. It insists that variations in the means of production result in variations in the nature of social formations and the forms of cooperation and conflict they experience, which often depend on whether elites are associated with an older or a newer mode of production.
2. It insists that the interests of economic elites usually conflict with those of non-elites. While personal and cultural variations may accentuate or retard the cupidity of elites, the fundamental sources of exploitation and inequality are rooted in the nature of economic relationships such as the pressures that capitalists face to lower costs.

Elite theory

An alternative to Marx's understanding of history is elite theory. Vilfredo Pareto (1935, 1968 [1901], 1976), Gaetano Mosca (1939 [1896]), and Robert Michels (1998 [1916]) produced the classical statements of this perspective. Its most elaborate form is probably best represented by Pareto. A small minority rules, and responsiveness to the masses is typically pragmatic or hypocritical. There is variation in the degree to which elites are closed to outsiders, that is, in whether elites "circulate." Mobility or circulation takes several forms.

First, in certain periods, political elites rule primarily by force (Pareto's "lions") and in other periods primarily by cunning (Pareto's "foxes"). This distinction, derived from Machiavelli, focuses on the means by which elites rule. These two approaches often involve different individuals who have dissimilar personalities rooted in different "residues," which are deeply held tacit sentiments.[1] A successful regime is one that has an effective mix of lions and foxes for the historical context in which they are located. History is characterized by continual cycles of lions being replaced by foxes only to be replaced in turn by lions, etc.

Second, all elites tend to degenerate over time, but they may be renewed by co-opting able and ambitious individuals from non-elites, which both strengthens the elite, and deprives non-elites of those who might lead revolts or revolutions.

A third type of circulation results from successful revolutions in which old elites are replaced by new elites. Rebellions and revolutions are especially likely if elites are both closed to talented non-elites and "humanitarian," that is, reluctant to use force and deceit. Regimes may fall from a revolution of non-elites (the "masses") or from a coup 'd'état by a small cadre. In either case, a society will soon be ruled by elites largely committed to their own interests.

In the economic realm, rentiers and speculators are roughly the parallel to the notions of lions and foxes. Rentiers want to maintain tradition and "play it safe," being concerned about maintaining their wealth, income, and established status. In contrast, speculators are often "newcomers," willing to take risks to expand their wealth.

In the cultural and ideological realm Pareto makes a less well-known distinction that focuses on variations in ideology or alternative "theologies": "two theologies will put in an appearance, one which will glorify immobility of one or another uniformity, real or imaginary, the other of which will glorify movement and progress in one direction or another" (Pareto 1935: 2173).

While other types of power and elites may be formally recognized, the focus tends to be on political power and who controls the state or the executive offices of organizations. Similarly, the role of non-elites is formally recognized, but seen as quite limited. History is made primarily by elites and the influence of the lower orders is downplayed.

The tendency to attribute most power and agency to elites is characteristic of contemporary elite theorists such as John Higley and his various co-authors (Burton and Higley 1987, 2001; Higley and Burton 1989; Higley and Moore 2001). They focus on the ability of modern nations to establish and maintain liberal democracies. Democracies require an "elite settlement" in which competing elites agree to the "rules of the game" for selecting those who control the government. This settlement must also include agreeing to limit the consequences of "losing the game," so that being defeated in an election and turning power over to others does not result in death, prison, or loss of private property.

Thomas R. Dye, who has written extensively on U.S. elites, makes a similar point: "Elites in all sectors of American society share a consensus about the fundamental values of private enterprise, limited government, and due process of law ... disagreement occurs *within* a consensus over fundamental values" (2002: 209–10). He notes, "A recognized source of factionalism is the emergence of new sources of wealth and new 'self-made' individuals ... a split between Sunbelt 'cowboys' and Eastern establishment 'yankees'" (2002: 210). The factionalism has increased, but even the Tea Party movement affirms the legitimacy of markets as the means to the key goal of economic growth.

The more pluralistic versions of elite theory (e.g., Dahl 1961; Lindblom 1965; Rose 1967; Verba 1987) emphasize that decisions are made by an ongoing process of negotiation and compromises that take a wide variety of interests into account. Virtually all elite theorists acknowledge that power is concentrated in a relatively small number of elites, but there is still disagreement about the degree of this concentration and level of consensus. Michels offered a more pessimistic version of elite theory, in his study of social democratic political parties; even in these avowedly democratic and egalitarian organizations, entrenched elites eventually monopolized power, producing an "iron law of oligarchy."

Some of the limitations of elite theory include the following.

1. It overstates the power of elites. The masses are always dominated by elites. What varies is the form and trappings of dominance. Whereas Marx saw change toward equality and justice as inevitable, elite theorists usually see progressive change as largely illusory. The less extreme versions – for example, Gaetano Mosca (1939 [1896]) and Joseph Schumpeter (1987 [1942]) – acknowledge that democratic institutions limit elites, but stress how often such limits are circumvented. In sum, a central theme of classical elite theory is that little changes with respect to the fundamental distribution of power.

2. It underestimates the ability of non-elites to mobilize and bring about change (e.g., the largely nonviolent Independence Movement in India, the American Civil Rights Movement, Women's Movement of the 1960s and 1970s, and the Arab Spring of 2011). These may be infrequent and they may be co-opted or diverted. Nonetheless, they are crucial phenomena and our theoretical models should not obscure such possibilities.

3. It usually focuses on political power and economic power and largely ignores cultural elites and the influence they exercise. Dye (2002) provides a useful and in many ways admirable overview of elites in the first decade of the twenty-first century. There is, however, virtually no discussion of significance of cultural elites or celebrities such as Oprah Winfrey, Steven Spielberg, or famous sports heroes or movie stars, of conservative Christian elites such as James Dobson, Jerry Falwell, or Pat Robertson and the network of organizations

they founded, not to speak of more traditional religious elites such as the U.S. Conference of Catholic Bishops. Elite theory tends to ignore whole categories of leaders, organizations, and cultural influences.

4. While its realism helps to unmask the highly unequal distribution of power, it can lapse into cynicism and nihilism.

Elite theory does have several key virtues useful in constructing a general model. It recognizes that:

1. Political power is not adequately understood if it is seen primarily as a derivative of economic power;
2. The emergence of elites is a virtual inevitability in any large organization or complex society;
3. Societies and historical periods vary in the extent to which elites are a self-perpetuating "aristocracy," but that there is a strong tendency toward domination of non-elites, social closure, and protecting elite power and privileges;
4. It recognizes that elites usually contain internal differentiations such as the differences between lions and foxes, rentiers and speculators, and conservative and liberal ideologues.

Max Weber

Weber certainly recognized the importance of economic power and ownership of the means of production, but he also saw the importance of other sources of power; for example, in some historical situations the control of the means of coercion might be more important than the means of production. In capitalist economies he thought that the basis of class differences was market power. Ownership of the means of production was only one source of such power. The notions of human, social, and cultural capital, developed in the last half of the twentieth century (Becker 1964; Bourdieu 1977; Bourdieu and Passeron 1977; Coleman 1990; Mincer 1958; Schultz 1963), can all become forms of market power.

While Weber saw economic power was typically central, political power and status power were each important in their own right. Each type of power tends to be associated with a particular type of social formation, namely, classes, political parties, and status groups. While the members of a given class tended to belong to the same parties and status groups, and vice versa, this correlation was by no means perfect.

The status of a particular activity can shape the likelihood of that activity being pursued. He famously argued that the "Protestant Ethic" played an important role in legitimizing and encouraging the emergence of bourgeois capitalism (Weber 1976b [1905]).[2] Similarly the prohibition against usury prevented Christians from becoming prosperous bankers, but Jews circumvented this limitation, arguing that the prohibition against charging interest only applied to loans to other Jews. This ethical dualism was likely to have been accentuated by the Jews' pariah status in medieval Christendom. Hence, some Jews were able to become prosperous financers to the Christian majority (Weber 1968: 612–14). In short, while ideology is often shaped by economic and political interests, an ideology that affects the status of different activities can also shape economic and political activities.

For Weber, elites had disproportionate amounts of power and influence, but non-elites also influence the nature and direction of social change. Moreover, he saw unintended contingent factors as "the great bulk of everyday action," and it was "often a matter of almost automatic reaction of habitual stimuli" (Weber 1968: 25). Nonetheless, the patterns of everyday action do change. While there is a strong strain of pessimism in Weber, he was not a cynic. History is not simply one elite replacing another, nor habit playing itself out.

Weber's writings are ambiguous about whether the future was determined and therefore predictable. On the one hand, he often emphasized the seemingly overriding power of the rationalization of social structure and culture. For Weber, "rationalization" refers to a process that involves making human action and ideas more rational, that is, the extent to which magical elements of thought and action are eliminated and replaced by ideas that are systematic and/or scientifically accurate. More generally, it involves the selection of effective means to a specified end. Rationalization affects law, religion, bureaucracy, politics, and most areas of life. His most familiar example of this theme is bureaucratization: the tendency of modern organizations to replace ad hoc sets of officials, which in pre-modern societies were often selected on the basis of kinship or personal loyalty, with trained professionals operating according to written rules. Religions are rationalized to the degree that magical rituals are replaced by systematic doctrines and ethical imperatives. Often rationalization is not only a dominant trend, but also a seemingly inescapable process. At close to the end of the *Protestant Ethic*, he notes that such rationalization may lead to an "ossification," and then he quotes an unknown author to describe what might be the state of the "last humans": "narrow specialists without minds, pleasure-seekers without heart; in its conceit, this nothingness imagines it has climbed to a level of humanity never before attained" (Weber 2009: 159).

Yet, charismatic power can always break through routinized patterns, and new prophets may arise or ancient traditions may be revived. Moreover, human actors and cultural variations can deflect dominant trends into more than one channel. Hence, the future is more open and contingent than in Marx or elite theory. Nonetheless, the thrust of his analyses suggests an increasingly rationalized and ossified future.

The limitations of Weber's work for our purposes include:

1. The trend toward rationalization is overemphasized in light of the Iranian revolution, the rise of the Falun Gong in China, Buddhist-led protest in Tibet, the rise of Hindu nationalism in India, the spread of Islamic fundamentalism in the Middle East, North Africa, Nigeria, Malaysia, Indonesia, Pakistan, Afghanistan, and Bangladesh, the Arab Spring of 2010, and the rise of the Christian Right and the Tea Party in the U.S. Ruling elites have certainly had to take these movements into account. Some of these are clearly forms of resistance to rationalization.
2. Weberian notions of charismatic authority, breakthroughs, and religious virtuosos seem inadequate to conceptualize these twenty-first-century phenomena.

Weber's contributions are that he recognizes:

1. The importance of non-political and non-economic power;
2. Different types of social groups and formations emerge from the possession of different types of power;
3. The Marxian concept of economic power, but broadens it to include more than the ownership of the means of production;
4. The significance of cultural differences;
5. That while the historical future is shaped by the past and present, it is open to alternative possibilities. In Weber there is an acute realism, but he avoids determinism and nihilism.

Bourdieu

While Pierre Bourdieu is not "classical" in the same sense as the previous theorists, he is probably the most influential social theorist of the last quarter of the twentieth century (e.g., Bourdieu 1977, 1984, 1990, 1996, 1998; Bourdieu and Passeron 1977) and his work continues to be very influential. Many articles and books have been written explicating and critiquing his work (e.g., Harker, Mahar, and Wilkes 1990; Lardinois and Thapan 2006; Susen and Turner 2011; Wacquant 1992). Here I can give only a brief outline of his key arguments and the implications and limitations of his work as a way of understanding elites. Scholars often disagree about how to interpret Bourdieu and this needs to be kept in mind.

Instead of starting with either the subject's perceptions of the social world (characteristic of various forms of phenomenology) or an observer's perceptions of structures found in a society or culture (characteristic of objectivism and structuralism), he wants to focus analysis on the actual practices of everyday actors.[3] The relevance of this argument for our purposes is that neither elites nor non-elites should be denied agency. Even the most powerful elites, however, are to some degree limited by the objective structures and their agency is shaped by the content of their subjectivities, much of which has been inherited from the structures of their society and culture.

Practices need to be seen in relationship to the notions of *structure* and *habitus*. Structures are the abstractions that emerge from the past history of practices. These abstractions (e.g., norms, conventions, and articulated values) shape, but do not determine subsequent practices (Bourdieu 1977: 95). Social structures shape subsequent practices through social institutions that place constraints on acceptable behavior. This, however, leaves open the question of how social institutions are reproduced or transformed since they are made up of the practices of other actors in a given social context. Bourdieu uses the notion of *habitus* to understand the link between structure and practices. *Habitus* refers to systems of tacit knowledge and deeply inculcated dispositions, which generate and organize practices (Bourdieu 1977: 78; 1990: 53).[4] These are not primarily conscious preferences and choices, but rather deeply instilled inclinations and reactions. They are analogous to the moves of an athlete rather than the conscious decisions of a chess player (1990: 66–8). Bourdieu wants to distance himself from what he sees as both a naïve structuralism and a naïve rational choice perspective. These notions have several implications for the understanding of elites and non-elites. First, elites want to inculcate a habitus that supports their interests. This takes at least two forms. One is creating social markers that distinguish elites from non-elites; more about this below. A second is instilling in the habitus of non-elites taken-for-granted assumptions that buttress the power and privileges of elites. Examples include the assumption that kings and priests are sanctified by God, or that markets are inherently efficient and governments are inherently inefficient. Elites also inherit a habitus that makes them take many things for granted; hence it is a mistake to see the legitimacy and taken-for-grantedness of the existing structure and habitus as simply the result of deliberate manipulation on the part of elites.

Central to Bourdieu's theorizing is the notion of *capital*. Following Marx, capital is accumulated labor. It becomes a form of power that biases subsequent exchanges in favor of those who have capital. Unlike Marx, capital is not limited to material capital in the form of economic and financial resources. It can also take a symbolic form and be embodied in humans as *habitus*. Capital takes a number of forms, but especially important is *cultural capital*, which is made up of the knowledge and dispositions that express the taste associated with various class positions. For dominant groups it is important that elite taste and style seem a natural part of one's identity (Bourdieu 1984, 1986). *Social capital* refers to social networks (including kinship ties) that give one access to, and alliances with, others who also have capital resources. Such connections may be more matters of an implicit consensus and "natural" solidarities of, for example, families and status groups rather than conscious real-politik alliances or specific favors for other elites.

Social institutions are crystallized practices that specify and legitimate some practices (and forbid or denigrate others). They also legitimate various credentials such as family lineage, citizenship, and educational degrees. Such credentials are in many ways parallel to religious ordination in pre-modern societies (1996: 71ff) and are one of the ways elites are set off from others. For example, it is presumed that someone with an Oxbridge accent and an air of confidence is a more educated and thoughtful person than someone with a Cockney accent who is deferential. Often these structures and presumptions become not only legitimate, but taken-for-granted "realities." Bourdieu calls these *doxa*, the presuppositions of the game, which is not a state of the mind, but more accurately a state of the body (1990: 64–8).

Any particular kind of capital primarily operates within a *field* of power in which conflict, struggle, and competition are the central reality. A field is roughly analogous to a particular social arena such as national politics, academia, the legal profession, or movie actors. Capital within a particular field does not necessarily give one power in another field; being rich does not necessarily make one cultured, or vice versa. Nonetheless, one kind of capital can often be converted into other forms of capital. The exchange rate between different forms of capital is an important attribute of different social contexts. In the first half of the twentieth century, it was easier to convert new wealth into high social status in Dallas than in Boston, in the Chamber of Commerce, than the Social Register. Power is always relational; what counts is an actor's relative capital and power (Bourdieu 1998: 31–4). The very identity of actors and groups emerge out of their common location in social space and the struggles for power within a particular field. These various fields also occupy a broader social space and much of the struggle that occurs in the broader social context is over the relative importance of different kinds of capital, that is, over the "dominant principle of domination" and hence the exchange rate for different forms of capital (1996: 265, 388).

Like Marx, Bourdieu makes the possession of capital virtually synonymous with domination and exploitation; the struggle for capital is the core of social reality. There are no disinterested actors, though actors can vary in the degree to which their efforts are directed toward particularistic versus more universalistic interests (Bourdieu 1998: 75–91). He wants to expand, not reject, the economic metaphor. Social analysis needs to "abandon the economic/non-economic dichotomy which makes it impossible to see the science of 'economic' practices as a particular case of a science capable of treating all practices, including those that are experienced as disinterested or gratuitous, and therefore freed of the 'economy', as economic practices aimed at maximizing material or symbolic profit" (1990: 122). Symbolic forms of capital are modes of dominance that are disguised or *misrecognized* – not only misrecognized by individuals, but also by the collectivity and its culture. For non-economic forms of capital and relationships to work, they must be misrecognized by "social alchemy"; there must be "learned ignorance" (1977: 12; 1996: 40). For Bourdieu, intimate and particularistic relationships are from an analytical point of view still exchange relationships that profit some and exploit others (1990: 159). Non-economic forms of dominance are rooted in "*symbolic violence*" – such as the situation of women in most societies. Emphasizing symbolic capital is not abandoning a materialistic analysis, but, like Weber, extending it, by identifying the misrecognized forms of capital, profits, and domination that it involves (1990: 27). Yet, honor, respect, and status are key motivations of human action, so what he means by "materialistic" is not economic or material in the usual sense.

While I can only mention it in passing here, Bourdieu also places strong stress on meta-theoretical issues. All social relationships are shaped by the location of the actors and groups in a field of power relations including intellectuals and social analysts, and they need to clarify the impact of such relationships on what constitutes knowledge. He emphasizes that the objects of social analysis are not simply found, but are in part constructed by the analyst and the discipline.

The notion of social reproduction may have been overemphasized in understanding Bourdieu, but it is nonetheless central to most of his empirical work, especially the way that the powerful and privileged attempt to maintain their capital and power across time and generations. His work on the Kabyle of Algeria analyzes how reproduction of capital occurs through marriage alliances (1977: 58–71). Tacit knowledge and the deeply inculcated *habitus* are the key mechanisms of the social reproduction of domination. This is also true of modern schools. Hence the sociology of education is not a specialization among many others, but the study of a core institution of social reproduction. He equates it with older forms of reproduction such as aristocracy and nobility. Modern education systems have not resulted in equality of opportunity and an unbiased meritocracy, but are a new mode of domination that largely reproduces elite power and privilege, which in the past were more tied to kinship and property (1996: 5).

This does not mean that he thinks nothing has changed. Rather in this new mode of domination the "circuits of legitimation" have been "lengthened" (1996: 382–9). For any individual or family, acquiring cultural and social capital is less certain than was the inheritance of nobility or property, but for the elite or class as a whole, capital, power, and privilege are usually secure.

It needs to be kept in mind that much of Bourdieu's writings on education pay special attention to the system of French *grandes écoles*, which are very selective and elitist institutions. In other societies the mechanism and outcomes may vary, though he is highly skeptical that modern education systems significantly reduce domination. He does not go as far as Pareto in seeing elite domination as inevitable or embrace Michels' iron law of oligarchy. Change and transformations occur; Algerian independence and the student and worker revolts of 1968 are examples in the contemporary history of France and Bourdieu's own experience. Nonetheless, elites typically reproduce the structures of power and privilege, and make these appear as not only legitimate, but a taken-for-granted *doxa*. His most extensive empirical study of the French business and governmental elite is entitled *The State Nobility: Elite Schools and the Field of Power*. The term "nobility" suggests continuity in the degree of inequality between the French *Ancien Régime* and modern France. The modes of domination and reproduction have changed, but the power of the elite and their ability to reproduce themselves continues.[5]

Bourdieu and colleagues did extensive fieldwork looking at lower-class and outcast groups (Bourdieu et al. 1999). Much of the reportage on this work involves excerpts from field notes. There is little systematic attempt to relate this material to his studies of elites. Even in his discussions of "The Abdication of the State" (1999: 181–253), the focus is on lower level state functionaries with little explicit analysis of the relationship between these field reports on low-status groups and the upper elites (i.e., "The State Nobility").

There are several key problems and lacuna that need to be remedied in order to relate his work to a model of elites that is relevant to a wide variety of societies.

1. There is no systematic identification of likely forms of differentiation within elites, and the type of cooperation and conflict that is likely to emerge.
2. There is no systematic typology of the likely subcategories of non-elites, nor of the types of relationships that might emerge between non-elites and elites. For example, how political elites relate to the middle classes may vary depending on whether elites stigmatize the lowest strata of society or whether they mobilize them as a populist movement.
3. Despite attention to symbolic forms of capital, these ultimately turn out to be misrecognized forms of material economic power – though this notion includes much more than usual notions of economic power.

The elements of Bourdieu that are useful for our present purposes include:

1. The identification of the strong tendency toward inertia in the distribution of power and privilege, without lapsing into an ahistorical notion of the inevitability of domination and exploitation;
2. The role of early socialization in the creation of *habitus* and taken-for-granted *doxa* in sustaining this inertia;
3. The identification of symbolic forms of capital and power;
4. The recognition that the dominant principle of domination can vary for different cultures and for different historical periods;
5. That changes in the dominant principle of domination lead to varying rates of exchange between different forms of capital.

Toward a More Adequate Model

How can we draw on these four traditions to create a more adequate framework for the analysis of elites and non-elites?

1. Following elite theorists, elites are almost certain to emerge in any complex society, but this "realism" should not lapse into the overly pessimistic or cynical view that "nothing ever changes."
2. The degree of inequality, ascription, and mobility varies, but following elite theorists and Bourdieu, most societies are biased in favor

of reproducing the structure of power and privileges and providing greater opportunities for those of privileged backgrounds.

3. Following Weber, there tend to be three types of power and elites who specialize in each form: political power, economic power, and what I will refer to as status/cultural/ideological power. While some elites may have multiple forms of power, most economic elites are not politicians; most warriors are not religious leaders; most religious leaders are not merchants.

4. Following Weber, the degree to which such elites coordinate their exercise of power or are in conflict with one another is historically variable.

5. Following Marx, different means of production produce internal variations and conflicts within economic elites, for example, between landowners and the bourgeoisie. Weber's important elaboration notes that in capitalist societies what is relevant is market power, which can come from a variety of sources. Weber also makes clear that within the same society alternative status groups (e.g., ethnic groups) may have their own elites with varying interests that conflict with elites of other groups. Bourdieu further elaborates this notion by identifying different forms of symbolic capital. Pareto notes several forms of differentiation within elites: lions vs. foxes, rentiers vs. speculators, and conservatives vs. liberals. These examples of differentiation suggest that there are likely to be such divisions within all three types of elites.

6. The significance of differentiations within non-elites is something none of these theorists adequately treat. For Marx, non-elites increasingly become homogeneous wage laborers. A partial exception is his notion of the lumpen proletariat, the down-and-out disreputable who retarded the class consciousness of the proletariat (e.g., Marx 1852, chap. 5). While Bourdieu studies "disreputable" groups, the significance of these for the broader structure of power is not well specified.

7. Several theories suggest that there are inherent conflicts of interests between elites and non-elites. Marx argues that the competition of the marketplace forces capitalists to pay laborers as little as they can or become uncompetitive. Bourdieu emphasizes that symbolic forms of capital are inherently scarce; for some to be high status others must have lower status.

8. On the other hand, non-elites may appreciate some of the services that elites provide, for example, law and order, economic entrepreneurship, and propitiation of the gods. This is suggested by Weber's recognition that legitimacy is important and variable. Bourdieu certainly recognizes this, though he tends to see it as domination "misrecognized."

9. Following Marx, we need to recognize that non-elites can shape and change history.

In sum, a better theoretical framework would include:

1. Three categories of elites.
2. A category of non-elites.
3. The identification of likely forms of differentiation within each of these categories.
4. Drawing attention to the types of cooperation and conflict that are likely to emerge between different types of elites and non-elites and within each of these categories, *without assuming* that the degree and precise nature of these relationships are predetermined.

A Note on Post-Classical Literature

There is of course a very sizeable post-classical literature that focuses on elites. Some of the most prominent writers are C. Wright Mills (1956), Robert Dahl (1961), William Domhoff (e.g., 1967, 1998, 2013), Thomas Dye (2002), and John Higley (e.g., Higley and Moore 2001). These and many other writers have made important contributions. I am not going to review this literature here, and hence it is appropriate that I state my reasons for this lacuna.

First, there are already useful reviews of this literature and to repeat much of what has already been said is redundant (e.g., Domhoff 2013; Dye, Zeigler, and Schubert 2012; Khan 2012).

Second, this literature deals with a variety of different analytical questions. Who rules America in a given decade is not the same question as what are the factors that lead to an "elite settlement" and viable democracy in developing nations. How much the concentration of power has increased or decreased over time is yet another question than who rules now. Whether directors of corporations are "interlocked" may be relevant to the above questions, but in different ways. Attempting to understand existing patterns or predict the future of politics and change by investigating the values and attitudes of existing elites is a different question from any of the previous ones. Whether there is (or is not) a new class in a given historical situation may or may not be relevant to all of these questions. My point is that what comes under the label of elite studies is a varied set of questions – and an even more varied set of answers. This is not to be dismissive of this varied literature. Rather, it is to point out that the question I am addressing – what are most common varieties of elites *and* non-elites, and the patterns of cooperation and conflict that tend to occur in a variety of societies and historical periods – is in many respects a different question. It is nonetheless a legitimate and needed endeavor in its own right.

Third, even the more contemporary literature tends to focus on economic and political elites and neglect the role of status elites.

These are the reasons I derive my model more from Marx, Weber, Pareto, and Bourdieu rather than the more recent literature; I think they are more helpful in pointing to the questions I am asking. This is not, of course, to suggest that more contemporary analyses have no parallels with my aims – and from time to time I try to point these out where I think it is especially relevant.

2

The General Model

The Theoretical Grounding

Drawing on the insights derived from the four traditions discussed in the Introduction, the aim is to develop a general model of the relationship of elites and non-elites. In addition to building on the discussions of Weber's multidimensional concept of power,[1] I will draw on some of my previous work on status systems, especially the notions that resources vary in their inalienability and inexpansibility.[2]

A key aim is to systematically identify the typical patterns, tensions, and dilemmas that occur in many very different historical situations. The focus is on the tensions and conflict between different types of elites. Equally important are the tensions and conflict that typically arise among elites of each type, and within the category of non-elites. Of course, many of these patterns have been previously observed and reported. There has not, however, been a systematic framework that aids in identifying similarities and differences across cultures and historical periods. Often these typical tensions present alternative historical possibilities. By itself, the model does *not* predict which of the possibilities will actually occur in any given historical situation, but it raises key questions and suggests that some outcomes are more common than others. The model can subsume class analysis within the proposed elite/non-elite model. The notion of elites should not be reduced to or confused with the notions of the upper class; one can be a member of the upper class and not be a member of the elite and vice versa.[3]

The Types of Resources and How They Differ

There are three key types of sanctions: force, goods and services, and expressions of approval and disapproval. The first is the elementary source of political power, the second of economic power, and the third of status (which is also a form of power).[4] These three types of resources vary significantly with respect to their *expansibility*, that is, in the degree to which they can be increased. At the collective level *political* power can be expanded enormously in absolute terms. Some societies have spears and some have nuclear missiles; some armies are a disorganized collection of individual warriors, and some are highly coordinated and disciplined. The relevant question in most political conflicts, however, is not absolute levels of power, but relative levels. One party may have nuclear bombs, but the other side could have even more powerful ray guns that disable nuclear weapons; one political party may receive 100,000,000 votes, but in a fair election they lose if the other party receives 100,010,000 votes – a one hundredth of one percent difference. *Economic* resources can be expanded dramatically; some societies have a much higher per capita income than others. Both relative and absolute amounts of economic power are of significance. It is an advantage to be in the top five percent of the income distribution. It is usually much more pleasant and healthful to live in a society with a per capita income of $10,000 per year than one where it is $1,000. This would be true even if most societies had a per capita income of $20,000. *Status* power, in contrast, is relatively *inexpansible* because it is primarily a relative ranking or positional good; if everyone receives A's, or drives a limousine, the status significance of these symbols is soon discounted. Similarly, if all of the kindergarten students receive some kind of ribbon or award at the end of the year, the children soon figure out that the "best-reader" ribbon is more valuable than the "quietest student" ribbon. Nonetheless, these implicit distinctions are not as demeaning as when a few students are made to wear dunce caps and are openly degraded. Likewise nations where everyone is a "citizen" are likely to be more egalitarian than nations where everyone is a "subject."[5] In modern societies superiors have reduced the amount of ritualistic deference required of inferiors and the levels of deference that they show to their own superiors. Stated another way, the absolute level of status available to most people was increased by decreasing relative status differences. To be more concrete, laborers stopped doffing their caps to bosses when bosses stopped doffing their caps to owners when owners stopped bowing to political elites when political elites no longer had to be consecrated by priests (e.g., bishops and popes) and the appointment of priests no longer had to be approved of by political elites.[6] In sum, compared to economic and political power, the total available status can be increased only to a limited degree, but the redistribution of relative status can give most people a sense that the absolute amount of status available has increased.

Resources also vary with respect to their *inalienability*. The material aspects of political and economic power can be transferred from one individual or society to another. Societies can, and frequently do, buy goods and services from one another. These may include weapons and mercenary soldiers. They can also use force to appropriate or extort wealth (or weapons) from other nations. In sum, the many features of political and economic power are expansible and alienable. Status, however, is relatively *inalienable* because it is "located" in other people's minds. A robber may say, "Your money or your life," but he is unlikely to say, "Your status or your life"; he knows you cannot give it to him no matter how much he threatens you. Hence, once status systems are *institutionalized*, they are relatively stable. The Indian caste system has existed for more than 2500 years. Once high school students are labeled or identified with a peer group, they have difficulty changing their status or their peer group. "Old families" maintain some of their status even after their wealth has declined. The status of categories also tends to be stable; cheer leaders are not the "popular crowd" one year only to be replaced by "band nerds" the next year. Of course, even well-institutionalized status is not absolutely stable.

Resources also vary in terms of their *immediacy* and *transience*.[7] Political power backed by force tends to have the most immediate effect; in the short run it usually overrides the other sanctions. But since political power is always relative to that of competitors and enemies, it can be very transient. The fact that you won the last battle does not mean you will win the next one. Stated in other terms, it is difficult to store political and military power; it must constantly be recreated. Many economic resources are generally less immediate and less transient. It may be months between the time a house is purchased and the time it is built or ready for occupancy. The time between paying tuition and being educated may be much longer. But once either a house or an education is acquired, they are useful indefinitely. Of course, goods deteriorate, but many of these can be stored for relatively long periods of time, in contrast to force or political influence. Status power can be very transient and

Immediacy

Transience

fleeting and hence individuals may have only "ten minutes of fame." Other forms of power can trump status in the short run: saints can be killed and celebrities can be bought. If, however, status becomes institutionalized, it can be extremely stable and even lead to a kind of immortality. Homer, Plato, Alexander, Jesus, Mohammed, and George Washington as well as Judas, Nero, Benedict Arnold and Hitler are remembered long after the political and economic resources of their time have ceased to exist. Moreover, their images and status may be drawn upon to affect contemporary efforts to gain status and legitimacy: "He's as trustworthy as Benedict Arnold," or "her philosophical ideas are as thought provoking as those of Plato."

The point is that while there are exceptions, in general the different types of resources vary in the extent to which they are inalienable and inexpansible and in whether their effects are immediate and their potency is transitory. Consequently, those who have one type of power often seek to convert some of it into other types of power. Warriors often seek wealth and legitimacy. Merchants support stable and friendly political regimes, and the blessings of religious authorities. Priests seek protection and contributions.

The Concepts of Power, Legitimacy, and Authority

Implicit in the discussion above is a particular concept of power, and the related concepts of legitimacy and authority. There are many discussions about the meaning of these terms, but a review of these would be a major tangent. Rather, I will simply try to outline clearly how I will use these terms. The conceptualization of power I draw on is what Scott calls the mainline tradition that focuses on social power as "an agent's intentional use of causal power to affect the conduct of other agents" (2001: 29). Perhaps more accurately, powerful actors at least have the potential to act in a way that changes the outcome of human actions. This includes the power to set agendas (and keep things off of the agenda), and to change or refuse to change institutional structures, but does *not include* taken-for-granted, often unconscious, biases that are built into the culture and social structure.[8] This is not to in any way deny the existence or importance of such biases and the need to identify and deconstruct them. If, however, such biases are included in the definition of power the concept becomes so expansive that it becomes nearly meaningless. This is the tendency of what are often referred to as structural concepts of power. Stated another way, the notions of structural power tend to collapse the notions of power/dominance and social order. All social orders in varying degrees privilege some behaviors and some social roles over others, but this is not the same thing as exercising power. Using English as a national language rather than some other language probably advantages some native born citizens over other native born citizens – not to speak of those whose mother tongue is not English. Nonetheless, it is beneficial to most people to have a dominant lingua franca, though it may be appropriate to make some concessions to those who do not have the lingua franca as their mother tongue. In the U.S. and much of Europe, people are supposed to drive on the right side of the road; in the U.K. and many of its former colonies they should drive on the left. Making people drive on the right (or the left) probably advantages some and disadvantages others, but it is beneficial to nearly everyone to have some rule. This is not, however, a matter of actors actively exercising power over others. A second way of saying this is that the notions of social control and socialization should not be collapsed. Certainly, socialization involves using certain kinds of social control and substitutes internalized controls for external controls; nonetheless, it is still useful to distinguish these two social processes. A third way to make the point is to indicate some of the limitations of Foucault's notion of discipline; it means shifting from explicit coercion to the creation of structures that result in a surreptitious manipulation and domination. For example, in *Discipline and Punishment* (1995 [1977]) he sees the modern reforms of the prison system not as a move toward more humanitarian forms of punishment, but rather as a new more effective (and insidious) form of the exercise of power.

Of course, more subtle forms of power and manipulation are often built into various institutional arrangements. But notions of such "discipline" in Foucault's sense (and to a lesser extent Bourdieu's notion of dominance) need to be linked with Giddens' (1984) notion that institutionalized structures *enable* as well as limit. Having national holidays helps everyone to plan ahead even if the specific dates are not especially meaningful to some. Foucault-like conceptions of power tend to lapse into a cynicism and even nihilism about social life that are not only inaccurate, but morally debilitating. Bourdieu does not in his writing or his life show as much pessimism as Foucault, but his notion of power is also subject to this same criticism. Structural notions of power have had the great virtue of making us aware of the built-in, often taken-for-granted structures of inequality. In my opinion, however, these very expansive notions of power increasingly handicap social analysis rather than facilitate it because they decrease our ability to see variations in the degree and forms of domination and the extent to which these are exploitive of the dominated. Let me repeat, this is not to deny the importance of identifying and critiquing taken-for-granted biases, much less deliberate efforts to institute or defend such biases, which are certainly attempts to exercise power. Dominating and enabling are in some respects two sides of the same coin. We certainly need to identify taken-for-granted structures and debate whether they enable and who they enable, but avoid seeing all order as dominance.

Legitimacy results when actions or social arrangements are taken for granted (a cognitive phenomenon) or are seen to have relatively high status in the eyes of non-elites (an attitudinal phenomenon). (It can also occur by approval from different types of elites – a matter I will take up shortly.) This approval usually occurs because these arrangements are seen to be justified in relationship to some more abstract notions of justice and/or sacredness shared by elites and non-elites. The percentage of a population that accepts a norm or value and the intensity of their support can obviously vary, but it must be substantial by this definition of legitimacy. Effective social control based primarily on raw repression and coercion is not legitimacy in the sense used here.

By *authority*, I mean the exercise of power that is seen as legitimate by most of those subject to that power. Obviously there are variations in the percentage of those who recognize an exercise of power as legitimate and in the intensity of their support.[9] Such legitimacy is usually related to the relationships between the holders of different types of power.

Relationship between the Different Types of Power

The different types of sanctions and power can be either mutually supportive or antithetical, or both. For example, if goods are constantly appropriated by force and workers are murdered and abused with impunity, the accumulation and exchange of goods and services are next to impossible. Therefore, force must be organized to repress the illicit use of force. Conversely, those who provide protection must have food, clothes, shelter, and amenities, which obviously require the production of goods and services. But an orderly exchange of goods and services for protection (and vice versa) does not occur automatically; legitimate rules about the terms of exchange are required. These "rules" may be largely unstated and most exchange may be implicit rather than explicitly contractual. This is the reason that, in some societies, exchanges of gifts are much more central than any kind of market exchange, and the aim may be to receive status and honor, political allies, or marriage partners rather than wealth.[10] This does not, however, mean that there are no norms about the terms of exchanges.

To a degree, the organizers of force can make the producers of goods and services do what they want. But even for simple tasks, not to speak of complex ones, the need for constant supervision often makes force inefficient as a way of gaining compliance. On the other hand, trying to motivate the wielders of force by proposing to give or withhold goods (or services) is irrelevant unless they respect property rights; otherwise, they simply take what they want. The actions of both protectors and producers are more efficient over the long run if they are legitimate.

Whose approval is needed for something to be legitimate? Obviously, the wielders of force and the producers of goods and services have some conflicting interests. Typically – though perhaps not universally – the former want to get as much as they can for the protection they provide, and the latter want to pay as little as possible. An acceptable compromise usually requires the assistance of some relatively neutral third party, someone whose main source of power is rooted in neither force nor wealth. This is the role of status elites and more specifically ideological elites.[11] For such legitimacy to be shared by non-elites, however, it is necessary that the elites offering approval be seen as having significantly different interests than the elites they are legitimizing. Religious leaders and intellectuals are the most important historical forms of status elites. Their power is rooted primarily in the status derived from their conformity to norms not directly concerned with the control of force or material resources. Typically, this is based upon the possession of esoteric types of knowledge including ideologies. Such elites are usually experts in the "other world." Even if they are completely secular, they are seen as living in "ivory towers." Somewhat ironically, this detachment gives them the power to provide approval and legitimization for the profane structures of this world. Since their own power is not primarily based on force or possession of material resources, they are others for protection and material necessities. As in the relationship between protectors and producers, there is always the question of at what cost.[12] Such inter-elite legitimizing is not restricted to religious and ideological elites. For example, economic elites may support being taxed by political elites in order to secure public services or protection of their property.

In sum, the different types of power can be mutually supportive, but they also offer much potential for conflicts of interest.

The Basic Model

I will now propose a basic model of elites and non-elites. The discussion of the relationship between the different types of power and sanctions implies the emergence of different types of elites with potentially common and conflicting interests. In turn, the notion of elites implies the category of non-elites. These notions suggest a simple analytical model of the key social categories relevant to most complex societies. The model will be based upon three variables: (1) the distinction between elites and non-elites, (2) differentiation of elites in terms of the three types of power we have been discussing, and (3) differentiation within both non-elites and each type of elite based upon the strains inherent in the possession of a particular kind of power. A fourth variable that cuts across these is the scope of the social system or arena in which these elites and non-elites operate.

The *first distinction* is between elites and non-elites. Contemporary studies of political elites focus on those who are in the top positions in powerful organizations, usually numbering a few thousand people.[13] Most people, even those who are well off, have relatively low levels of political, economic, and status power; hence they are non-elites. (The matter of the definitions and operationalization of elites and non-elites are discussed in the Appendix; in part this depends on the society being studied.)

The *second distinction* is between different types of elites based on the type of power they use most frequently. *Political elites* may or may not be warriors, but the underlying form of power that they have is force. In modern societies political elites normally vie for control of the state and use its monopoly on force to back up their policies and orders. This is not, of course, to deny that they also use other forms of power. *Economic elites* typically own or control the means of production. The concrete form of these means of production varies depending on the period and the society. The mode of control may involve the orders of medieval lords (or their stewards), the decisions of officials in a planned economy, or exchanges in the market. In the latter case market power takes various forms such as ownership of property, union solidarity, or human and cultural capital. *Status elites* have accumulated high levels of approval. This may be tied to the individual or to the office they occupy, or in some cases both; Jesus represents the first, many popes are examples of the second, and Pope John XXIII is an example of the third. Historically most status elites have been religious elites and intellectuals who played a key role in articulating and inculcating ideologies.

The *third distinction* points to tensions and alternatives within each of the four key categories. This usually involves alternative roles and strategies that are pursued by those who are members of a given type of elite, and a nearly universal segmentation that occurs within non-elites. For example, among economic elites there is usually some differentiation and tension between those who are primarily engaged in alternative modes of production (e.g., farmers vs. merchants, or merchants vs. bankers). These tendencies toward internal segmentation will be elaborated on shortly.

The *fourth distinction* (or variable) points to variations in the scope within which elites (or non-elites) operate, and the extent or depth of their power. In the U.S., for example, there are local elites, state elites, national elites and elites that operate on an international level.

Now we return to the issue of the internal differentiation or segmentation within each of the four main categories: political elites, economic elites, status elites, and non-elites. We begin with non-elites.

Non-elites

A study of prisons that largely ignored the prisoners would be considered inadequate, or at least incomplete. Yet many of the analyses of elites and ruling classes pay scant attention to non-elites. One of the virtues of the proposed model is that it draws attention to these less powerful actors – both the respectable and the unrespectable.

Obviously many strata and cleavages may exist within this broad category of non-elites. The most fundamental cleavage separates respectable, "decent" members of the society who receive at least a minimum level of respect from those who are in varying degrees not respected and excluded. The disrespected may or may not include relatively well-off non-members such as foreign aliens. More typically it includes those who are considered disreputable. Most striking are outcast groups, but other examples include the *lumpen proletariat*, under-classes, political prisoners, slaves, stigmatized racial or ethnic groups, foreign aliens, recently arrived or illegal immigrants, and religious minorities. The size of such "outcast" groups varies by society and depending on the definition used by the analyst. For example, in India the groups that were traditionally outcasts make up about 15 percent of the population, though this varied by region. During the sixteenth and seventeenth centuries in Europe the urban poor constituted between 10 and 25 percent of the population (Jütte 1994: 56). In the Stalinist era from 1929 to 1953, there were approximately between one and two percent of the population in the Gulag at any one time. In the U.S. in 2013, about seven percent of the population were in jails or prisons, 14 percent of the people were below the poverty level and about one percent experienced homelessness each year. In short, the disreputable members of society usually run between one and fifteen percent of the total population.[14]

The usual effect of stigmatizing and excluding the "undeserving" is to create higher levels of solidarity between elites and "respectable" non-elites. Outcasts are a reminder to respectable non-elites that their situation could be much worse. The recurring dilemma for respectable non-elites is whether their antipathies are best directed at elites or at outcasts. Elites, especially those I will refer to as conservative elites, often emphasize the distinction between the respectable and unrespectable to maintain the support or acquiescence of the former.

The disreputable are not the same as opponents. Opponents may (or may not) be despised, but they have enough power to be considered adversaries. Of course, the disreputable may become opponents, usually through some kind of social movement. The African-American Civil Rights Movement in the U.S. is an obvious example, which in turn spawned other movements by disadvantaged groups.[15] Conversely, opponents who lose power struggles can become disreputable.

Most elite theory pays relatively little attention to non-elites, especially "unrespectable non-elites," and sees them as largely irrelevant to future developments. Marx, of course, emphasizes the role of the working classes, but tends to be dismissive or derisive about unrespectable non-elites such as the lumpen proletariat. In contrast the model I am proposing reminds the analyst that it is important to at least consider the role of the most powerless social categories – even though these groups may have little intentionality and agency in carrying out the part that they play. Often they perform the role of increasing solidarity between elites and respectable non-elites by being defined as a threat to social order. For example, in Victorian Britain the unrespectable non-elites were often seen as "dangerous classes."[16] There are, of course, cases where they become the base for important social movements such as various slave revolts, the Welfare Rights Movement in the U.S., and the political mobilization of Dalits (Untouchables) in India. Protest and reform movements that mobilize the unrespectable non-elites are often instigated and led by those who are at least relatively educated and privileged individuals, but seldom are they elites in the early days of these movements.[17]

Why not three kinds of non-elites?

As indicated above, elites will be differentiated by the primary type of power they wield (i.e., economic, political, and status). Why not differentiate non-elites into political non-elites, economic non-elites, and status non-elites? The reason is that most non-elites in most societies cannot be seen as either specializing in or even primarily concerned about only one of the three forms of power. It is true that in complex societies there are non-elites whose occupation makes them specialists, e.g., policemen, lower level clergy, stockbrokers, etc. But neither in their own view of themselves or the way others view them are they seen as specialist in a particular form of power in the same sense that terms like "politician," "capitalist," and "archbishop" or "public intellectual" suggest. Certainly the nature of non-elites' relationships with elites varies for the different types of elites. For example, non-elites may be especially resentful (or appreciative) of one type of elites, but not of another. In Communist Poland they were more appreciative of bishops than cabinet ministers. In the contemporary U.S., non-elites are generally more critical of members of Congress than they are of directors of corporations. This does not, however, differentiate non-elites into separate social categories. In some instances non-elites may be more concerned about changes in one sector or another (e.g., more concerned about gay marriage than declining real wages). This should not be ignored. For some analytical purposes and in some historical cases, it might be useful to disaggregate non-elites into three subcategories, but in many cases this would make the conceptual scheme more complex than the empirical reality and needlessly complicate the analysis and exposition. Having added these clarifications about the nature of non-elites, we turn to the conceptualization of the three kinds of elites and the tensions and alternatives within each type.

Political Elites

Experts in force have the potential to both protect and exploit. Warrior elites are often seen as little better than those they supposedly protect against. To slightly rephrase a Rogers and Hammerstein song from *The King and I*, "they may 'protect' you out of all you own." Among sociologists, it is Charles Tilly who frequently articulated the link between protection and extortion (e.g., Tilly 1985). So the category paired with police-warrior is that of robber-invader (or sometimes robber-rebel). The potential link between protection and extortion or protection and repression is well known; consequently telling the cops from the robbers is sometimes difficult. "Robbers" in this context includes political thugs and secret police.

Often the general population will complain about the failure of the authorities to protect them from criminals, and in democratic societies this can become a major issue. But historically robbers are politically relevant primarily when they become bandits, an organized group of marauders. If they become guerrillas, they not only reject the legitimacy of the existing state, but offer an alternative ideology, a new vision for organizing and running the society. Hobsbawm (1959) has used the terms "primitive rebels" and "social bandits" to refer to those on the margins of society who resist the established authorities.

Of course, there is no clear-cut line between robbers, bandits or guerillas, or between these and the police or army. When a distinction can be drawn between the cops and the robbers, it is based upon some notion of legitimacy. The legitimate use of force is associated with defending against external enemies and upholding the norms of the group, which frequently are embodied in law. This may be customary or traditional law rather than modern rational-legal statutes. Of course, different subgroups in a society or nation-state may disagree about what is legitimate and hence whether the actions of political elites are legitimate.

A common means for gaining the support of non-elites is by starting wars or exaggerating their likelihood. Of course, this risks defeat by outsiders and alienation of non-elites. Rulers may also seek legitimacy by identifying themselves with other high status entities. Most often this took the form of deference to gods and respect toward religious elites, but in contemporary societies associations with celebrities – including sports stars, movie stars and renowned intellectuals – may also be useful. The ruler's dilemma is how to use force to achieve elite and societal interests, and, at the same time, avoid antagonizing powerful neighbors and maintain internal legitimacy by showing restraint and respect for traditions, laws, and the gods.[18] The dilemma of the ruled is whether the threats of outsiders, criminals, and bandits are worse than the demands of political elites and their subordinates.

The classical functions of political elites are maintenance of internal order and protection against external enemies.[19] With respect to *internal order* another dilemma emerges: to what degree is social control directed at the lower strata and concerned with law and order, or to what degree is it directed toward elites themselves and aimed at placing some limits on the exploitation of non-elites. This latter concern is a case of limiting the interest of a subunit to protect the viability of the larger unit; for example, a king tries to limit the exploitation of peasants by local nobles in order to avoid peasant rebellions. With respect to *external relations* the dilemma is to what degree does a group rely on a large, heavily armed military for protection as contrasted to developing relations of trust and cooperation with outside groups? The former course can increase the level of mistrust, lead to an "arms race," and increase the probability of conflict. The latter course can lead to disaster if a society's external neighbors are aggressive and duplicitous. These alternative concerns provide the bases of differentiation within political elites. The labels vary by historical context, but, typically, "conservatives" or "the right" are preoccupied with internal "law and order" and external "defense," while "liberals" or "the left" give more attention to limiting internal exploitation and maintaining "good relations" with other societies.[20] The terminology used to describe these differences of course varies with the historical and cultural context.[21]

Common sources of political elites' inability to adequately carry out the above responsibilities are polarization and stalemates between "conservatives" and "liberals" or some more complicated fracturing among political elites. This can lead to a civil war, in which one or both of the parties not only become defined as guerillas and traitors, but de facto become external enemies. The obvious example in American history is the stalemate over the future of slavery, which eventually led to the Civil War. Short of civil war, such segmentation and polarization can lead to the inability of political elites to reach working compromises, which can result in a decline in the legitimacy of politics per se. The following quote describes this situation:

> Presidential elections between the two major parties (the Republicans and Democrats), were so closely contested that a slight nudge could tip the teeter-totter to the advantage of the opposition party, and Congress was marked by political stalemate. Mudslinging became an increasingly popular way of gaining advantage at the polls ... The negativity and ambiguity of politics began a shift in the press to ... sensationalism and sentimental stories took as prominent a role as factual news.

This is not a description of the politics of the first decade of the twenty-first century. Rather it describes the period following the American Civil War that became known as The Gilded Age.[22]

Of course, such segmentation, polarization and stalemates are not limited to U.S. history. Other modern examples include Lebanon following the end of its civil war in 1990, the political stalemate in Northern Ireland following the 1998 Good Friday Agreement, the stalemate in Europe during 2011–12 over how to resolve the debt crisis, and the civil wars in South Sudan and the Central African Republic in 2013–14. The key point is that polarization and stalemate within political elites may or may not lead to civil war, but nearly always erode the legitimacy of the political system.

A note on military elites

For some analyses it would be appropriate to distinguish between political elites and military elites. While such a differentiation can be useful, in my opinion, it should not be part of the basic typology of elites. When the military and the police decline to enforce the orders of civilian political leaders, the latter have de facto ceased to be political elites; conversely, when this occurs, military leaders have de facto become political elites, or at least would-be political elites. In pre-modern societies the line between political leadership and military leadership is often obscure; kings and nobles were often warriors on the battlefield as well as politicians. Even in modern societies the upper levels of the military and the police are quasi politicians; they spend as much time dealing with budgets, legal procedures, public relations, etc., as they do with military strategy and logistics. This is the reason I have not treated the military as a distinct elite in the general model, but I acknowledge that it might be useful to do so for the purpose of some analyses.[23]

Economic Elites

In the realm of material production, a cleavage often arises within *economic elites* between those who control different means and modes of production. Typically, this involves a conflict between traditional and emerging forms. In agrarian societies, there were often conflicts between agriculturalists and herders.

It is telling that the Old Testament story of the first murder was when Cain, who was a "tiller of the ground," killed his brother Abel, who was "a keeper of sheep," because Abel's offering to God had been acceptable and Cain's had not (Bible, Genesis 4: 1–16). That is, the product of one mode of production had more religious legitimacy than the other. In this archetypical story this difference was the origin of the first violence and conflict. The Cain and Abel story is obviously prominent if not central to Christianity and Judaism, and has been retold many times in various forms of literature, music, and modern media. A condensed version is also given in the Koran of Islam, though the occupations of the two brothers are not mentioned (5: 27–31).

Conflicts rooted in alternative means of production are not limited to the ancient past. I grew up watching Hollywood Westerns. It is striking how most of these revolve around conflicts between those who are associated with different modes of production: cowboys versus Indians, ranchers versus farmers, cattlemen versus sheepmen, etc. As society became more complex, those who controlled and managed land were threatened by the increasing importance of those who specialized in more moveable forms of resources, e.g., merchants, traders, and bankers. In contemporary industrial societies much of the debate over class formation has been over whether a new class is emerging, whose power is rooted in knowledge and human capital rather than ownership of physical capital.

It is important to stress that such shifts in economic power usually involve both new technologies and new forms of cultural and social institutions. The shift from hunting and gathering or herding to more settled forms of agriculture was based in part on new technologies like plows and draft animals, but it also involved new patterns of settlements, kinship relationship, notions of property, and mechanisms for conflict resolution. In hunting and gathering societies, serious conflict usually led to one or more of the parties simply moving to another area (Woodburn 1982). To some degree this is the case for herding societies, though moving a large number of animals is more problematic and organized conflict between groups is more frequent (Lenski 1970: 295–9). When much time and labor is invested in particular plots of land, moving becomes an unattractive solution and new forms of conflict and conflict resolution are necessary to make the new technologies productive. A modern example of this interaction between newer technology and social institutions is the conflict that emerged between those who owned the copyrights for music and those who developed new technologies for disseminating music such as Napster. Such technologies often allowed consumers to transform commodities, such as copyrighted music, into non-commodities, which became a virtually free good shared by vast networks of users. In the Napster case, however, court rulings, new laws, and other means of social control were soon implemented that limited such sharing.

Ironically, those who control the older dominant form of production in any given historical period usually need the assistance of those who control new forms of production and vice versa. The landed nobility and gentry of pre-industrial societies needed the goods and services of commercial elites if they were to have anything but the most provincial of lives. Conversely, a main market for the luxury goods and money lending of commercial elites was the landed aristocracy. The case of Napster offers a contemporary example of such compromises. The record companies initially fought most forms of Internet distribution of their music. While they won in the courts, it was less clear that they could in fact prevent illicit sharing if the costs of recordings remained as high as they had been. Consequently, they have increasingly negotiated various arrangements to charge relatively low prices for the distribution of copyrighted music over the Internet. It seems likely that this compromise will erode the long-term profit margins and economic power of record companies.[24] Similar pressures and trends are affecting newspapers, periodicals, book publishers, video retailers, and movie studios.

Therefore, while old and new economic elites often are in competition (both within the economic realm and in seeking the support of political and religious elites), they also often need each other. But it is difficult for established elites to utilize the goods and services of rising elites without at the same time contributing to their legitimacy and wealth. Rising economic elites face a mirror image of this predicament. So, the dilemma of each group is how to develop terms of cooperation without harming their long-term interests. Rarely is there a solution; the typical outcome is that old elites make a series of short-term accommodations that eventually undercut their dominance. This is not to suggest any kind of ironclad technological determinism; in specific historical circumstances other outcomes are, of course, possible.

Status Elites

First, it is necessary to elaborate the category of status elites. Status elites vary in terms of the key role that they play. Some are primarily exemplary individuals; some are cultural elites such as admired authors or famous performers; some are noteworthy because they are articulate in advocating how their society and culture should operate.

Status, culture, and ideology

The concept of *status elites* can be elaborated by introducing the notions of *cultural elites* and *ideological elites*. Elites in general have relatively high status. Economic and political elites usually have status because of their economic and political power, respectively. Status elites are in some respects a residual category – but a very important one – referring to status not primarily derived from economic and political sources. Such status is typically based on extraordinary levels of beauty, bravery, knowledge, virtue, or eloquence. For example, Jim Thorpe, Rosa Parks and World War I hero Sergeant Alvin York were status elites because of their skill or bravery, but had little wealth or political power, and they were not cultural elites.[25] *Cultural elites* are status elites whose status is rooted in their knowledge, skill, or eloquence. Helen Hayes, Laurence Olivier, Martha Graham, Arthur Rubenstein, Louis Armstrong, Frank Sinatra, Leontyn Price, James Thurber, and Walter Cronkite were famous and highly respected cultural elites, but they were not ideological elites.[26] *Ideological elites* engage in cultural and political debates and propose (at least implicitly) various visions of the way things should be or are supposed to be.[27] These visions may be of either an earthly world or a heavenly world; they can be progressive, reactionary, or for the status quo. Ayn Rand, Arthur Miller, John Steinbeck, Billy Graham, Harriet Beecher Stowe and George Bernard Shaw were ideological elites, as well as cultural and status elites. These concepts are additive or nested: all ideological elites are cultural elites and all cultural elites are status elites, and all status elites are "elites in general," but the reverse is not necessarily the case. Of course, some ideological elites are not considered as accomplished in the purely cultural realm as others and vice versa. For example, George Bernard Shaw was probably more of a great dramatist than a great ideologue, Harriet Beecher Stowe more of a great ideologue than a great novelist. These distinctions are, of course, ideal-typical concepts that actual cases more or less approximate.

The patterns of status relations

Within the literature on elites, status and status elites tend to be relatively ignored or neglected. Most studies focus on economic and political elites. Moreover, there are distinct disciplines that focus on economic and political power (i.e., economics and political science), but there is no discipline devoted to the analysis of status power. Within sociology there are formally organized sections named "Political Sociology" and "Economic Sociology," but not a comparable section devoted to the analysis of status – though, of course, status and prestige are frequently discussed across a variety of subfields within the discipline. Because of this relative neglect I will briefly outline my own understanding of the nature of status and summarize what I have in earlier work referred to as a "theory of status relations."[28]

By status I mean the accumulated expressions of approval and/or disapproval that others express toward an actor, group, activity or object. It is roughly the same as notions of prestige, rank, honor, or dishonor, though each has its own nuances. A prerequisite to status is social *visibility*; the individual, group, or object that has no social visibility has no social status. The theory outlined below attempts to explain the typical patterns of relationships that tend to emerge when status is a highly valued attribute, especially when it is not simply a reflection of economic or political power. Hence, status-based relations are more likely to appear among religious devotees than among stockholders or members of a political party.

The theory has four key elements. The first two elements of the theory are about the nature of status compared to other resources. Status is relatively *inalienable*; it is not easily transferred or appropriated, and hence once institutionalized is relatively stable. Status is also relatively *inexpansible*. Hence upward mobility tends to be carefully restricted or regulated and "putdowns" of competitors and inferiors are common.

The second two elements of the theory focus on the sources of status. One obvious source is *conformity* to the norms of the group; hence, higher status groups tend to elaborate and complicate the norms in order to make it difficult for upstarts to conform. Brahmins create elaborate rules about purity and pollution, upper classes are often distinguished by accent, demeanor, and style, scholars must acquire erudition to be taken seriously, and the "popular crowd" frequently changes what is "in" with respect to dress, music, language, etc. Another source of status is *associations*; associating with those of high status improves your status, with those of low status lowers your status. This is especially the case with respect to *intimate expressive* relationships; eating and romantic relationships are key forms of intimacy. Hence, upper castes cannot eat with or marry those of lower castes, though they can interact with them in work situations. Teenagers care about "who eats with whom in the lunchroom" and who "goes with" or "hooks up with" whom, but are less concerned about who sits next to them in class – especially if seats are assigned by the teacher.

This is a very cryptic account of the theory that leaves out many nuances and complexities. Now we turn briefly to the notion of celebrities, which is an increasingly important category of status elites.

Celebrities

While most complex societies have had some celebrities, this has become an especially important type of status elite in contemporary societies. In part, this is because changes in technology and social networks have resulted in the greater significance of celebrities. As societies become larger and more complex, it is very difficult for elites to be socially visible by physical presence – and as the theory of status relations argues, social visibility is a prerequisite to status. Even the largest stadiums hold only a small percentage of the population of contemporary societies. Economic elites can often operate behind the scenes and may prefer to be socially or politically invisible. Political elites in electoral democracies must become highly visible when campaigning, but many of the key activities of politicians can be done behind the scenes. For status elites, however, social visibility is a prerequisite to rank and power.[29] Hence, it is not surprising that elites, especially status elites, would be concerned about the resources that give them access to the means of public visibility. In contemporary societies this usually means the mass media. This structural change has accentuated the creation and importance of celebrities. Celebrities are status elites, but not necessarily or usually what I have earlier referred to as cultural and ideological elites, that is, religious or intellectual leaders. Since celebrities play an increasingly important role, it will be necessary to elaborate the typology of elites to take this into account when we consider contemporary U.S. society. Now we turn to the type of tension that is most characteristic of status elites in both pre-modern and contemporary societies.

Priests and prophets

For status elites who are ideologically oriented, a cleavage often develops between those who support (and legitimate) existing activities or elites, and those who are more critical of these. The ideal-typical distinction here is between priests and prophets (or renouncers). Priests focus on mediation between this-worldly and otherworldly perspectives. Normally many of their efforts are directed toward the legitimization of worldly structures. In contrast, prophets tend to be critical of existing structures or to renounce them as being irrelevant and of no value.[30] Intellectuals and religious elites who are too involved in political and economic structures forfeit an independent basis of status and legitimacy. Preachers who live too lavishly become suspect; professors who become cabinet members soon have their objectivity questioned. Conversely, complete detachment and rejection of the world makes the status of religious and intellectual elites largely irrelevant to worldly matters; their status is restricted to cloisters, ivory towers, or the world-to-come. Hence, cultural elites (e.g., artists, intellectuals, and religious elites) who are interested in also being ideological elites are constantly under cross pressures to be both worldly and otherworldly, to support and criticize existing patterns. When the Rev. Jerry Falwell became closely associated with conservative politics, it tended to increase his support among his core constituency, but it reduced his religious stature among more liberal evangelicals. In given historical situations, this frequently produces social cleavages within ideological elites.[31]

Summary

This simple model suggests that there are typically three types of elites in addition to a large population of non-elites. Both cooperation and conflict are possible between each of these four categories. In addition to possible conflicts between different elites or between elites and non-elites, each of these four social categories has internal tensions, strains, and contradictions that make further cleavages likely. Note that these internal cleavages suggest both potential antagonists (e.g., police vs. bandits, priest vs. prophets) and alternative social roles (e.g., bandits instead of police, prophets instead of priests). Thus far, the argument has been that all complex societies have a tendency to develop four basic

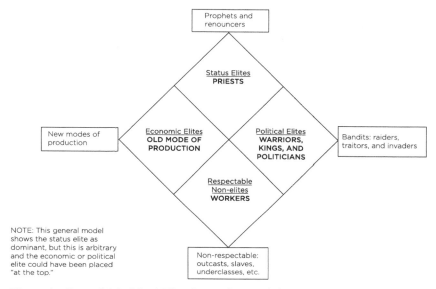

Figure 1: General Model of Elites/Non-elites and their Antagonists

categories and these have internal tensions that potentially will produce a further differentiation of each (i.e., a total of eight categories). Of course, each of the eight categories can undergo further internal differentiation. These are simply the minimum number required to illustrate the logic of the model. Special attention has been paid to the nature of status and status relationships because this is the kind of elite that previous models have tended to neglect. The model is summarized in Figure 1.

Deep Structure

The concept of deep structure refers to an underlying structure that can take alternative forms but has a common foundation. It is derived from linguistics. For example, "George hit the ball" and "The ball was hit by George" use a different grammatical structure, but mean roughly the same thing. Noam Chomsky and others have argued that these sentences are alternative forms of an underlying deep structure. Whether or not this is correct, the notion of deep structure has been used analogously to refer to underlying structures that take different concrete forms. Anthropologist Claude Levi-Strauss used a version of this notion, especially in his analysis of myths. He famously sees deep structures as located in the human mind, and focuses on myths because he sees these as the elements of culture that are least constrained by the material or political contexts (Levi-Strauss 1963: chap. 11; 1975: 1–32). However, he recognizes that some underlying structures may be shaped by the historical and cultural context and are "merely the reflections in men's minds of certain social demands that have been objectified in institutions" (Levi-Strauss 1975: 10). It is this latter version of deep structure that I want to draw upon here.

The general model I have proposed can be usefully thought of as an underlying deep structure. I do *not* mean to suggest that it is rooted in the structure of the mind (much less the brain) or some notion of human nature. Rather, I mean that the set of relationships it identifies are common in most complex societies, though the specific historical forms that it takes varies by period and culture. Such deep structures are relevant on at least two levels of analysis. The first is the *analytical level* such as the general model I am proposing; this is theorizing by specialized observers such as social scientists. Such social scientists may or may not consider themselves as members of the social unit they are observing. Of course, to some degree they bring with them the assumptions and biases of the societies and professional groups from which they come, but in principle both the assumptions of their societies and those of their professional group are subject to criticism and revision. The second level refers to *indigenous models*, which serve to help the members of a social unit make sense out of key features of that particular unit, and usually to legitimate some patterns and define others as illegitimate. Some of these models may also serve as boundaries for what is taken for granted or what is considered legitimate discourse. In this sense they are similar to Goffman's (1974) notions of social framing or Bourdieu's (1977, 1990) notion of doxa. The line between analytical models and indigenous models is not a fixed one. Analytical models can become indigenous models and analytical models draw on indigenous ones. In the next chapter we will consider the Indian varna system as one such indigenous model and in subsequent chapters indicate some of the deep cultural structures of Classical Athens and the contemporary U.S.

The Mode and Logic of the Analysis

Let me clarify the nature, benefits, and limits of the model and the type of analysis I am proposing. I am not claiming that this typology is all that is needed to analyze elites and the sources of social change, much less is it some kind of general theory of social change. Rather, I am suggesting that the typology will be useful for analyzing a wide array of societies as a way of identifying key social and cultural categories and relationships between different types of elites as well as their relationships to non-elites. The typology points to a kind of "deep structure" that takes different forms in different cultural and social settings. The model is in some respects simply a complex checklist. An analogy from anatomy may be helpful. Suppose we want to dissect a newly found species or compare several species. If we just start cutting into them, it is hard to know what it is we see. Common sense or conventional wisdom may help us to find the heart or the stomach, and we may recognize the liver, but have little idea of what it does. We may miss the lymph nodes and many of the nerves altogether if we do not know to look for them. On the other hand, if we have a general model we have a tentative map and some idea of the relationship between the various organs. It makes it much easier to recognize and understand what we are seeing. This does not mean all organisms are the same and that we can skip the details of how they differ, but it does mean that we have a perspective that guides our analyses. A map of the organs, however, does not by itself tell us how everything works, enable us to diagnose a particular disease, or spell out its prognosis.

To shift to a sociological example, Weber's famous ideal-type models of classes, parties, and status groups are not primarily causal models. These categories enable us to see similarities and differences across cases. The status groups associated with European aristocracies are not the same as those of the Indian caste system or American teenage peer groups, but Weber's model helps us to see similarities and differences across these cases. That is a key purpose of the model I am suggesting.

Particular historical circumstances and cultural traditions will determine (1) whether all of the categories are fully differentiated or sub-differentiated, (2) the relative importance of categories (e.g., which categories are dominant or degraded), (3) the elaboration and importance of particular segments within a category (e.g., priest vs. prophets, or the emergence of celebrities) and (4) how changes in one category affect power relations with the other categories as well as within these categories. Finally, the model allows the analyst to acknowledge that the arenas within which different types of power and elites operate may vary. Through global markets many contemporary economic elites may impact extensive parts of the world; the influence of most political elites is usually restricted to smaller areas. Some celebrities are of international renown; most are known primarily in particular cultures or subcultures.

The consequences that result from these common dilemmas and contradictions are not simply the result of the factors that this model identifies, but also of exogenous and intervening variables. (These notions are discussed in more detail in the Appendix.) It is the combination of the typology and the specification of such variables that can lead to useful hypotheses. Some of these exogenous variables are near world-wide processes that are affecting many, if not most, societies. Examples include technological innovations such as the cell phone and the worldwide web; ideological innovations such as the human rights movement; and the recognition of certain physical and social trends such as global warming. Others are rooted in the specific history and past experience of much more limited groups of people, as well as specific concrete decisions that are made by both elites and non-elites. For example, the decision of the George W. Bush administration to go to war in Iraq was not simply the consequence of universal exogenous variables or the general tendencies that are identified by the model of elites and non-elites. Rather, it was rooted in the dilemmas identified by the proposed model *and* by the particular history of the U.S. and the choices made by the leaders who were in power at the time. In other words, the model is a lens that is helpful in identifying common tendencies; it is not a substitute for more detailed historical and social analysis. It is intended as a useful way to begin our studies, not a way to end them. The aim is to provide enough theory to guide research and more parsimoniously organize findings, but not so much that we misapprehend and misrepresent the social reality that we seek to understand.

What is to Follow

The next three chapters use the model to provide an analysis of the three cases: pre-modern India, ancient Classical Athens, and the contemporary U.S. A word is needed about the reason for choosing these disparate cases. They vary greatly with respect to the *nature of the unit of analysis*. The units of analysis vary with respect to (1) the time period considered, (2) the geographical location, (3) the culture and its traditions, and (4) the abstractness of the phenomena analyzed. In India I focus on an abstract, but deeply institutionalized cultural model and ideology that emphasized hierarchy, and helped sustain a caste system for probably 3,000 years, and deeply penetrated the culture in a variety of ways. In ancient Classical Athens I identify the key social categories and relationships that created and sustained a radical form of direct democracy for approximately 200 years, and contributed to accomplishments in art, drama, and philosophy that continue to shape much of Western civilization. For the contemporary U.S. I look at much more concrete structures and events from approximately 1980 to 2008, and then more briefly at the financial crisis of 2007–8. That is to say, I have deliberately chosen cases where there are significant differences in the units of analysis.

These societies also vary with respect to which *type of elite is culturally dominant*: status elites in pre-modern India, political elites in Classical Athens, and economic elites in the contemporary U.S. These variations in the time spans, the units of analysis, and who is dominant are intended to demonstrate the usefulness and flexibility of the model. If it is a "general model," then it is important to use it to analyze a wide range of variation in the types of societies.[32]

Finally, it must be acknowledged that this model, like all theories, simplifies and leaves out much that actual humans experience. The crucial question for any theoretical concept or model is not whether it fully grasps social life. Rather, the test is whether the simplifications it proposes are more adequate and more useful than our previous perspectives.

3

Traditional India:
the Varna Scheme[1]

Traditionally, Indian society is divided into four main castes. At the top Brahmins, as priests and teachers; second came the Kshatriyas, the warriors and rulers; third, Vaishyas, who were merchants; last, Shudras, the laborers.

Lavana Sankarn, *New York Times*, June 16, 2013

Introduction

The above description of Indian society is by a highly respected Indian short story writer and novelist in a relatively recent opinion essay. She is from Bangalore, the center of India's high-tech industries. She notes, "Caste is not a word that modernizing India likes to use. It has receded into the unfashionable background." She goes on to argue that instead of being associated with occupation or even wealth it is now associated with marriage partners and politics. The first is a traditional pattern, the second is new. She says, "Indians, it turns out, are passionate about the caste of their politicians. Nearly half of the voting population of even a highly educated city like Bangalore considers caste to be the No. 1 reason to vote for a candidate." So while caste is still relevant in India and has maintained some of its traditional features, it is also changing significantly. Yet when she starts to explain the nature of the caste system, she begins with a description of the traditional varna scheme of four categories. This scheme is described in ancient Vedas, which are usually dated c. 1500–900 B.C.E., and hence are at least 3,000 years old.

According to some scholars, the varna scheme may not have initially referred to a caste system per se (Habib 1995: 165). It is, however, clear that it does refer to such a system by the time of the "Laws of Manu" (*Manusmriti*), which is usually dated between 600 B.C.E. and 200 C.E. This means that the varna scheme has been used to describe and legitimate the caste system for at least 2,000 years and probably much longer – even if it has not been a very accurate description of the actual organization of castes.

There have been numerous languages, religions, and kingdoms that have come and gone during that period. Nonetheless, there has been a caste system throughout most of this period, and it is generally recognized as the signature institution of India.[2] While it has certainly changed over time, there is a recognizable continuity between the earliest descriptions of the system and the contemporary structures.

The varna scheme has served as the longtime ideological foundation of the caste system. As the opening quotation indicates, it contains four categories: Brahmins who are priests and teachers, Kshatriyas who are warriors and rulers, Vaisyas who are farmers, merchants, and artisans, and Shudra who are laborers and servants. Varnas are not actual social groups, but rather categories of groups.[3] The actual social organization of most villages was based on *jatis*, usually translated as "castes." These are actual networks of families that would intermarry and were usually identified with a particular occupation – though individuals might or might not perform their traditional occupation. There are hundreds, perhaps thousands, of different jatis scattered over India and often a dozen or more in any local area. Jatis are usually identified as being associated with one of the four varnas. This is analogous to the relationship between the notions of upper, middle, and lower class to the myriad of occupational categories or gradations of wealth.

Stated another way, the varna scheme has been the India-wide ideological blueprint of the Indian caste system. People in one region may not be familiar with the names and relative ranks of jatis in another region, but if the jati is categorized as belonging to a particular varna, this gives a rough approximation of the likely status and lifestyle of that jati. Less obvious, but equally important, the varna scheme also serves as a model for the categories used to understand a wide array of other things, including the classification of gods, space, time, and flora and fauna (Smith 1994). For example, different gods, seasons, and body parts are associated with particular varnas. Hence, the varna scheme shapes the very categories that Hindus have to make sense of the world around them.

Change and Stability of Ideological Models

"Ideological model" refers to a reasonably systematic idealized description of a particular social reality and how it is "supposed to" work. Some of the places such models are found include folk tales, religious and philosophical texts, and legal documents. Examples of such ideological schemes include the Chinese "four occupations," probably created by Confucian gentry around the second century B.C.E., the medieval European concept of the "three estates" of clergy, nobility, and peasants, and the European doctrine of the divine right of kings in the sixteenth and seventeenth centuries.[4] A more modern example is the notion of equality of opportunity, which is core to the notion of the "American dream."[5] Examples of more formal ideological models include the U.S. Constitution, the Declaration of the Rights of Man and the Citizen of the French Revolution, the charters of corporations, and the constitution and by-laws of voluntary associations. An emerging model is the notion of human rights, formalized in the U.N. Universal Declaration of Human Rights; many regimes fail to live up to this model, but very few if any publicly reject the legitimacy of some notion of human rights.[6] Such ideological models are primarily an element of culture rather that the social structure. Human rights are in the process of becoming institutionalized. The other cultural models that I have mentioned have for the most part been deeply institutionalized and hence tend to be much more stable than the actual social structure. This is not, of course, to argue that they were uncontested or do not change or that all elements of such models are taken-for-granted.

Ideological models usually limit the range of behaviors that are considered acceptable. They vary in the degree they attempt to bias the distribution of power and privilege. The doctrine of the divine right of kings was more biased than the Declaration of the Rights of Man – which is not to say the latter had no biases. Social units vary in how closely their behavior matches the ideological model. The government of the Soviet Union departed from its constitution more than was the case in the United States – which again is not to say that the latter always conformed to its constitution.

Such models also vary in how old they are and how long they continue to be relevant. The modern concept of equality of opportunity is relatively new; according to the *Oxford English Dictionary*, the first known use of the phrase "equality of opportunity" was in 1891. The doctrine of the divine right of kings had many antecedents, but as an articulated doctrine relevant to European politics it lasted less than 200 years. The U.S. Constitution has lasted about two and a quarter centuries.

In contrast, the Indian varna scheme has served as an important ideological model for at least 2,500 years. Such longevity and pervasiveness certainly call for analysis and explanation.

Exogenous Variables

By exogenous variables I mean those characteristics that are not part of the model that I will outline. They are likely to affect the characteristics of the model or in combination with the factors in the model are likely to have a significant impact on historical outcomes. Since parsimony is desirable, I will introduce only four exogenous characteristics relevant to India. The first is ecological, the second about the economic mode of production, the third about the nature of politics, and the fourth about the culture and ideology of Brahminism.

1. **Terrain and climate:** The bulk of the population was located along alluvial plains of significant rivers in a semi-tropical climate.
2. **Agrarian society:** For the period of concern, India has been primarily an agrarian society, and the base of economic activity was plow agriculture with cereal grains being the most significant crop.[7]
3. **War lords and honor:** As in most agrarian societies, war lords were very important, with the most successful ones becoming kings of various kinds. Honor, which is a particular form of status, and deference toward those with high status were very important.
4. **Brahminism:** Brahmins maintained an ideological visibility, and during most periods an ideological dominance, for approximately 3,000 years, with three consequences:
    a. They formulated the varna scheme that was their conception of the proper composition and role of elites and non-elites.
    b. According to this formulation Brahmins where to eschew political power.
    c. They institutionalized an unusually strong cultural emphasis on status based upon ritual purity and the importance of following the *dharma* (i.e., law, way of life) of the caste into which one was born.

Like most agrarian societies, it assumed gender inequality and patriarchy. The ecological, economic, and political factors are not particularly unique to India. What is distinctive is the emphasis on status and the *intensity* of the ideology of hierarchy linked to notions of purity and impurity and the importance of each social group following its particular way of life, that is, their *dharma* (Dumont 1980).[8]

The varna scheme is the idealized Brahminical view of how Indian society is "supposed to be" organized, downplaying crucial contradictions, conflicts and tensions. There is disagreement about the extent to which Indian society was ever actually organized in the prescribed fashion. There is no doubt, however, that this scheme has been an important part of Indian culture since the first millennium B.C.E. and that it has shaped Indian society in a number of ways.[9]

Now let us consider in more detail the various categories of the varna scheme.

Status/Cultural/Ideological Elites: Brahmins

In the terms of the general model, Brahmins are the status/cultural/ideological elites. Between the Aryans' arrival in India (second millennium B.C.E.) and what is often called the Brahminical synthesis (200 B.C.E.– 900 C.E.) represented in the Dharmasastras, the Brahmins made ritual status the core of their identity and the fundamental basis of their power. Violence and physical labor were viewed as degrading, and thus compromised their religious purity. Accordingly, they formally assigned political and military power and economic activity to other varnas.[10] Brahmins did, however, own land, often participated in the rule of the various kingdoms, and on occasion even became warriors. But their genius was to avoid making the control of land and labor, or the control of force – which are intimately related in agrarian societies – the primary basis of their power. For these are the resources that are most alienable and hence easily appropriated by outside conquerors or upstart discontents and, in India's long and complex history, frequently were. In contrast, the highly elaborated lifestyle, emphasizing among other things ritual purity, was nearly impossible for outsiders to copy or appropriate.

In addition to making ritual status the fundamental basis of their power, the Brahmins had another genius: they rejected the notion that ritual purity required renunciation and life-long otherworldliness. While they adopted many of the characteristics of ascetic renouncers (*sannyasins*), the key actor and most central social role in the Brahminical synthesis was the married householder. This enabled the Brahmin to combine legitimately in one social position the power of the exemplary religious life and still participate actively in the worldly affairs of an agrarian society. Moreover, they could biologically and socially reproduce themselves, and hence outsiders did not have to be recruited to a monastic order or a special "calling." It also geographically dispersed the religious elite and made them an integral part of the agrarian infrastructure. Consequently, conquerors who might be motivated to destroy these religious elites could not do so without the risk of disrupting the agrarian infrastructure that provided taxes and other crucial resources. In contrast, more monastic religions in India, such as Buddhism, had greater vulnerability (and were largely exterminated). As priests, Brahmins could demand gifts. At the same time they could become landholders and hence not be solely dependent on the petty gifts of the masses.

In short, the genius of the Brahmins was combining a highly regulated and esoteric lifestyle, which gave them a relatively inalienable religious status, with a legitimate opportunity for many of their members to have substantial local control over the crucial resources in an agrarian society – land and labor. They were not usually the dominant economic and political group, but they maintained a cultural prominence, and in most periods and locales a cultural dominance, for much of 3,000 years. Nonetheless, the Brahmins' social identity is full of difficulties. Relegating force and secular power to others meant that their relationship with those who wielded such power was often problematic. Relationships with inferiors are also potentially corrupting. Unsurprisingly, the Brahmins' sense of religious superiority, frequent disdain toward the worldly tasks of others, and their dependence on others for protection and labor were all rich sources of potential conflict.

Let us now consider the other key social identities, focusing on their relationship to Brahmins.

Political Elites: Kshatriyas

This is the varna of warriors, rulers, and kings. The Brahmins' dilemma was how to translate their religious status into other resources, including wealth, without undercutting their religious status – the fundamental basis of their power. The king's dilemma was how to become associated with the religious elite so that their status and rituals legitimize his political power without either becoming too dependent upon the religious elite or having to reward them too handsomely. Brahmins were, however, ambivalent about entering into such associations because it compromised their purity. Yet, most Brahmins did not completely shun associations with land controllers and kings. Nor was the Brahmin the only possible source of legitimacy for the Indian king, and he could, and on occasion did, decide to abandon Brahmins for other religious elites such as Buddhist monks. Hence the Brahmin and the Kshatriya are involved in a relationship that is usually vital to both and yet full of contradictions, and various kinds of conflict were frequent.[11]

Economic Elites: Vaisyas – the Anomalous Category

Vaisyas are the third "twice-born" varna, which means those who are allowed to study the sacred texts known as the Vedas – Shudras and Untouchables supposedly are not. Compared to the other varna distinctions, the Vaisya category is ambiguous and anomalous. First, the older sacred texts suggest that a large portion, if not most, of the population fall into this category, yet for hundreds of years it has been the varna category that contained the smallest number of people. Second, while in the early stages of Indian (Vedic) society most Vaisyas must have been farmers or herders, for at least 1,000 years the category has referred primarily to merchant castes. Third, even in pre-modern India many of those engaged in trading and commercial activity belonged to other varnas. These are anomalies within the culture itself. In addition, on the analytical level the fit between the general model's category of economic elites and category of Vaisyas is not very good; clearly in an agrarian society those who control land and agricultural labor must be considered part of the economic elite.

In agrarian societies, the main economic activity is agricultural production and this is controlled primarily by local political elites; land and crops are inherently dispersed and difficult to secure and defend. Pure economic elites develop only for those commodities and services that are relatively easy to concentrate and defend, or in areas where peace and order are reasonably secure. Moreover, since anyone can acquire physical commodities, it is relatively easy for caste groups who are not traditionally Vaisyas to undertake such economic activity when conditions are favorable. Hence, we would expect the referent of the category Vaisya to be relatively ambiguous compared to political and religious elites. As already indicated, in modern India this category is usually thought of as referring primarily to some (but not all) of the merchant castes.

Alternative modes of production: right and left castes

Our general model argues that usually there is at least an implicit or latent differentiation within economic elites based on alternative modes of production – and a set of categories to represent this. As we have just seen, over time the category of Vaisya has shifted from referring primarily to the producers of agricultural products to merchant castes – probably indicating the increasing importance of this alternative form of production. There is, however, another historic indigenous distinction that indicates tension between those associated with alternative modes of production, that is, the difference between right (*valangai*) and left (*idangai*) castes in South India. (The contrast between right and left is obviously used in many societies and symbolizes a variety of social differentiations and concerns.)

In South India, right castes were nearly always the local controllers of land and the castes that were closely allied with or dependent upon them. Left castes were typically artisan and merchant castes and others who engaged in various exchanges with the dominant land controllers and their dependents, but were less subject to their direct authority. In addition to differences in economic activity and local alliances, dissimilarities in lifestyle and status criteria are apparent. Right castes admired the ability to associate with and dominate others. They often followed a diminutive version of a kingly model of status. Left castes showed a reluctance to be associated with anyone other than their immediate family members and rarely sought to directly dominate others outside of their family. Even if they were wealthy, their demeanor was restrained and controlled. Tendencies toward asceticism, vegetarianism, and unorthodox religion were common.

In North India, the categories of right and left are more ambiguous and were never explicit but these distinctions seem latent. As Brenda Beck notes, "throughout the subcontinent the artisan communities have attempted to counteract the power of the landed castes with the assertion of superior status on the grounds of the exclusiveness of their caste customs and the orthodoxy of their ritual" (1973: 402). In addition, throughout northern India merchant castes were often relative outsiders in the place they lived and were thought to have originated in some other specific region. They were roughly equivalent to the Armenian, Jewish, and Lebanese merchants so common in many parts of the world.

In short, the left and right distinction seems to have been primarily rooted in alternative modes of production, which were then often intertwined with other bases of conflict such as sectarian religious disputes. This is what our general model of elites would predict and parallel phenomena are seen in many societies. For example, Weber famously argued that the ascetic lifestyle of Protestant merchants, in contrast to the ethic of conspicuous consumption of the nobility, contributed to the emergence of bourgeois capitalism. So the contrast between left and right caste illustrates the tensions that are common between groups who are engaged in different modes of production. Hence the ambiguity and changing meaning of the category of Vaisyas reflects the tensions between alternative modes of production.

Non-elites: Shudras

Some scholars have suggested that originally those classified as Shudras were the indigenous populations that were conquered by the invading Aryans, but the evidence for this is sketchy.[12] Whatever the origin of Shudras, twice-born castes and especially Brahmins could not have led exemplary religious lives, requiring high levels of ritual activity, if they had to be self-sufficient in an agrarian society. The solution was to create a class of laborers and servants to relieve them of the onerous aspects of production. This is one of the key roles of Shudras. Brahmins stabilized the availability of this labor by enlisting the ruler's support in the demands for such service, and by providing ritual services to at least the higher-status Shudras. Yet this makes the Brahmins more dependent upon the ruler, involves them in the morally ambiguous exercise of power and domination, and brings them into regular contact with those who are less pure. In short, the exemplary lifestyle requires appropriating the labor of others, but, ironically, this involves Brahmins in relationships that undercut their purity.

Missing Categories

One of the purposes of the general model I have proposed is to point out the lacuna that exists in previous models – both the models of modern social theorists and indigenous models such as the varna scheme or the Confucian "four occupations." The varna scheme has only four categories, but the general model I have proposed has eight categories. Does this mean that the general model is not useful in understanding the varna scheme and hence traditional Indian society? I will argue that the opposite is the case: as we shall see the "missing" categories have in fact long been present in Indian culture and important in understanding that culture. Moreover, the general model brings this to our attention and helps better understand both the varna scheme and Indian culture. Now let us consider categories of the general model that seem to be missing.

Prophets: renouncers

"Renouncers" refers to individuals who have withdrawn from conventional society and are ascetic mendicants who in principle give up all their possessions, are celibate, and beg for their food; the most ascetic also go naked. Women can also become renouncers, but this is less common. They may or may not be members of various monastic orders or networks. If they are members, they are often referred to as "swami." Many gurus, who are usually teachers and are founders or leaders of particular religious movements, are renouncers. Since Louis Dumont's essay on renouncers, it has generally been conceded that they constitute a crucial social category for understanding traditional Indian social structure and culture (1980: App. B). In India, the highest religious status went to renouncers: those who gave up worldly comforts and security in their quest for salvation. Any involvement with worldly life is considered an impediment to salvation. Hence, household priest (*purhoit*) or temple priest (*pujari*) are compromised because priestly activity necessarily involves mediating between the sacred and the profane and hence decreases the purity of the mediator. In contrast, the Brahmin pundit scholar has a higher status, in part, because he has the least contact with the conventional world and more closely resembles the renouncer.

Brahmins have had a highly ambivalent relationship to renunciation. Their strongest competitors for religious status were the renouncers and monks of Buddhism, Jainism, and numerous other anti-Brahminical movements. Yet, ideally all Brahmins should, in the fourth and last stage (*asrama*) of life, become renouncers (*sannyasa*). This is so because being tied to this world – as householders necessarily are – is detrimental to one's spiritual well-being. The great dilemma for the Brahmins has been how to create a lifestyle that gives them religious virtue comparable to the renouncer's, without becoming asocial and otherworldly like these competitors. The austere and otherworldly life of the renouncers has been both a serious competitive threat to Brahmins and a source of much of their creativity and capacity for religious renewal. Of course, there are renouncers that are, and are perceived to be, charlatans, just as there are immoral priests and superficial intellectuals. This does not, however, void the social and cultural significance of the category.

Obviously, Hindu renouncers are in many ways different from Hebrew prophets, but what they have in common is that they offer a rejection of, and severe critique of, existing conventional life.

The disreputable: untouchables

I should begin by making clear that "Untouchable" is a Western term used in colonial India for a variety of outcaste groups.[13] In contemporary India many of these groups have adopted the name Dalits and strongly reject any notion of their religious or social inferiority. I use the old-fashioned term "Untouchable" because this analysis is not about contemporary India, but rather a central element of pre-modern Indian culture – and it is the term most non-Indians recognize as referring to Indian outcast groups.

While the classical texts are full of references to "Untouchables," this category is not part of the varna scheme. Yet, like renouncers, they were a crucial structural category in the Indian social structure for thousands of years. Why has this been the case? First, because of the relative inexpansibility of status, the extraordinary purity and status of the Brahmins is in part due to the extraordinary impurity of the Untouchables. For some to be pure, others must deal with the excrement, waste, and dead bodies that are an inextricable part of live organisms. Second, the poorest of the poor must often subsist on substances that others consider impure. Third, like all pariah groups, the existence of Untouchables both raised the social status of Shudras and warned them that things could be far worse. Though many Shudras competed with Untouchables for employment as laborers, they were not inclined to identify with the lifestyle of those who were closest to them in the mode of production. There were very real, tangible advantages to being even a landless Shudra as compared to being an Untouchable. Just as the renouncers were both a crucial and yet "unofficial" and implicit part of the varna scheme, so were Untouchables. All of this is suggested by and compatible with the general model.

Bandits: dacoits

Robbery and other forms of thievery are present throughout Indian history and are discussed in many of both the earliest and latest religious texts. Theft involving violence (*sahasa*) was considered especially reprehensible.[14] As Das (1977: 14–15) reports:

> A study of the Vedic literature reveals that from a very early period Indians were disturbed by the ... activities of thieves and robbers. The *Rig Veda* made specific mention of thieves (*Tayu* or *Stayas*) and robbers (*Taskaras*). The harmful activities of thieves and robbers are also reflected in the *Mahabharata*. From the works of the early law givers it is clear that the activities of these criminals affected the society in such a way that people considered them major evils of the society and wanted to get rid of them.

Robbery and banditry have been an important cultural category throughout Indian history.[15] It is noteworthy that Buddhist and Jain sources, many of which are critical of Hinduism, probably discuss this more than the "official" Brahmin sources.[16]

The category of robber or bandit is not, however, part of the varna scheme. Nonetheless, it is an integral element in the system of categories, which identifies key actors in this culture. The bandit is significant both because he threatens the conventional social order, and because he has the potential to transform himself into a king, the chief guarantor of that order. The bandit, however, need not be concerned with anything other than force and extortion – until he wishes to be king.

The distinguishing characteristic of the king and the legitimate warrior is that he upholds the law (*dharma*) and honors the gods. As in most societies, this is what distinguishes the king (and his various agents such as the police) from the bandit. Nonetheless, Indian culture recognizes the ambiguity of the distinction; the king or the police are always in danger of degenerating into the bandit. In traditional India and many parts of even contemporary India, people have been very reluctant to call on the police because they think that it is as likely to lead to some form of extortion as it is to result in meaningful assistance. On the other hand, the bandit has the potential to become a ruler, and this is precisely the intent of some of the armed guerilla groups in contemporary India.

In sum, renouncers, Untouchables, and bandits are the potential antagonists of Brahmins, Shudras, and Kshatriyas respectively, but they are also their alter egos. Many of the dynamics and conflicts of pre-modern Indian culture (and contemporary India) resulted from the inherent internal contradictions of these key cultural categories.

Prominent Categories – Brahmins, Holy Men, and Untouchables

One of the assumptions of the general model is that in varying historical periods and cultures the relative importance of different types of resources and power may vary. Such variations help explain why some categories of elites and non-elites have higher visibility than others in a given historical setting.

I have argued that most complex societies have some equivalent of priests, prophets (or renouncers), and at least quasi-outcasts, but these categories are especially prominent in Indian culture. If you ask either foreigners or Indians what social categories are most distinctly Indian, the answer would not be bandits, merchants, farmers or kings. Nor are the non-Brahmin categories of the varna scheme likely to be mentioned. What India is "famous for" are Brahmins, holy men, and Untouchables.[17] The pivotal role of Brahmins has already been discussed. In India, the role of renouncer-guru is highly visible and the traditions of renunciation have greatly elaborated the techniques and importance of asceticism. (It is not accidental that many Westerners have gone to India to learn relatively ascetic modes of meditation and spirituality, nor that Indian gurus have developed extensive followings in many Western societies.) Highly degraded groups are present in many societies, but nowhere else has the rejection and control of such groups been so dependent upon the creation of negative social status. Slave societies and modern concentration camps were more brutal. But nowhere else has such an extensive and indispensable outcast group developed whose forms of exclusion and inclusion were so dependent upon ritual status. It is not accidental that India's lower social strata were "outcasts" excluded from religious temples, rather than prisoners, slaves, paupers, or the unemployed. In short, the greater salience – relative to other societies – of these three social categories was rooted in the unique importance of status as a source of power and powerlessness.

In sum, many of the key categories of Hindu culture make sense when placed in the context of a general model of elites–non-elites. These categories and relationships are summarized in Figure 2. While I have not

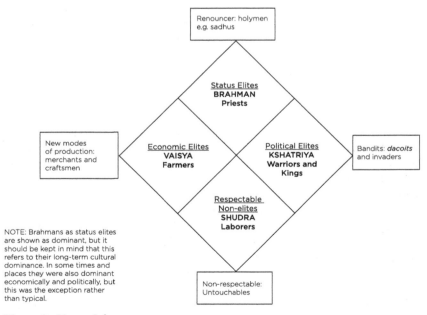

NOTE: Brahmans as status elites are shown as dominant, but it should be kept in mind that this refers to their long-term cultural dominance. In some times and places they were also dominant economically and politically, but this was the exception rather than typical.

Figure 2: Varna Scheme

systematically dealt with contemporary India, some of the same dynamics can be seen there.

Some caveats

The ideological dominance and centrality of the varna scheme and the relative power of status of its various categories have almost certainly varied in different historical periods and across different regions and subgroups. I have not attempted to explain such variations and it is doubtful that our present levels of empirical knowledge make possible any kind of sustained or systematic description and analysis of these historical variations. Recognizing these qualifications does not negate the assertion that the cultural dominance of the Brahmins for over 3,000 years, and the role of the varna scheme in legitimating that dominance, is an extraordinary social fact that needs to be explained.

Comparison with Other Models

What are the advantages of the general model I have proposed over earlier sociological models? To make a start on answering this question, I will compare the proposed general model to two of the alternatives, Marxism and Bourdieu.

Comparison with Marxism

During much of the twentieth century Marxism was the predominant perspective among Indian intellectuals including historians of Ancient India. While those sympathetic to Marxism produced some fine studies, Marxian models tend to reduce caste to class and to see notions of pollution, karma, etc., as a ruling-class ideology that perpetuates false consciousness among the disadvantaged. There are plenty of historical instances of resistance to Brahmin dominance throughout Indian history, yet the caste system has persisted. And how is it that contemporary writers still use the varna scheme to describe and explain castes, even though it has long been empirically inaccurate? Of course caste and class tend to be correlated, but reducing the former to the latter is too simple a model that fails to explain the cultural prominence of renouncers, Brahmins, and Untouchables – much less the persistence of the system over at least 2,500 hundred years.

I will illustrate both the strength and weaknesses of the Marxian model by focusing on the analysis of caste by one of India's most renowned Marxian historians, Irfan Habib (1995). He begins his analysis by a critique of Louis Dumont's explanation of caste in *Homo Hierarchicus* (1980). Habib points out – rightfully in my opinion – that Dumont's focus on the ideology of purity and impurity lapses into a kind of cultural essentialism that largely ignores the material and economic elements of the caste system.

On the other hand, Habib tends to reduce caste to class exploitation by pointing to a series of historical developments that supposedly explain the emergence of castes. These include the shift from herding to agrarian agriculture, the related increase in "labor surplus" that makes possible an increased division of labor, which Habib sees as the basis of the varna scheme – rather than notions of hierarchy and purity. He sees the caste system as largely the result of incorporating various tribes – tribe is one meaning of *jati* – into a broader dominant society. He sees the incorporation of the even less developed hunting and gathering societies as the origin of those who became known as Untouchables. The development of craft and service caste such as blacksmiths, weavers, and barbers is rooted in another round of the increasing division of labor. He mentions several other developments, but his conclusion is, "The caste system, in its classic form, could therefore function as much in a natural economy as in a market-oriented one. In either case it helped essentially to maintain not a fabric of imagined purity (if it did this it was incidental), but a system of class exploitation as rigorous as any other" (1995: 172). Habib's Marxian analysis is the mirror image of Dumont's – both are erudite and sophisticated analyses, but they seem determined to leave out or de-emphasize what the other sees.

A key problem with Habib's argument, and most other Marxist analyses of castes, is that the processes they identify are characteristic of the stages of development of many societies; the emergence of plow agriculture, increased surpluses, and a greater division of labor was hardly unique to India. Yet, nowhere else in the world did there develop anything approaching the scope and intensity of social separation, endogamy, commensality, and an aversion to what were seen as impure substances; this cannot be understood simply as a matter of disguised economic and political power.

Marxists also tend to be dismissive of the varna scheme as either an irrelevant historical anachronism or obfuscating Brahmin ideology. This, however, fails to explain why the varna scheme is still a well-known cultural model after more than 3,000 years.

Comparison with Bourdieu

Unlike most forms of Marxism, Bourdieu recognizes that culture and ideology are not only ways to disguise economic and political power. They are sources of power in their own right, even though the actors may misrecognize that these are forms of dominance.[18] His strong emphasis on the reproduction of social and cultural capital through habitus and doxa offers insights into how the caste system has sustained itself across history. He does not, however, *systematically* suggest the forms of differentiation that are likely to occur within each type of elite and within non-elites, or the most likely forms of conflict and cooperation between such subcategories. He emphasizes the importance of cultural capital and style, but does not explain the strong emphasis on endogamy, commensality, and purity. Nor does he offer any particular insights into why the varna scheme continues to be used to describe and explain caste, even though it has been empirically inaccurate for at least 2,000 years.

The proposed general model

To begin with, my general model offers an explanation of why the varna scheme has remained culturally import for so long, despite its inaccuracy. The varna scheme is a deep structure of Indian culture not only because it is an ancient model for the Indian caste system and associated with Hinduism's most sacred texts, but also because it has served as a model for so many other forms of classification from gods to plants. There is, however, another level of deep structure. Instead of dismissing the varna scheme as an anachronistic relic as Marxists tend to do, or explaining its persistence by reference to the intergenerational transmission of habitus as Bourdieu's theory would suggest, I want to suggest an alternative hypothesis: the varna scheme is a version of the very general set of social categories and relationships that the proposed general model identifies. It is a version of the genera model that has been "edited" by Brahmins to downplay or ignore potential competitors and dissidents. When the actual social categories used in Indian society are identified, it becomes apparent that these "missing categories" are also relevant. Stated another way, the general model identifies a "deep structure" of power relationships, and the varna scheme is a particular cultural version of this deep structure. None of this is to deny that the varna scheme was also an ideological tool that dominant elites used to perpetuate their power and privileges. Nor am I claiming that historical outcomes are completely determined by such deep structures.

Second, the proposed model takes status power seriously in a way that Marxism does not. It does this without making the metaphor of capital theoretically central, as Bourdieu does; capital is at best an analogy when we are talking about a form of power that was used centuries before capitalism emerged.[19] Nor does my model commit one to Bourdieu's arguments that all forms of power and exchange are really misrecognized "economic" relations in a broader sense than that used by economists. Moreover, Bourdieu's theorizing offers no particular hypotheses or insights about the most striking characteristics of the caste system: highly restricted mobility, endogamy, and commensality. Instead, the general model, supplemented with the theory of status relations, suggests parsimonious explanations – without resorting to the kind of cultural essentialism that is characteristic of Dumont's arguments.

Conclusion

The key ideological categories that were used in Egypt, Mesopotamia, China, and Mesoamerica 3,000 years ago are often not known, much less used, by people in the contemporary societies located in these regions. Yet, many contemporary Indians are familiar with the varna scheme.

How is this to be explained? First, traditional India is close to unique in the centrality of status based on religious purity as a form of inequality and stratification. Since status is relatively inalienable, well-institutionalized status systems tend to be relatively stable and resistant to change. Second, there were no major changes in the predominant economic modes of production and the political modes of coercion. When India became politically independent in 1947, plows pulled by bullocks formed the most common mode of production; kings and their courts ruled many areas of the country – which is not to deny that there were many changes, especially in the nineteenth and twentieth centuries. This relative stability of economic and political forms of power, *wedded with* the centrality of status as a form of power, helps to account for the stability of the varna scheme. Third, the varna scheme was not only a set of categories relevant to caste, but was a "deep structure" of the culture that was used to categorize a wide array of social, material, and spiritual phenomena. Fourth, the varna scheme is a particular cultural version of the set of categories and relationships present in most complex societies.

In the last 50 years there have been dramatic changes in the first three of the factors mentioned above. While notions of hierarchy are still deeply entrenched in Indian culture, the nature and significance of the caste system have been significantly transformed, though the system has not disappeared. I suspect that in 100 years the categories of the varna scheme may be as anachronistic in India as the notions of lord and serf are to contemporary Europe – but that analogs of the categories of the general model will be present.

Having looked at how the general model can be useful in analyzing and systematically organizing the social categories of a very ancient culture whose ideology emphasized hierarchy, we now turn to an ancient society most noted for emphasizing equality and democracy.

4

Athens in the Classical Period

Introduction

If India is "famous for" holy men, Brahmins, and Untouchables, and certain forms of cultural stability, we now turn to an ancient society that is famous for democracy, for drama and philosophy, for slavery, and for dramatic changes during its ancient past. I refer to Athens during the fifth and fourth centuries B.C. I choose to contrast ancient Greece with ancient India because these are often seen as significantly different societies and cultures. Greece has long been considered the seedbed or cradle of Western civilization. In contrast, India is seen as decidedly "the East," the home of the non-Abrahamic religions of Hinduism, Buddhism, Jainism, and Sikhism. My point is that Athenian Greece and India are contrasting and perhaps polar cases, in the ancient world.[1] The application of the model to such varying cases provides a more rigorous test of its utility than if it were applied to more similar societies.

The analysis of the varna scheme focused on a longstanding cultural model and ideology that was used across 3,000 years by diverse subcultures in India; except for a few comments about recent changes, I did not attempt to analyze a more specific time and place or the many empirical versions or deviations from this scheme.

The following analysis is relatively speaking more specific and concrete; it focuses on Athens in what has come to be called the classical period. This is often dated from the establishment of democracy under Cleisthenes in 508 B.C. to 322 B.C. when Athens and her allies were defeated by the Macedonians at the Battle of Crannon.[2] These 186 years are, of course, an extended time period, but with the exception of two brief oligarchic coups in 411 B.C. and 403 B.C., democratic Athenian society was relatively stable.[3] It is this period for which I will provide an ideal-typical description guided by the general model of elites and non-elites. But if the period that is our focus was relatively stable, it was nonetheless a striking departure from previous and subsequent societies, for it was during this period that history's most radical form of popular direct democracy was created and sustained for nearly 200 years. It has never since been replicated for any extended period, and it was another 2,000 years before modern representative democracy would emerge. Hence, if our general model can help us to organize the data about this society in this period – which differs so much from traditional India – then this is further evidence of the model's potential generality. Before applying the model to this case, a few basic facts about Classical Athens are required.[4]

Athens refers not just to the city, but to the surrounding district of Attica, which was about the size of Luxembourg. Reliable data about population is limited, but estimates of the total population range between 100,000 and 400,000.[5] Of these, approximately 20,000–50,000 were adult male citizens who could participate in the Assembly (*ecclesia*) and its political decisions (Ober 1989: 128; Raaflaub 2007: 98). The wealthy leisure class was approximately 1,200–2,000 citizens plus their families, totaling perhaps 4,800–8,000 persons (Ober 1989: 128). There were at least 50,000 slaves (Patterson 2007: 156) and perhaps double that number. The number of resident aliens (*metics*) was probably between 20,000 and 60,000 with about half being ex-slaves, usually of foreign origin, while the other half were voluntary immigrants.

In addition to Attica, Athens in effect established an empire in the eastern Mediterranean. Initially this was through the Delian League, which was an alliance of more than 150 city-states, formed in 477 B.C. to resist Persian invasions. In part by creating a powerful navy, Athens became the hegemonic power within the League. She often demanded tribute and favorable trading terms and these significantly contributed to Athens' prosperity.

Exogenous Variables

1. **Ecology and Resulting Social Units:** A terrain suitable mainly for dry-land agriculture that was composed of numerous valleys divided

by rugged mountains and hills, but had easy access to the sea, and, in the case of Athens, the sheltered harbors of Piraeus. The ecological setting did not determine, but tended to encourage, relatively local solidarities and city-states, rather than more expansive land-based kingdoms such as those in Egypt and Mesopotamia.[6]

2. **Political and Military**: The ecological setting and local solidarities meant that hoplite infantry, which required relatively inexpensive equipment and extensive non-elite participation and solidarity, was often more effective than cavalry units, which were expensive, and generally the weapons of the rich. (This is not to say that the Athenians and other Greeks did not use cavalry, but only that this mode of fighting was less central than in many other societies.) In part because the rich did not have to invest as heavily in cavalry, they could and did use private and public resources to invest in a powerful navy that was the basis of its empire.

3. **Economic**: Because of its success in establishing an empire that brought significant tribute from client regions, its ability to acquire and utilize large numbers of slaves, and its silver mines in Laurium, Athens was quite prosperous. Hence, without significantly diminishing the wealth of the elite, its citizens could afford to participate in the Assembly and the other institutions of popular democracy (Osborne 2010: chap. 5; Sinclair 1988: chap. 1).

4. **Cultural**: In the warrior societies of archaic Greece there was a long tradition emphasizing honor, competition, dominance, pride, and expressions of pre-eminence bordering on braggadocio. This often lapsed into personal and family feuds, and civil wars. Stability often hinged on a careful balance of opposing forces. This competitive tradition continued to be evident in Classical Athens in many areas of life including athletics, drama, and oratory. These diverted competition from its more violent forms and channeled it into political persuasion by means of rhetoric. Hence the long period of relative stability within Athens contained nearly constant internal competition, tension, and conflict as well as conflict and war with other city-states, but relatively little violent conflict within Athenian politics.

Key Social Units

Traditionally most local life was organized around a relatively large household called an *oikos*. These usually included extended family members, dependents, servants, and slaves, and were the basic, relatively self-sufficient units of production, consumption, and expressive relationships. These were grouped into 139 districts called *demes* that were subunits of the *polis* or city-state; they were roughly comparable to a large village and its surrounding region. "These demes were miniature republics, issuing documents, handling finances, copying institutions of the wider polis, enjoying political life of probably a highly personal kind ... and running some cults and festivals" (Davies 1992: 293). *Demos* originally referred to the common people in contrast to the aristocracy, but it came to refer to all citizens within a deme or a polis – and was the root of the word "democracy" (*demokratia*). Attica was divided into three regions: coastal, inland, and urban. As part of Cleisthenes' reforms, the demes were grouped together into ten larger districts called *trittyes*. By selecting one tritty from each region, ten *phyle* or "tribes" were created. These "tribes" served as the constituencies that selected council members, magistrates, and generals and provided military brigades. This linking of demes from different regions of the country created solidarities that cut across locality and kinship and strengthened the solidarity of the polis. There were also *phratries* that had roots in ancient brotherhoods probably linked to kinship; they conducted some cult practices, but their exact membership and nature is unknown.

The Constitution and Its Development

The creation of democracy in Athens was a gradual process, not a revolution. Hence, it is necessary to sketch out its development over time.[7]

Like many complex pre-modern societies, Athens had a history of being dominated by a set of aristocratic families, or on occasion by individual tyrants. Usually power was wielded by various coalitions of elites that formed an oligarchy, often through the *Areopagus*, which was the traditional council of noble elites. Athenian democracy evolved from various reforms over two centuries. Three of the early reforms by Solon began in 594 B.C. One was the agreement of the Areopagus to give up much of its decision-making power and restrict itself to a limited set of judicial functions. A second was the canceling of debt bondage; a citizen of Athens could no longer be made a slave because of debt. As the model suggests, this reduced the status schism between traditional elites and citizens. It probably created a stronger sense of identity and solidarity between elite citizens and non-elite citizens, and accentuated the distinction between citizens and non-citizens. This was increasingly expressed in terms of the contrast between Greeks and barbarians, the latter term initially meaning a non-Greek speaker, but taking on the broader notion of foreigner. The third key reform was a change in the prerequisites for holding state offices; nobility of birth was eliminated as a requirement. The population was divided into four categories based on wealth, and the two highest categories were eligible to become *archons*, who were the key magistrates or officers of the state. While obviously wealth was correlated with nobility, these changes provided the opportunity for newly wealthy elites to gain political power, that is, for the circulation of elites. Under the quasi-populist tyrant Pisistratus (ruled 561–527 B.C.), the people of Attica developed a greater sense of identity and solidarity. He established the Panathenaic Festival that became one of the key events in popular culture. He also promoted a standard version of Homer's epics, arranged for small farmers to receive loans from the state, and set up rural courts to hear petty disputes. The latter two made families less dependent upon local nobility. All of these forged closer ties to the Athenian state, and gave people a greater sense of a common cultural identity.

In 508–507 B.C. there was a revolt against the unpopular archon Isagoras and the foreign occupation of the Spartans that kept him in power. After the revolt succeeded there was no recognized authority that could maintain order and justice. Cleisthenes (c. 570–508 B.C.) led the masses in a series of reforms that initiated Athenian democracy. The males of each deme became responsible for deciding who was an Athenian citizen. All male citizens were now considered formal political equals, undermining (but not eliminating) the deference shown toward the traditional nobility. Both before and after Cleisthenes, women were largely excluded from public political life. As noted previously, Cleisthenes divided the population into ten "tribes" (*phyle*), but each tribe was required to have members from the city, inland areas, and the coastal areas. This reduced the possibility of a geographical area becoming dominant and increased the solidarity of Athens as a whole. Each "tribe" selected fifty representatives by lot to form the Council of 500 known as the *Boule*. The Council met every day except feast days and days considered inauspicious. Moreover, the year was divided into ten periods or "months" called *prytanies*. The representatives of each tribe served as the executives of the Council for one of the prytanies (and that "month" was named for that tribe). Those who served in these offices were also known as prytanies. This rotation of executive responsibility meant the Council was no longer dominated by traditional elites or by any one tribe or region. The Assembly, which was often attended by as many as 6,000 men, met about forty times a year. They made the final decisions about most matters. It was open to all male citizens and each had a right to speak, though most did not. Another significant change was a formal procedure for ostracizing: each year at a special session of the Council, which required a quorum of at least 6,000, citizens could vote to send one person into exile for up to ten years. This was sometimes used against the wealthy and noble to discourage them from displaying arrogance or exercising power and privileges too blatantly. It was also used against politicians, archons, and generals who had displeased the Assembly in some way.

In 487 B.C. members of the Council and the archons (and other magistrates) became chosen by lot from a pre-screened set of 100–500 candidates. This procedure, and the one-year terms for which they served, almost certainly reduced the power of these officials – as well as increasing the diversity of their social backgrounds and their political sympathies. In 462 B.C., under the leadership of Ephialtes, the influence of the Areopagus was further reduced by annulling its authority to declare acts of the Assembly unconstitutional. The amount of property one had to have to hold office was reduced, and magistrates and other government functionaries became paid officials. This made it possible for those with limited amounts of wealth to take on such responsibilities. In 457 B.C. all wealth and status qualifications for government offices were eliminated for male citizens. In 451 B.C. under the leadership of Pericles, the most famous military and political leader of Classical Greece, citizenship was limited to males with both an Athenian father *and* an Athenian mother. Circa 440 B.C., pay was introduced for jurors, which greatly expanded the pool of those who might actually participate. Through much of the fourth century B.C., citizens who attended the assembly received a subsistence level payment, encouraging participation of even the poor. These payments may have been limited to the first thousand or so to arrive.

In addition to the Assembly and the Council, the courts (*dikasteria*) played a crucial role, not only in dispensing justice, but in sustaining democracy. Athenians of the period were highly litigious. The court system was complex and evolved over time, and I will mention only a few key features. What is striking to the modern person is the extent to which it was not professionalized. Prosecutions usually had to be brought by the injured party. There were arbitrators who could hear cases, but these were usually ordinary older citizens who served for one-year periods of time. If the two parties did not accept the arbitrator's decision, then the case was tried before a jury of either 201 or 401 jurors. This meant that many were needed to serve as jurors and each year 6,000 persons were selected as a panel of potential jurors. These large numbers discouraged attempts to bribe jurors. The judiciary was not as clearly differentiated and insulated from politics as is the case in most modern democracies; a person's ideology or established reputation might influence the decision of a jury as much as the facts that were presented. This meant that the rhetorical skills of those involved were important. Professional writers (*logographers*) often provided the speeches used in courts and the Assembly. Gradually some individuals made accusing and prosecuting others into an occupation; these semi-professional prosecutors (*sycophants*) attempted to make money by prosecuting others or threatening to do so. To discourage frivolous suits, prosecutors who did not received at least one-fifth of the votes of a jury, were liable to fines or loss of citizenship rights.

A distinction was drawn between routine personal suits (*dikai*) and those that involved the public interests (*graphe*), though this difference only vaguely matches modern notions of this distinction. In the fourth century B.C., use of the *graphe paranomon* became important to politics. This specified that anyone who proposed a decree in the Assembly that was antithetical to democratic principles or established laws could be sued and prosecuted in court. This, however, presumed a relatively clear distinction between established general laws (*nomoi*) and the much more common decrees (*psephismata*) passed by the Assembly to deal with current exigencies. Accordingly, a related development was the creation of boards of Lawmakers to review and classify decisions of the Assembly. In part, this was probably an attempt of elites to limit and control the acts of the Assembly, but the Lawmakers included about 1,500 citizens chosen by lot and paid for their service, so it is doubtful that this greatly increased elites' ability to limit the Assembly. The key point is that the courts played a vital role in maintaining popular sovereignty.

A probably unintended development was the professionalization of military leadership and the separation of the political and military elite. During this period the Greeks were frequently engaged in wars with Persia, Sparta, and various rebellious elements of their empire; often much was at stake and outcomes were uncertain. Consequently, by the fourth century B.C., generals were usually selected primarily for their military ability. Moreover, since they were often away from Athens for extended periods, rarely could they participate effectively in politics. No general after Pericles had his political influence.

The state's finances became more complex. In addition to the central state treasury, which had existed during much of the fifth century B.C. and dealt with routine expenditures, the Theoretic Fund was created to disperse surplus revenues. The elected directorship of this fund gained more bureaucratic power, though there is little evidence that this significantly compromised the democratic nature of the regime.

This brief summary of the development of the Athenian Constitution ignores many complexities and disagreements among scholars about various points. Its intent is simply to give the reader an overview and flavor of the laws and procedures under which Athenian democracy operated.

Differentiation in Classical Athens

There has been a longstanding debate about the degree to which economic activity was differentiated from other aspects of household social
life. In *The Ancient Economy* (1985) M. I. Finley famously argued (1)
that in ancient societies it was misleading to speak of an economy as if
it were a separate kind of activity than the operation of the household
(*oikos*), (2) that the rudimentary markets handled a very small proportion of the distribution of goods and services, (3) generally land, which
was the key means of production, was not bought and sold in markets,
(4) that ancients were much more preoccupied with accumulating honor
than they were with securing wealth, and (5) hence that Marxian perspectives tended to distort our understanding. He argued for a conceptualization of production, consumption, and distribution along the lines
suggested by the work of Max Weber (1968) and the economist-
anthropologist Karl Polanyi (1957 [1944]). In contrast, G. E. M. de Ste.
Croix develops a much more Marxian analysis in his *The Class Struggle
in the Ancient Greek World* (1981), which focuses on forms of exploitation and class struggle. While less Marxist in perspective, Lisa Kallet
(2007: 70) also departs from Finley and draws on the picture given in
Aristophanes' *Wasps*, saying it "encapsulates a fascinating feature of
fifth-century Athens: the place of money, economic activity, and numer-
acy in the life of citizens from rich to poor, urban to rural. It suggests
an audience with a fondness for calculating and counting, one attuned
to economic advantages – in short, an Athenian economic mentality."
As these different perspectives indicate, there is disagreement among
specialists about how differentiated economic activity was from the rest
of social life.[8]

Fortunately, these issues do not have to be resolved for the purposes
at hand. Even if economic life was not well differentiated from the rest
of social life, this does not mean that the Athenians had no sense of the
difference between status power, economic power, and political power
or between status elites, economic elites, and political elites. Generally
non-citizens were rigidly excluded from political activities; in contrast,
nearly all citizens could participate in political decisions. On the other
hand, *metics* and slaves could engage in the same occupations as citizens.
Moreover, many wealthy foreign aliens (*metics*) had no meaningful political power and relatively little status in the eyes of many Greek citizens.
This certainly indicates that political power and status were conceptually
and actually differentiated from economic power. Similarly, winners of
Olympic events had considerable status, and were allowed to build
public monuments commemorating their victory, but often they did not

have substantial economic or political power. In Thucydides' version of Pericles' famous Funeral Oration he specifically contrasts "gain" or "making money" with "respect" or "honor." He talks about Athens' wealth and about the extensiveness of imports that made available a wide array of foreign goods. He notes that citizens who spend most of their time on "industry" or "their own affairs" nonetheless participate in politics. My purpose in citing these themes is to point out that Athenians had a relatively clear sense of different kinds of activities and different kinds of power – even if ancient economies were quite different from modern ones.

This is not to deny that like most social categories the boundaries are sometimes fuzzy and that some individuals will have multiple forms of power and hence fall into more than one category. Nonetheless, it is possible and useful to distinguish three kinds of elites.

Political Elites

Rhetores

In a democratic society in which major decisions are made by an assembly of several thousand citizens, and in which most officials are elected or chosen by lot annually, who are the political elites? They were primarily those who could persuade the Assembly, the Council, or particular juries to follow their recommendations. As Ober (1989: 123) succinctly states the matter, "The most important political linkages in democratic Athens were not between politicians and generals but between public speakers and mass audiences." This was a group, most often referred to as *rhetores* (i.e., orators), who spoke relatively frequently before Assemblies, juries and other decision-making bodies. This term was usually used in contrast to *idiotai*, those who were not habitual speakers in the Assembly and the courts.[9] Rhetores had no special legal privileges and this was not a formal category or a restricted status group. Other citizens could and did speak from time to time, but the rhetores were in a sense the "professional" politicians (*politeuomenos*) of their time. Most were skilled orators. They frequently disagreed with one another and their exchanges were often rhetorically ferocious. While there were certainly coalitions that supported particular policies or decisions, there were not established political parties.

Unsurprisingly, rhetores were disproportionately wealthy, noble, educated, and urban, but this was also a route for the upward mobility of those from relatively modest backgrounds. Obviously, to regularly attend the forty or more Assemblies per year, to address juries, and to keep up on current issues required time that could not be devoted to earning a living. Coming from a privileged background was both an asset and a liability to a politician. Most citizens were well aware that men of talent and education were more likely to offer good advice than others. It was also assumed that the wealthy were less tempted by bribery. Nonetheless, wealth and privilege were often resented, and especially if speakers displayed arrogance toward idiotai or expressed disdain toward the demos. Consequently, effective politicians often included in their orations affirmations of their commitment to democratic government. To express solidarity with other citizens they used such phrases as "you all know ... " or "everyone knows ... " They also tended to downplay their own wealth and stress their commonality with the demos. Those who sought influence by pandering to the demos became known as *demagogues*. Unsurprisingly, a speaker's critics might question the authenticity of such expressions of solidarity and commonality, pointing out their opponents' privileges and accusing them of hypocrisy and demagoguery. It is not accidental that it was during this period that rhetoric increasingly became an established discipline and that many rhetores had formal training in these skills.

We have already noted that rhetores were not a formally established office or role. This was in part because the political realms were less clearly differentiated from the rest of life than is the case in modern societies. Hence, rhetores could also be status elites, and were in some respects analogous to modern celebrity politicians. Similarly, some would be very wealthy men who were also economic elites. The wealthiest citizens certainly had more political influence than the typical citizen, not to mention the poor. Nonetheless, the demos in the form of the Assembly had the ultimate power over most political decisions. Hence, rhetorical skill was usually a key requirement for being a political elite.[10]

Generals and bureaucrats

By focusing on rhetores as leaders of political decision making and oratory as the means of persuasion, I do not mean to suggest that the exercise of force and coercion were not important aspects of Athenian political life. While the military and the bureaucracy were much less professionalized than in modern societies, generals were nonetheless important actors, especially in executing the foreign policy decided upon by the Assembly. The archons and their various assistants were de facto police. Most of those who actually kept order and arrested people were foreign slaves acting under the direction of the various magistrates. So while it is important to recognize the significance of these officials, it is unwarranted to think of them as a power elite or to see their increased power in later years as the inevitable operation of Michel's iron law or oligarchy.

Raiders, invaders, and traitors

Pirates are a classic form of raiders or bandits. As Thucydides makes clear in the first chapter of his famous *History of the Peloponnesian War*, piracy had long been prevalent in ancient Greece. For some areas it was considered a more or less normal occupation. By the fifth and fourth centuries the more developed city-states and their navies had significantly repressed piracy, but it was not eliminated. The line between piracy and various forms of hegemonic domination was not always a clear-cut distinction. In what Thucydides records as the "Affair of Epidamnus," Corinth is in conflict with its former colony Corcyra [modern Corfu]. Corinth accuses them of de facto piracy:

> [T]hey are constantly being visited by foreign vessels which are com-
> pelled to put in to Corcyra. In short, the object that they propose to
> themselves, in their specious policy of complete isolation, is not to
> avoid sharing in the crimes of others, but to secure monopoly of crime
> to themselves – the license of outrage wherever they can compel, of
> fraud wherever they can elude, and the enjoyment of their gains
> without shame.[11]

This is probably a very biased view and from the point of view of Corinth, and for Epidamnus is a matter of legitimate control of port facilities. The key theoretical point, however, is that the line between being bandits/raiders/pirates and police is often an ambiguous one and is to some degree affected by the observer's cultural perspective.

Of course, more threatening than pirates and robbery were foreign invaders. During the fifth and fourth centuries Athens was engaged in several crucial foreign wars. The most important were repelling Persia, Athens' defeat by Sparta, and its defeat by Philip II of Macedonia. The first of these laid the groundwork for the flourishing of Athens and the creation of its empire, the second drained Athens and led to its decline, and the third severely compromised Athenian democracy and made it vulnerable to various foreign and oligarchic pressures. Of course, decisions about how to handle these conflicts were central issues in the democratic politics of Athens. Advocating a policy that became a failure could lead to being sued, exiled, or worse. Sometimes invaders were assisted by discontented members of the political elite. As Rhodes (2007:

37) says, "we have evidence from many places at many times in Greek history that, whatever the attitude of ordinary citizens may have been, leading politicians frequently preferred being on the winning side in their city thanks to outside intervention, ... to being on the losing side in a city that was free from outside intervention." Two famous cases in Classical Athens of elites siding with outside enemies are Alcibiades' defection to Sparta and the Thirty Tyrants installed by Sparta after Athens' defeat in 404 B.C. To sum matters up, the frequent threat and counterpoint to the democratic regime in Athens were a combination of pirates, invaders, and traitors.

Of course, democratic Athens was by no means an innocent party. Frequently it was the invader, not only of other states in Greece, but of Asia Minor, Egypt, and Syracuse. Athens was viewed by some of those subject to her domination as almost like a pirate, raider, or tyrant. Of course, attempting to be an aggressor can lead to defeat. This was certainly the case for the Athenian expedition to Sicily and Syracuse in which it lost approximately 200 ships and most of its large army was killed or captured. This failed attempt to be a raider and invader was the prelude to its loss of the Peloponnesian War to the Spartans and Athens' general decline.

Non-elites

Respectable citizens

Non-elites were made up of a complex mosaic of citizens, metics (i.e., resident aliens), and slaves. Individuals from any of these categories could do the same work. There were wealthy metics and poor citizens. Agriculture was still the foundation of the economy, though shipping, shipbuilding, construction, crafts, manufacturing, and trade became increasingly important as the empire expanded.

Citizens had both privileges and responsibilities. Younger male citizens were required to serve in the military, usually either as hoplite infantrymen or as oarsmen in the navy. Hoplites had to arm themselves, usually with shield, spear, sword, and breastplate, so were composed of citizens who could afford these items. In contrast, oarsmen required no costly equipment and they included poorer and middle-class citizens, as well as metics and slaves. This meant that warfare was not primarily conducted by professional warriors; rather military service was a part-time activity and a key basis of citizenship. (The counterpoint is Sparta: citizens were virtually fulltime professional soldiers.) Athenians had pride in their citizenship both because of Athens' economic, architectural, military, and political accomplishments *and* because they were not slaves or metics, but free citizens, who participated in key political decisions.[12] In the middle of the fifth century Athens created a cavalry of 300 and 1,000 horsemen. The sons of the aristocracy were predominant and it was often perceived as anti-democratic, because it supported the Thirty Tyrants' coup of 404–403.[13] Nonetheless, the core of Athens' military power was in the hands – literally and figuratively – of what I have called respectable citizens.

Political outcasts – foreigners and slaves

Metics composed a substantial portion of the population. Athens' prosperity attracted many non-Athenians. To become a resident, however, metics had to be sponsored by a citizen. Some were engaged in import and export trading with citizens as partners. Others provided various services. Some became wealthy and were accepted as friends by the Athenian economic elite. Special courts were created so aliens could bring suits against Athenians and other metics. Metics could lease real estate, but could not own, inherit, or pass it on to their children, probably discouraging their participation in agriculture. Wealthy metics were expected to fund social, religious, and governmental activities. Many served as hoplites. With rare exceptions, they could not become citizens or openly participate in politics.

Large numbers of slaves worked for the larger landowners and in the mines. Many more families owned one or two slaves who assisted then on their farm or in their business. Scholars are divided about how far down the economic ladder families owned slaves. It is clear that slaves were numerous and central to economic activity. Frequently they had been captured in various wars and were chattel property bought and sold in local, regional, and international markets, which could split up spouses or children from parents. Some were prosperous enough to buy their freedom – usually the skilled or educated.

A note is required about the relationship between slavery, freedom, and democracy. In his book *Freedom*, Orlando Patterson's central thesis is that "the very ideal and valuation of freedom was generated by the existence and growth of slavery" (1991: xiv). While slavery usually stimulated some notion of freedom, only in Western culture did freedom become a widely held institutional value. This occurred initially in Athens because large-scale slavery created an urban class who were *neither* slaves nor aristocrats and took pride in their freedom, (i.e., they were respectable non-elites). Most were not economic dependents of the aristocracy and they frequently owned slaves themselves. Because slaves were assigned much of the heavier work, women became more confined to the household and in close contact with slaves. Consequently, women frequently became a voice for personal freedom both in everyday life and Greek drama. According to Patterson, these structural developments of large-scale slavery and differentiated gender roles interacted with political democracy and the emphasis on rationality in Greek philosophy. This combination of circumstances made possible the social construction of freedom. Large-scale slavery, however, was the crucial stimulus.

Status/Cultural/Ideological Elites

The priests

In ancient India, status/cultural/ideological elites were typically differentiated from political elites. The recruitment and support of Brahmins or other religious elites was a primary way that rulers sanctified their rule. Classical Athens is distinctively different.

Rhetores

Politician orators (*rhetores*) were key ideological elites. Orators such as Demosthenes, Pericles, Isocrates, and Antiphon were both famous cultural elites and important ideologues. They advocated particular policies, shaped the assumptions of their period, and created the rhetorical techniques used in debate. Generally, rhetores were "priests" who claimed or feigned support for Athenian democracy. Some, such as Theramenes (d. 404 B.C.) and his contemporary Antiphon of Rhamnus, were sympathetic to forms of oligarchy, and on occasion surreptitious prophets opposed to the existing social order. Ironically, the first was killed by more extreme oligarchs and the second by democratic Athens.

Other groups were also part of the ideological elite: religious priests and oracles, dramatists and poets, athletes, and philosophers.

Religious Elites

Few leaders of cultic activities were full-time priests (*hiereis*). Most made their living doing other things.[14] Their religious responsibilities were limited to leading the rituals and sacrifices of a particular cult in a particular location. The Greeks had many gods and each god could have multiple functions. For example, Demeter was the goddess of crops, especially of grains, and more generally of wealth and prosperity. She was also, with her daughter Persephone, responsible for the kind of afterlife the dead experienced. There could be separate priests for the different functions that gods performed and cultic centers in multiple locations. Greek religion of this period was not centrally organized, nor had Weberian rationalization of religion proceeded very far. To use an analogy, Greek religion was not like the Roman Catholic Church with an organized hierarchy and an articulated orthodoxy. It was more like Pentecostal sects with considerable variations in leadership, doctrine, and ritual. There were official state cults, such as those to Athena, who was in a sense the "official" goddess of Athens. The priests and other officials were appointed by the government, often after being chosen by lot. Income and expenditures of these religious leaders were carefully audited by government officials. Stressing the multiplicity of cults is not to deny the existence of some full-time priests or to discount the significance of pan-Hellenic religious activities. The oracle at Delphi and the religious ambiance of the Olympic Games are obvious examples.

Earlier periods were largely ruled by kin-based aristocracies and clergy were probably less diverse and perhaps part of the aristocracy. In democratic Athens religious authority was diffused through a variety of priests and lay committees. In his essay, "Priests and Power in Classical Athens," Robert Garland (1990: 91) summarizes his findings:

> [T]he diffusion of religious authority in Classical Athens mirrors the diffusion of political authority in the same period through large numbers of boards of magistrates with many members performing minor, routine tasks. In matters that count in ... the religious sphere, the *demos* arrogated to itself as much power as possible. Thus the study of the evolution of Athenian religion provides a novel, yet complementary perspective to the study of the same process by which the citizen body came to establish a unique degree of control over its own affairs.

Which priests in which periods were supervised by the Assembly and city officials is unclear. Much of the evidence involves interpreting inscriptions and texts that can be ambiguous. Classical Athenian democracy was probably preceded and followed by more oligarchic forms of religious leadership. Earlier it was probably linked to long aristocratic traditions such as those portrayed in Homer. Later it was probably influenced by Macedonia and Rome. In all of these periods there was probably a complicated mix of religious leaders chosen by a variety of means.[15]

In addition to priests who organized and led sacrifices, there were specialists in the sacred law (*exegetai*) who advised about correct ritual procedures to avoid offending the gods and to insure the efficacy of rituals. Seers, oracles, and diviners (*chresmologoi* or *manteis*) advised about the auspiciousness (or inauspiciousness) of, and the timing of, activities. Some specialized in recommending the timing of military actions. Divinations were available to individuals for a fee or gift. Respected oracles were seen as the voice of the god and could call for innovation in cultic activities. Nonetheless, all of these actors were in varying degrees subject to the demos gathered as the Assembly. In such a situation the usual effect of cultic activities is legitimation and not critique.

Drama and Literature

Drama and other kinds of performances flourished in this period.[16] Henderson (2007) reports: "In the fifth century alone [Athens] supported the production of some 2,000 dithyrambs, 1,250 tragedies, and 659 comedies."[17] These were elaborate and expensive undertakings. While early comedies poked fun at contemporary politicians and issues, most of the dramas were not explicitly ideological. Their narratives and imagery typically drew on pan-Hellenic myths and dealt with near universal themes facing human beings, such as conflict, betrayal, and death. Tickets had to be purchased for most productions. Most performances were open to virtually all members of the community, though how many women attended is unclear. The famous dramatists such as Aeschylus, Aristophanes, Euripides, and Sophocles were celebrities who competed in contests that were associated with various festivals. Other poets wrote odes of praise for whoever would pay them for their efforts. The long famous historians Thucydides and Xenophon were well known as military leaders, but it is unclear how famous they were for their writings during their own lifetime. Most dramatists, poets, and historians were more cultural elites than ideological elites in the narrower sense. As with religious activities, a well-ordered and widely shared popular culture was a likely source of the relative social stability of the period.

Athletes

Most people know that the modern Olympics were modeled after the Olympics in ancient Greece, but are unaware that this was only one venue that could convert an athlete into a celebrity. A Metropolitan Museum of Art publication (Hemingway and Hemingway 2002) succinctly summarizes the significance of these events for the distribution of status:

> By the sixth century B.C., other Panhellenic ... games involving Greek-speaking city-states were being held at Delphi, Nemea, and Isthmia.

Many local games, such as the Panathenaic games at Athens, were modeled on these ... The victors at all these games brought honor to themselves, their families, and their hometowns. Public honors were bestowed on them, statues were dedicated to them, and victory poems were written to commemorate their feats. Numerous vases are decorated with scenes of competitions and the odes of Pindar celebrate a number of athletic victories. At the core of Greek athletics was an individual's physical endeavor to overtake an opponent. For this reason, sports in ancient Greece generally excluded team competitions.

This is another example of the highly competitive nature of ancient Greek culture and the centrality of the quest for honor, which like all forms of status is relatively inexpansible – and hence the outcome produces losers as well as winners. While this made athletics relatively agonistic, it probably deflected aggression and dominance into realms less destructive of social order and peace than the forms of military conflict they probably echo. In the fifth century B.C., athletic contests were an elitist affair, but it is unclear whether these became more democratic over time.

The prophets

Ancient Greece's most obvious influence on modern society is through its philosophers.[18] Bryant (1986) has argued that, in part because of the non-hierocratic and fragmented nature of Greek religion, Weberian rationalization did not occur in that realm, but in the realm of philosophy. Socrates, Plato, and Aristotle are still "gods" of the philosophical world. While they were well known in their time, they were not "gods" to all of their contemporaries. They were ideologues as well as cultural elites, but were in many respects out of step with Athenian democracy. It was democratic Athens that condemned Socrates to death for sacrilege. Plato took slavery for granted, voiced hostility toward democracy, proposed that societies should be run by philosopher-kings. If Gouldner (1965: chap. 5 and p. 344) is correct, Plato sought to abolish politics altogether, or more accurately restrict political debate to the elite philosopher-kings. Aristotle was also critical of democracies, sympathetic to aristocracies, and an out-and-out defender of slavery. He was a metic and, in the eyes of some of his contemporaries, was a traitor and supporter of the Macedonians; ironically, his former pupil who became Alexander the Great also thought he was a traitor to the Macedonians.

In the terms of the model, many of the Greek philosophers were prophets, not priests; that is, they were critical of existing institutions rather than supportive of them. They illustrate well that there can be prophets of the "right" as well as of the "left." With the possible exception of Socrates, they did not publicly confront their rulers in a manner that was characteristic of the prophets of Israel, but they were nonetheless highly critical of the society of their time. According to Plato, his chief opponents were the Sophists.[19] One of Plato's chief accusations was that Sophists were unprincipled relativists who used rhetorical skills to support specious arguments that are all too easily accepted by the demos. This implicitly criticizes many of the rhetor politicians and the functioning of democracy. Not all philosophers or all prophetic voices of the time were opposed to democracy. It is important to remember, however, that philosophical and intellectual brilliance, and the secularized rationality often associated with these, are not necessarily supportive of democracy.

The key point is that in Classical Athens it is fairly easy to identify what I have called status/cultural/ideological elites and analogs of such concepts as celebrity, priests, and prophets – and to see the role they played in legitimizing (or delegitimizing) classical Athens.

Economic Elites

In all societies, control of the means of production is an important form of power, but it is not always the dominant form of power. Moreover, there are typically tensions and conflicts between various groups of economic elites.

The old

Who were Athens' economic elites? Obviously they included 1,000–2,000 wealthy families. Most owned relatively large tracts of agricultural land outside the city, usually managed by stewards and worked by a combination of peasants and slaves. These were predominantly, but not exclusively "old families" of aristocratic origin. Some of these economic elites were heavily involved in Athenian politics and some were not. A noble lineage was both honored and resented in Athens. Most wealthy families were not famous or status elites per se. Obviously, there were exceptions such as the famous orators Demosthenes and Isocrates, who came from wealthy families. Attica was not a land of slave plantations. Most of the land in Attica consisted of small plots worked by individuals and their families, and perhaps a slave or two. They usually grew a variety of crops. Barley was the common staple grain and olives the most valuable crop. Most Athenians lived relatively independently of large, rich land owners. Certainly, this relative economic independence of most non-elite citizens is one of the contributing factors to political democracy.

The new

If land was the source of old money, mining, manufacturing, construction, and shipping were the "new" means of production and the source of much new wealth. Some became extremely wealthy by using thousands of slaves to work silver mines leased from the city. Money from the mine leases also flowed into the government's coffers and helped fund the enormous building projects of the classical period, of which the Acropolis and the walls protecting the route to the port at Piraeus were especially notable. These building projects were a source of new wealth for contractors. Some who started out as skilled craftsmen became relatively wealthy. Ship building for the Athenian navy and the trade the empire made possible were another source of new wealth. Some traders imported huge amounts of grain from the Crimea, which was crucial to the city's expanding population prior to the Peloponnesian War. A few seers and diviners became wealthy. The point is that, while owning agricultural land was still the most honorable form of wealth, new sources of wealth were a crucial part of Athenian society and its empire.

Tension and conflict

The general model suggests that there are usually tensions, and potentially conflict between those controlling the traditional modes of production and those associated with new modes of production. While the Athenian evidence is not definitive, there is good reason to think that this was the case. Focusing on the period after the Peloponnesian War, Strauss (1986: 11–12) says:

> A half-century earlier, democratic Athens was governed by the sons of aristocratic families ... Even Pericles, eulogist of democracy, came ... from the proud and ancient house of the Alcmeonids. Now in 400 [B.C.], after the social and economic changes that came from empire, world war, defeat, and revolution, aristocrats in Athens politics were the exception, not the rule. The men who governed Athens c. 400

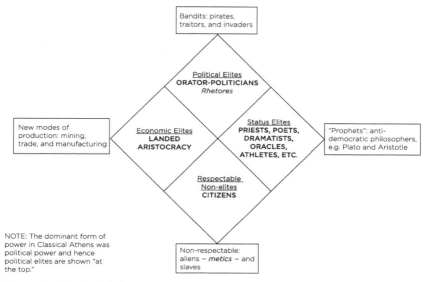

Figure 3: Classical Athens

[B.C.] generally made up in wealth what they lacked in lineage. They were men who could afford to subsidize the cost of a warship or a statue in a temple ... who could afford to be educated by Sophists. Often they came from families that had made their money in commerce or manufacturing, which led to the ancient slander that they were mere potters or lampmakers ... In other cases their fortunes rested on the traditional source of Athenian wealth – the land.

I certainly do not mean to suggest that source of income was a perfect predictor of whether a politician supported oligarchy or democracy, but it is probable that many of the supporters of the oligarchic coups of 411 and 404 where those whose wealth derived primarily from traditional forms of agriculture.

The model as applied to Classical Athens is summarized in Figure 3.

Comparison with Other Models

In the previous chapter I compared the ability of Marxism and Bourdieu's theories with that of the general model with respect to their ability to understand the caste system and the role of the varna scheme in ancient India. Now I will compare the usefulness of elite theory and Weber with the proposed model in their understanding of Classical Athens. Elite theory is the most abstract and general of previous theories seeing all complex societies as ultimately controlled by a small elite. Weber, in contrast, is most sensitive to historical specificity. Hence, by using these alternative frames as the basis of comparison, we increase the possibility of identifying inadequacies in the proposed general model.

Comparison with elite theory

First, elite theory tends to gloss over important differences. In Classical Athens it was certainly the case that wealth was distributed in a highly unequal fashion, that political elites had disproportionate amounts of influence and power, and that those from aristocratic families were over-represented among elites. Nonetheless, many and perhaps most political elites were not from aristocratic families. Moreover, there were often substantial differences in the policies different elites pursued. Even more important, significant powers were exercised by ordinary male citizens in the Assembly and juries. The pessimism inherent in elite theory does not help to grasp the complex system of checks and balances and the qualitatively different role that non-elite citizens played in shaping important collective decisions. The contrast in the treatment of political enemies and non-elites in democratic Athens with the two oligarchic coups or in later Roman Athens is strong evidence that an elite model tends to understate the significance of important social and moral differences between democratic Classical Athens and more oligarchic regimes.[20] Second, most elite theory tends to ignore or understate the significance of the relationship between respectable non-elites and unrespectable non-elites. The crucial difference between citizens and non-citizen metics and slaves is a clear example of this. Third, elite models tend to concentrate on political and economic elites and neglect the analysis of status, cultural, and ideological elites. This is an important shortcoming in the analysis of a culture and society that is most famous for its dramatists, philosophers, athletes, and religious temples. This is not to say that those who start from elite models are necessarily guilty of the above shortcoming, but rather that elite theory often handicaps the analysis rather than sensitizing the analyst to the complexities of the situation.

Comparison with Weber

In some of his earliest work, and especially in *The Agrarian Sociology of Ancient Civilizations*, Weber wrote extensively about ancient societies and specifically about ancient Greece including Classical Athens (Weber 1976a: esp. 147–219). He uses examples from Classical Athens in many places in his more synthetic works like *General Economic History* (1981) and *Economy and Society* (1968), but this early work focuses largely on economic institutions. While Finley (1985) is strongly influenced by Weber, Weber tends to see more economic activity occurring beyond the realm of the oikos than Finley does. In his work that actually focuses on Greece, Weber tends to only cursorily treat political and status elites (1976a: 147–219). Of course, it would be possible to draw on the more mature Weber and his emphasis on different types of power, but there is a strong tendency in Weberian perspectives to overemphasize the trends toward rationalization. Nor does Weber offer any systematic delineation of the differentiations that are likely to occur within each type of elite and within non-elites. While Weber is probably a less distorted theoretical perspective than elite theory or Marxism, it remains theoretically underdeveloped.

The proposed general model

How is the deep structure that the model identifies, which is characteristic of all complex societies, useful in understanding this society and time period? First, it is useful in organizing much of what we know about the social categories and actors in Classical Athens and their relationship to one another. Second, while the abstract categories of the typology are useful, the *content* of such categories as *rhetores*, *logographers*, *demos*, and *medics* can be made relatively specific to this particular historical setting. Hence, the typology does not require ignoring the specific historical patterns and institutions of Athens of this period.[21]

Third, it helps to recognize and explain the relative stability of this specific city-state over a period of 186 years.[22] Once direct democracy emerged following the reforms of Cleisthenes, its institutionalization for this extended period was largely successful. What are some of the sources of this stability? One is the taken-for-grantedness of treating some as unrespectable and of trying to dominate and exploit outsiders (i.e., non-Athenians); this is what I have referred to earlier as a deep structure on the cultural level. This takes the form of slavery and empire: the right to force a "social death" upon slaves and foreigners – to use the imagery of Orlando Patterson (1982). This meant that there was more wealth for respectable non-elites without reducing that of elites. A second source of stability is political in the broad sense, but more specifically military: the importance of hoplites and rowers meant that non-elite citizens had a central role in military matters. It also gives them greater solidarity with one another, and makes elites dependent upon them. A third source is political in the more usual sense: the rights of citizens to participate in decisions through the Assembly, the *Boule*, and the courts. A fourth source is the flip side of citizenship: the exclusion and diminished status of much of the population – women, metics, and slaves – contributed to greater solidarity between "respectable non-elite" male citizens and political elites. A fifth source is the diversion of the emphasis on competition and dominance – rooted in an earlier warrior ethic and ideology – into the non-violent realms of athletics, drama, literature, and religious ritual. The sixth and the most important source of stability was the centrality of another form of non-violent competition: the reliance on rhetoric to persuade the Assembly and juries of the wisdom of what one advocates.

Fourth, the model helps to take the substantial inequalities that existed seriously, and still recognize the real benefits of Athenian democracy. (These are seen when contrasted to the tyranny that occurred during the brief periods of oligarchy.) While there were constant conflicts over both policies and personalities, and two brief coups, the radically democratic structure of Athens was relatively stable.

Fifth, the general model also helps to understand the eventual decline of democratic Athens. What was unique about Athens of the period was the extent of non-elite political participation and power. Yet, non-elites still needed political leadership. Crucial was the relationship between political elites and respectable non-elites, and in turn their relationship with other city-states. The success of the empire was due in part to the relative social solidarity between Athenian elites and its citizen soldiers and sailors, which in turn was rooted in prosperity *and* a well-institutionalized egalitarian, democratic ideology. The irony was that these factors also contributed to a collective arrogance. The empire, pride in being Athenian, and condescending attitudes toward non-Athenians led non-elites to be supportive of an aggressive foreign policy in which ambition outstripped resources and good judgment. This led to conflicts with other Greek states. Some of these were avoidable and led to serious defeats and losses, especially the calamitous expedition to Sicily. These conflicts contributed to the decline in population and prosperity, and the eventual downfall of both the empire and Athenian democracy.

Conclusion

A key challenge of the last chapter was to explain why the varna scheme had continued to be a key ideological model for so long when it so poorly represented the actual structure of social relationship. The key challenge in understanding Classical Athens is to explain how such an anomalous structure as Athenian direct democracy emerged, maintained itself for approximately 200 years, and then virtually disappeared from human history – though of course modern representative democracy emerged 2,000 years later. The proposed model helps to organize the data in such a way that we see some of the sources of its emergence, the mechanisms that sustained it, and the causes of its decline. Of course, the elements of this analysis have been carried out previously by others without this theoretical tool, but the model helps to organize the broader picture and place it in a useful comparative perspective.

5

The U.S. 1980–2008: Economics and Politics

Is the model useful in identifying and understanding the relationships between the various types of elites and between these elites and non-elites in contemporary American society? We will focus on the period c. 1980–2008. Most analyses concentrate on economic and political elites – and that is the focus of this chapter. In the next chapter we will take up the actors who often get ignored.

Exogenous Variables

Many things have impacted U.S. society in the last quarter century, but I will focus on three key variables.

1. **From Processing Objects and Substances to Processing Symbols:**
   Computers, optic cables, and satellites have enormously increased the capacity to process and communicate symbols. This has created new industries and companies such as Yahoo, Google, and Facebook, and facilitated the transfer of information, money, and capital. This is not to say that the processing of objects and substances are no longer important, but to note that such activities are increasingly

automated – and automation is dependent upon the processing of symbols.

2. **Expansion of Networks:** Due largely to our increased ability to process symbols, people and organizations now communicate much more frequently and quickly, often with others at great distances from themselves, and quickly receive or provide information to much broader audiences than before.[1] This has greatly facilitated the exchange of information, money, and capital, which in turn has increased the exchange of goods and services. But ironically, operating in a broader network that involves many more actors means that it is harder to gain visibility in such networks than it was in smaller networks. It also means that individuals are dealing with a much more complex, and hence difficult to comprehend world.

3. **American Exceptionalism:** Seymour Martin Lipset (1963: chap. 3; 1996, 2000) argues that the core values of the United States are exceptional. "Exceptional" does not mean good or virtuous, but rather that when compared to other countries, the U.S. is a statistical outlier. (Perhaps a better term than "exceptional" would be "deviant.") Americans are unusually religious and moralistic. This is reflected in their attitudes about sex, especially the sexual behavior of politicians. They see themselves as going to war against evil, not to defend their national interests. Americans are more patriotic and more willing to serve in the military. In other respects, they are suspicious of and resistant to the power of the state, with a stress on individual rights that the state cannot violate. Historically they supported mass public education and equality of opportunity more than most countries. This is linked to a stress on individual responsibility. The result has been less public funding to assist the poor, the stigmatization of those who receive public assistance, but high levels of charitable giving. In the economic realm, the U.S. is strongly capitalist in its ideology and economic structure. Lipset's characterization refers not to public opinion, which is often fluid and shaped by short-term factors. Rather he refers to deep-seated values and assumptions, which evolved out of a particular historical experience, and continue to shape private behavior and public policies.[2]

Exogenous variables can have direct effects on the categories of the general model, but typically they affect the relationships between various elites and non-elites through intervening variables. For example, computers and automation have made women more competitive in the labor market since physical strength is less important than in the past.[3] The ability to process symbols has also increased the use of images (rather than texts), and the significance of good looks, which in turn affected the use of cosmetics, plastic surgery, and exercise, and the selection of politicians. (The evidence for such indirect effects will be traced out in the discussion of each category of the model.)

Economic Elites

Much can be said about contemporary U.S. economic elites, but I will deal with only four key points: the ideological dominance of economic elites, the relationship between old and new economic elites, the significance and limitations of knowledge as a source of power, and the emergence of global elites.

Ideological dominance of economic elites

One type of elite (and one type of power) usually has more legitimacy than other types; in India it was Brahmins who were status elites and in Classical Athens it was orator politicians who were political elites.

In the U.S. economic elites are paramount, and this is one of the deep structures of capitalist culture in general and American culture in particular.[4] "Entrepreneur," "businessman," and even "capitalist" are generally positive terms, while "government official," "politician," and "bureaucrat" are categories looked upon with suspicion and even derision. Shoddy levels of performance are described as "good enough for government work." Ideological elites also are on average inferior to economic elites. Such terms as "preacher," "intellectual," and "professor" often carry connotations of not being quite in touch with the realities of life. "If you can't do, then you can always teach or preach." The "private sector" is presumed to be more efficient and legitimate.[5] The government, voluntary associations, and churches should be "run like businesses." No one ever suggests that a business should be run like a church or a government agency. Those who are economic failures are often degraded – especially if they are perceived to avoid work. Hence the derision expressed toward "welfare chiselers," "welfare queens," "freeloaders," "loafers," "bums," etc. (Boushey 2004; Gilens 1999). Ironically, living off of inherited wealth is seldom considered a moral lapse.

I want to further illustrate this by the way U.S. society is handling the use of "big data." In 2013 a great controversy arose when it was revealed that the national security agencies collected vast amounts of data on foreigners and citizens to detect possible terrorist plots. Investigations have not revealed any abuses where individuals not engaged in terrorism were negatively impacted. Nonetheless, the result was numerous

Congressional hearings, lawsuits to stop the program, a federal judge ruling the program unconstitutional, and the Obama administration's review and scaling down of the program.

Another concern has been educational and research data. Nearly all educational and research institutions are subject to intricate rules and scrutinized by Institutional Review Boards. These significantly limit what can and what cannot be done and require elaborate consent procedures to protect subjects' privacy and confidentiality. Violations can bring an institution heavy fines and an end to federal funding.[6]

In contrast, much more inclusive and intrusive collection of data for advertising and marketing purposes has been largely ignored. This not only involves metadata that identifies patterns of communication, but also includes detailed information about individuals such as what they buy, their credit rating, the value of their home, what they look at on the Internet, who they communicate with, the state of their health, whether they are pregnant, their exercise routines, and numerous other pieces of information. This has been subject to no systematic oversight and has gone largely unnoticed and undiscussed.[7]

Another example of the bias in favor of the private sector and against the government sector is the conventional wisdom about the sources of innovation. It is generally assumed that the private sector is the source of most technological and economic innovations. Often the government is perceived to limit or stifle such innovation through onerous regulations or taxes that reduce the willingness of private investors to take risks. This is at best a debatable assumption. Many of the most important innovations, including the bases for the Internet, satellites, and various modern drugs are rooted in the entrepreneurial actions and policies of the government, and it is unlikely that these developments would have occurred if left to the private sector.[8]

My point is not that we should be unconcerned about government regulations that might stifle private sector innovations, or government surveillance programs, or the treatment of research subjects and data. It is rather the different standards. The market sector and economic elites have a taken-for-granted legitimacy, whereas other sectors are looked upon with suspicion and are subject to extensive scrutiny and supervision. This is rooted not only in the power of economic elites, but in the deep structure of cultural and ideological assumptions that give some types of elites dominance relative to others.[9]

Old and new elites

The model suggests that significant tensions are likely between those associated with different modes of production. The first exogenous variable suggests that now this is likely to distinguish those who primarily process objects and substances from those who primarily process symbols and images. The former's power is rooted in ownership of physical capital and goods in traditional industries and services such as agriculture, mining, manufacturing, cleaning, and maintenance services. The power of the new elite (sometimes referred to as the "new class") is based on specialized knowledge, especially about processing symbols and images. This includes companies that produce computers, software, social networks, communications, mass media, and information, especially information useful in the marketing of both physical and symbolic products. The technologies and knowledge used by "old" and "new" firms are not mutually exclusive; chemical companies rely heavily on scientific knowledge and computers, and computer companies manufacture and sell a particular kind of object. Nonetheless, there is a significant difference between DuPont and Microsoft, between United Airlines and Facebook, in types of capital and organizational culture. These differences shape a company's internal processes and external orientations. For example, elites in more traditional industries such as agriculture, construction, and food services usually favor liberal immigration policies to insure a supply of cheap labor.[10] Leaders of high-tech industries usually support easy immigration of the highly educated and technically trained, but are more ambivalent about low-skilled immigrants since these industries want quality schools, good housing, low crime rates, and advanced infrastructure (Sengupta 2013).

The nature of capitalism has shifted over the course of history, for example, the shift from merchant capitalism, to monopoly/oligopoly capitalism, to industrial capitalism, to post-industrial capitalism. At different points in time, some problems are more central than others to the success of a firm and to a capitalist economy in general. The last couple of decades has seen the development of "investor capitalism." Managers are under increasing pressure from large stockholders such as mutual funds, hedge funds, pension plans, insurance companies, and investment banks to maximize profits and raise the company's stock price; those who don't are often replaced (Lounsbury 2001). Salary and bonuses are often linked to increases in stock values, motivating them to maximize this even when it is not in the company's long-term interest. One technique is for companies to buy back their own stock, reducing the number of stockholders and usually increasing the return to each remaining share – but this reduces the resources available for long-term investments.[11] Companies are also split up and sold off if this results in greater returns for large stockholders. In short, power has shifted from managers to outside board members whose primary interest is in relatively short-term gains (Froud et al. 2008). Closely related is what has been called "financialization": the increased proportions of economic activity based on banking, insurance, and investment (Davis 2009; Krippner 2011; Lewis 2010; Phillips 2008; Tomaskovic-Devey and Lin 2011). It also refers to the tendency to increased "leveraging," that is, financing economic activity using borrowed money. Large investors may gain control of boards by using borrowed money to buy large blocks of stocks. A key aspect of financialization and leveraging has been the proliferation of new complex types of financial instruments. It is not accidental that the origins of the recession of 2008–10 were financial institutions. I will consider these issues in more detail in chapter 7.

The consequences of these developments, especially the political proclivities, are complex. Professionals working for government and nonprofits are more likely to be liberal, while those who are employed in businesses are only slightly less conservative than managers (Brint 1994). While it seems clear that knowledge provides a new basis of economic power, it is by no means clear that the so-called knowledge-based new class will simply replace the owners of physical capital as the most powerful economic elites. Nor does power based on knowledge necessarily lead to more liberal political opinions; the often distinguished scholars at conservative think tanks negate this assumption. Likewise, the wealthiest individuals are not necessarily conservative on every issue. Warren Buffett supported higher U.S. tax rates for the rich and Georg Soros advocated government stimulus spending in Europe. Nonetheless, there are tensions between those oriented to older modes of production and those who use newer modes of production.

Knowledge and property

Because of variations in inalienability and inexpansibility, some resources can be more quickly accumulated and transferred to others; you can become a millionaire overnight by winning the lottery, but it takes much longer to become well educated. Moreover, the effective uses of physical capital and human capital are often interdependent. You had better get a lot of training before you try to fly a modern jet airplane; even a brilliant chemist needs a lot of expensive equipment to manufacture modern plastics.

The above factors have implications for the distribution of power. The increased centrality of knowledge, human capital, and processing symbols does not necessarily lead to more economic independence. Many members of the "new class" increasingly require large amounts of physical capital that cost too much for individual practitioners. Consequently, more centralized and socialized modes of organization may make them more subject to hierarchical authority. For example, physicists, astronomers, and physicians increasingly work with elaborate networks of colleagues to utilize extremely expensive technology that they do not own. But this trend primarily applies to the lower levels of economic elites, for example, even renowned physicians and engineers.

While the upper elites of the new class need high levels of human capital, extensive wealth is still rooted in the control of property. Bill Gates, who founded Microsoft, knew this; Steve Jobs, who founded Apple – and lost control of it for several years – had to learn this the hard way. It is not accidental that the richest people in the U.S. are primarily those who founded computer, media, and financial companies.[12] They may have initially relied on their human capital, but they soon converted this into enormous amounts of private property.

Older more traditional industries – such as simple manufacturing – have been moving to overseas economies where human capital is less central and wages are lower. Many of these, such as steel and automobiles, have had significant reductions in their workforce and operations. As developing countries became more prosperous and wages increased, some manufacturing moved back to developed countries, but this was often in industries with high levels of automation, and therefore employing fewer people.

A global economic elite

The general model indicates that elites vary in the scope of their influence: local, regional, national, etc. The second exogenous variable points to the increasing scope of networks. Hence it follows that both economic networks and economic elites are likely to become more global in their orientation. For example in 2012 the percentage of the total earnings that came from international operations was 41 percent for General Motors, 53 percent for Google, and 58 percent for Citibank.[13]

International trade has long been important, but it is clear that business activity is now even more internationally oriented. U.S.-owned assets abroad increased from $457 billion in 1976 to $20 trillion in 2010. During this period foreign-owned assets in the U.S. increased at an even faster rate from $294 billion to $22.8 trillion in 2010 (U.S. Department of Commerce 2010; see also Mataloni 2005). This globalization of business is apparent in multinational corporations such as Chrysler,[14] Microsoft, Sony, USB, and Shell. For example, The Shell Group operates in 140 countries, is incorporated in the U.K., is headquartered in the Netherlands, and in October 2006 had an executive committee of five:

two were Dutch, and one each was Swiss, British, and American. The executive director for oil and chemical products speaks "English, Dutch, French, German and, to a lesser degree, Swedish and Italian." According to their websites, Citibank operates in 160 countries, Wells Fargo in 130, JPMorgan Chase in more than 100, and Bank of America in more than 40.

An array of international organizations has become economically very important and highly visible, including the European Union (EU), the International Monetary Fund (IMF), the World Trade Organization (WTO), and the World Bank.

The increased power of internationally oriented elites is hardly debatable, but the details are hotly debated. Multinational corporations have increased from 3,000 in 1900, to 7,000 in 1970 to about 63,000 in 2000 (Gabel and Bruner 2003). The development of the World Economic Forum, based in Geneva, is famous for its annual meeting in Davos, Switzerland. It is an indicator and symbol of a socially integrated and self-conscious international elite. They are not, however, of one mind or engaged in a conspiracy. The sponsors and participants of the Forum see themselves as well-intended global citizens, while many critics see them as a self-serving, non-elected ruling class.[15] The obvious importance of such organizations as the World Bank, International Monetary Fund, and the European Union is another indicator of an economic elite whose focus is well beyond a particular nation-state. While the leaders of international non-governmental organizations (INGOs) are not usually economic elites per se, they do contribute to the development of a world culture (Boli and Thomas 1999). There are a burgeoning number of both profit and non-profit INGOs that are hired by donor governments to carry out various kinds of technical assistance programs in developing nations (Cooley and Ron 2002). In addition to the top elites, there is a much larger group whose interests and interpersonal networks often cut across national boundaries.[16] Hence, attempts to analyze the contemporary U.S. must take into account the widening arena within which economic elites operate.

Obviously, the above discussion deals with only a few of the key features of contemporary economic life and economic elites. What it does do is put the discussion of widely observed and commented upon phenomena in the context of a general model. This discourages the tendency to see economic elites and economic issues in isolation from other types of elites and forms of power. It also helps us to see both the similarities and differences between the U.S. and other societies and between the past and the present. We will come back to economic matters when we analyze non-elites.

Political Elites

Unsurprisingly the changes in the nature of technology and the structure of the economy discussed above have modified the kinds of resources that are important in the domestic political realm and the international arena.

Politicians as economists and social workers

Increasingly politicians are held responsible for the society's economic prosperity. In part this is due to the ideology that assumes that the private sector is efficient, that the government is not, and that it often handicaps economic productivity. Politicians are also seen as responsible because of the increasing role of the government in managing the macro economy. It is supposed to sustain consumer demand by means of *neo-Keynesian policies* that manipulate government spending and taxation, and *monetary policies* that manipulate the money supply and interest rates. (In theory the government should increase spending, cut taxes and lower interest rates during downturns and do the opposite during periods of high growth and prosperity.) The problem is that both politicians and economic elites are reluctant to dampen economic expansion by raising taxes and interest rates, but are usually supportive of stimulating the economy during downturns by deficit financing and lower interest rates. The result has been alternating periods of growth and recession and the accumulation of government debt. In 1980 the Federal debt was $900,000 billion, which was 33 percent of GDP. By 2008 the debt was $10.7 trillion, about 75 percent of GDP.[17] In addition, the development of large corporations and banks who are "too big to fail" means that the government and political elites are virtually forced to "bail out" such businesses when they have made bad investment decisions. Letting them fail can devastate the economy as a whole and hence ordinary people. Bailing them out, however, often creates more debt or increases taxes, which again makes politicians vulnerable at the ballot box.

In addition to managing the economy, the state and political elites have had to take on additional welfare activities. As people have become more urbanized and mobile, as women have joined the paid labor force, as people are living longer, and as medical care has become more expensive, it is much more difficult for families or charitable groups to care for sick, aging, or unemployed kindred and neighbors. It is not the case that previous societies did not have "welfare"; it was that it was carried out by less differentiated social institutions such as families and churches.[18]

The U.S. has actually been a laggard in expanding state-based welfare systems. Since these programs are publicly funded, they have increasingly become the responsibility of political elites. In this sense political elites have had to become social workers as well as economists.[19]

The expanded and weakened state

There are other sources of an expanded state. Governments are now responsible for acquiring and managing vast amounts of data including the decennial census, unemployment and job statistics, estimates of crop production, weather records and forecasts, highway and auto safety statistics, balance of trade data, crime statistics, not to speak of the vast amounts of data collected by intelligence agencies. The state has taken on more regulatory responsibilities as it has become apparent that many of the desirable products and services of modern societies have harmful side effects. Some expansion may be due to the self-interests of government officials who gain stature as their subordinates and their budgets increase. Much of it, however, is due to pressures from the private sector for data and services crucial to businesses or civic organizations. For example, dairies, feedlots, bakeries, cereal companies, ethanol manufacturers, distillers, and breweries have a vital interest in knowing whether the grain crop is likely to increase or decrease and how this is likely to affect their costs; farm equipment manufacturers, railroads, trucking companies, and barge companies want to know how this will affect the demand for their services. The tourist industry and consumer groups want airlines made safe, the National Parks kept open, and damaged beaches restored. The point is that the modern state expands because of political pressures from non-governmental sectors.

The responsibilities of political elites are made even more difficult because of the declining relative power of the nation-state, which in large part is due to the increased span of networks.[20] Dealing with rising sea levels and increasing levels of carbon dioxide requires the cooperation of many nation-states, which in turn requires increasing the span of networks and reductions in national sovereignty through international treaties and organizations.

Factors affecting the economy are often beyond the power of any one state to manipulate.[21] The U.S. economy was made more volatile by the European debt crises of 2011–12, but there was little the U.S. could do to alleviate this. Similarly, the Chinese could do little to prevent the U.S. recession of 2008, but this had a significant negative impact on their economy. So the irony is, just as political elites are held responsible for more areas of the collective life, their power to affect these has declined.

This is probably one source of the polarization and impasses characteristic of contemporary political life.

The power of the political elites is also circumscribed by such things as human rights and international trade agreements. The increasing powers of international institutions such as the World Trade Organization, the International Monetary Fund, NATO, and the International Criminal Court are additional constraints.[22] People's consumer taste are also shaped by an increasingly globalized culture, for example, the adoption of jeans as the near-universal "uniform" of young people, and the "McDonaldization" of both work and consumption.[23] Social media also weaken political elites as shown by the Arab Spring's demand for less authoritarian government.[24] Political elites may be able to suppress such demands, but they seem unable to silence them for long. The same media may make democratic politicians more sensitive to short-term pressures, further reducing the ability of the state to solve core problems. The evidence about any one of these effects is often mixed and there is considerable debate about how responsive U.S. politicians are to public opinion.[25] Nonetheless, the basic trend of states having more responsibilities and yet being more affected by factors beyond their control is pretty clear.

Politicians as fund raisers

The high cost of political advertising has made politicians increasingly dependent upon funding from special interest groups and economic elites. While Internet fundraising has increased contributions by small donors, even they are very much above average in wealth and education.[26] In 2010 the Supreme Court ruled that individuals, corporations, and labor unions could contribute unlimited amounts to (supposedly) independent political action committees (so-called super PACs) that supported a particular candidate or cause.[27] This greatly increased the influence of "big money" on politics. Politicians now spend a substantial portion of their time raising money to purchase access to the media. There is debate about the consequences of the increased attention to fundraising (Bailey 2004), but the need for money has on occasion led to bribery and corruption of public officials, and has changed the way elected officials spend their time.

The key point is that these changes, which are widely lamented, are rooted in the changing nature of political resources. As societies have grown in size and complexity, the importance of interpersonal networks and party organization has decreased and the importance of media has increased. While much of politics and governing may be behind the scenes, in democratic regimes making a good impression on voters through the mass media – or making sure your opponent has a more negative image than you do – is crucial. Many of these tendencies are seen in other societies, but they are accentuated by private ownership of most media, a capitalist culture committed to minimizing government regulation, and the veneration of private wealth.

Conservatives and non-elites

As we have pointed out, in most complex societies established political elites seek the support of priestly religious and cultural elites to add to their legitimacy. Only rarely do political leaders embrace prophetic religious leaders. Similarly economic elites are seldom enthusiastic about political elites who want to raise taxes. Frequently they support those who are committed to "law and order" (and especially the protection of property), and to the expansion of territory and markets.

In most societies, and especially democratic ones, a key issue is how conservative political elites gain the support of respectable non-elites – especially for policies that often benefit elites more than non-elites.[28] I argued above that the key functions of political elites were, on the one hand, to deal with external enemies and to create internal order, which primarily involved suppressing deviance from traditional patterns (especially among the lower classes), and, on the other hand, placing limits on the exploitation of the lower strata by economic elites. World War II and the Cold War contributed to a kind of social solidarity that allowed both high expenditures on the military and modest expansions of the welfare state.[29] Whether the expansion of defense spending by the Reagan administration bankrupted the Soviet Union and led to its demise is highly debatable (see Chernoff 1991). It seems very likely, however, that the military buildup and the characterization of the U.S.S.R. as an "evil empire" were effective in creating an alliance between conservative political elites and majorities of the non-elites. This was accentuated by high levels of patriotism and commitment to capitalist ideology characteristic of American exceptionalism. During this period conservative elites could not be totally negative about the state because it was the key organizer of the military and the related industrial complex. With the end of the Cold War, this rationale for non-elite support collapsed and a new basis of solidarity between elites and respectable non-elites was needed.

Internal enemies

One response was a "war" against the unrespectable non-elites. This ideological attack identified welfare chiselers,[30] illegal immigrants,[31] urban gangs,[32] and foreign drug cartels as responsible for many of society's problems.[33] Welfare reform and "law and order" were proposed – some would say touted – as the solutions. There were, of course, real problems with welfare programs, immigration, crime, and drug use. Yet, the stereotypical vilification of welfare recipients, illegal immigrants, urban youth, and drug dealers was not unrelated to the need of political elites for support from respectable non-elites.[34] The state, that is, "the government," also became a stereotyped and vilified enemy. There are, of course, differences between liberal and conservative politicians over these issues, but even "New Democrats" like Bill Clinton gave strong support to welfare reform, and law and order, and declared that the "era of big government is over" (Clinton 1996).

Unsurprisingly, at the height of the anti-government, anti-poor rhetoric, and as the initial impacts of economic globalization began to be felt, "bandits" and "guerrillas" became relevant to American life. The marginalized increasingly resorted to force to secure economic resources and status. Urban gangs and drug organizations were obvious examples. A government report noted, "The last quarter of the 20th century was marked by significant growth in youth gang problems across the United States. In the 1970's, less than half the States reported youth gang problems, but by the late 1990's, every State and the District of Columbia reported youth gang activity. In the same period, the number of cities reporting youth gang problems mushroomed nearly tenfold" (Miller 2001).[35]

Other groups were alienated because of what they saw as the abandonment of traditional values. This was sometimes linked to white supremacist and anti-feminist ideologies. Militia groups implicitly threatened to use violence as a form of resistance.[36] Some resorted to crime to secure the money needed for political activities. The most spectacular example of their violence was the 1995 bombing of Alfred P. Murrah Federal Building in Oklahoma City. Overlapping with, but not identical to, militias were "survivalists," many of whom were millenarians of various types (e.g., Lamy 1996). The best-known is the standoff between federal agents and Randy Weaver in Ruby Ridge, Idaho in 1992. Another overlapping category was religious cults willing to use force to resist government agents, the most famous case being the Waco Branch Davidians in 1993. A variety of relatively left-wing movements also emerged, including radical environmental activists such as the Earth Liberation Front (ELF), which carried out at least 21 serious acts of sabotage between 1996 and 2000 (Young 2005), and animal rights groups such as the Animal Liberation Front (ALF) (Munro 2005).

These right-wing groups were generally condemned for offering violent resistance to government officials that sometimes resulted in their being killed. The eco- and animal-rights radicals were frequently referred to as "terrorists," though most contemporary uses of "terror-ism" imply violence against officials and civilians, rather than crimes against property. Those convicted of crimes were given extraordinarily harsh sentences.[37] The intense reactions to these groups were not just because they violated the law (like ordinary criminals). Far worse, they rejected the legitimacy of the existing social order and violated core values like patriotism and "law and order." While none of these "bandits" threatened to topple the existing political regime, urban mayors did confer with gang leaders to reduce urban violence and federal officials negotiated with armed militia in Waco and Ruby Ridge (Bell 1993; Tucker 1992). In some areas, gangs provided quasi-police protection by keeping out other gangs.[38]

Unrespectable non-elites are often rooted in various domestic prob-lems such as high unemployment, poor Veteran benefits, secularization, or the reactions to the loneliness and alienation of socially and economi-cally marginal individuals. Some see themselves as resisting an intrusive government, and various external threats and conspiracies. Accusations have ranged from "sell outs" to the Communists, to world-wide Jewish and Zionist conspiracies, to "black helicopters" taking over the U.S. and establishing a "New World Order" (NWO).

The key point is that the intensity of the reaction to these groups was related to the need of conservatives for a new "enemy" in order to strengthen the support of the respectable non-elite. This in turn was due in part to changes in the international context, especially the end of the Cold War.

External enemies

Throughout history, elites (especially conservative elites) have invoked the menace of external enemies – real or fabricated – to secure the support of non-elites. Obviously, 9/11 placed terrorism at the center of political discourse. It revealed an external enemy that actually killed several thousand people within the borders of the U.S. and avowed a goal of killing many more. They also killed people in Spain, Bali, India, Northern Ireland, Iraq, Afghanistan, and Pakistan. These terrorists are a particular type of bandit: a guerrilla group, who attack not only the institutions and officials of the state, but non-combatant civilians.[39] In contrast to the mafia, terrorists' motives are more political than eco-nomic, but like mafia they are secretly organized – though this may be a very loosely coupled form of organization.

Predictably, active terrorist groups strengthened the power of con-servative political elites, and economic sectors dependent upon military expenditures. Because conservatives in a capitalist society usually oppose state regulation of economic elites, conservative control impacted much more than security issues. This included relaxation of environmental regulations, consumer protections, and labor laws. It brought large tax cuts that disproportionately benefited the wealthy.[40] Increased defense expenditures and tax cuts led to bigger deficits and a higher national debt – an ironic outcome for a conservative administration. Such changes would have been unlikely without 9/11 and the definition of the response as a "war" on terrorism rather than a hunt for criminals.

Conservatism was accentuated by the invasions of Iraq and Afghanistan. Being "at war" usually increases support for the military and the government in power. Political elites are able to set aside economic issues in the name of security and national honor. When foreigners criticize a nation's political elite – the dominant foreign response to the invasion of Iraq – this often strengthens the government's legitimacy and makes it less necessary to respond to the domestic concerns such as wage levels and job security. Unless a war results in a defeat or stalemate, political elites typically have higher levels of internal legitimacy than in peacetime. There may be internal dissent and protest, but, until the war seems lost, these are typically trumped by increased patriotism, loyalty, and chauvinism by the bulk of the non-elite.[41] This pattern was clearly seen following the 2003 invasion of Iraq.[42] The failure of such actions, however, produced splits within political elites and eroded non-elite support. It became apparent between 2005 and 2008 that the U.S. occupation did not result in a friendly and effective new government. Predictably, conservative elites began to fracture. Critics of the Bush administration's handling of the war in Iraq included retired top commanders, the Iraq Study Group co-chaired by longtime Republican James Baker, and key Republican Senators such as John Warner and Chuck Hagel (Baker et al. 2006; Cloud and Schmitt 2006; Gray and Roberts 2007; Ricks 2006). Violence in Iraq began to decline in 2009, but the prospects for long-term stability and a democratic government continued to be problematic. The key point of this discussion is not, however, about Iraq, but about the use of external enemies as a way political elites gain the support of non-elites.

Liberals and the disadvantaged

Liberal politicians have tried to mobilize political support from disadvantaged groups. Since the Civil Rights Act of 1964, African-Americans have usually supported Democratic candidates. On the whole the Democratic Party has been more active in reducing gender inequality, and predictably women disproportionately vote Democratic. Democrats have been more open to immigration reform that would give millions of illegal Latino immigrants a possible path to U.S. citizenship.[43] It is possible that the combination of these three groups – African-Americans, women, and Latinos – may eventually give the Democratic Party a ruling majority. Ironically, it was generally conservative businessmen who sought low-wage workers and attracted illegal immigrants. The key theoretical point is that just as conservative politicians have often mobilized respectable non-elites against unrespectable non-elites, liberals often try to transform disadvantaged groups into political supporters.

Decline of local elites

People on the East Coast regularly eat vegetables grown in California, Florida, Texas, and Mexico, and talk with call centers in Utah, Kansas, and India; people in the Midwest and the West Coast regularly deal with banks, insurance companies, and brokerage houses on the East Coast. One result is that local economic elites like bankers and owners of local businesses have declined in significance. Between 1990 and 2010, the number of bank branch offices increased from 50,858 to 87,732, while the number of main offices declined from 12,342 to 6,676 (U.S. Census Bureau 2010a). Most banks are part of a chain and the success of managers and loan officers is not primarily dependent upon the prosperity of their local community. Community prosperity is increasingly dependent upon large companies building facilities in the vicinity. This has eroded the position of local economic and political elites. Corporations look for areas that have a favorable "business climate": low taxes, weak trade unions, low labor costs, and deferential local officials.[44] Corporations often pressure local politicians to give them tax moratoriums or to provide infrastructure and buildings at public expense – and it is made clear that a given community is in competition with several other communities. State governments are also subject to the same pressures. In at least one case a governor has called a special session of the legislature to propose that the state give a corporation $150 million in tax breaks and incentives (Wilson 2013). The winner of the contest is often the community or state that offers the corporation the best deal. Of course, this argument can be overstated; local politics and local elites can shape the attractiveness of their cities to business investment, and can vary in their skill at bargaining with business interests. Nonetheless, local areas are more affected by global structures and trends, and the power of local elites is circumscribed by such factors.[45]

Local status and cultural elites face similar pressures. Opera fans can now watch live broadcasts of the Metropolitan Opera at their local movie theatre – for less than the cost of a ticket to hear an inferior regional opera company. Local ministers must compete with national and international televangelists. Local radio stations and disk jockeys have been replaced by national chains whose programming is often done at the company's headquarters. For example, Clear Channel Communications Inc. owns and operates more than 850 radio stations in the U.S.[46] Minor league sports teams have fewer fans because it is easier to watch the national and international teams on TV. In short, the relative power of local elites has declined.

A note on the elite solidarity

While the model points to the importance of identifying different types of elites, their varying interests, and their patterns of conflict and cooperation, this is not to deny the importance of mechanisms that build solidarity across elites. These include similar social backgrounds, levels of education, levels of income, shared social and cultural institutions such as clubs, museums, orchestras, etc., and "revolving door" patterns of recruitment between government, businesses, and universities. I have paid less attention to these mechanisms, because they been extensively discussed and emphasized by previous analysts (e.g., Domhoff 2013; Dye, Zeigler, and Schubert 2012). In some historical periods they explain much of what goes on. My point is that the degree of elite integration is more likely to be adequately accessed only if our models focus on forms of differentiations, varying interests, and areas of conflict – as well as mechanisms that produce cooperation and solidarity.

I will postpone summarizing the above discussion, comparing the proposed model to earlier models, or stating general conclusions until we take up the actors often neglected by previous analyses.

6

The U.S. 1980–2008:
Other Actors

Economic and political elites have great power and exercise enormous influence, and many analytical models limit their analyses to these groups. In this chapter we will consider the "other actors" who are important for understanding what is going on: status elites and non-elites.

Status Elites

When we consider contemporary status elites in the context of the general model, it is apparent that there are those who are roughly equivalent to prophets and priests. But before we take up these conflicts, it is important to point out how the nature of status elites has changed.

Celebrities

The greatly enhanced processing of symbols made possible new communications media, expanded networks, and new cultural arenas. These increased the importance of celebrities. Larger more complex societies make it more difficult for an individual to be widely known. In a village or small town, nearly everyone knows everyone else; in a major city a person knows only a small percentage of the residents. Hence visibility has become more scarce and valuable and celebrities with high visibility have increased in importance and power. Greater cultural pluralism has interacted with this trend. The category of celebrities is more consequential than ever, but because there are more celebrities, their relative average worth has decreased. At the beginning of the twenty-first century no movie star had the near-universal visibility of earlier stars such as Humphrey Bogart, Cary Grant, Kathryn Hepburn, Ingrid Bergman, Frank Sinatra, or Elvis Presley.[1]

Widely known celebrities probably contribute to cultural and social integration. Not everyone liked Elvis Presley, but virtually everyone knew who he was. Status elites commonly bolster the legitimation of political and economic elites – and the institutions they use and shape. In the U.S. celebrities are central to this process. Celebrities advertising beer, fast foods, tennis shoes, watches, credit cards, and automobiles are only the most overt example. More important is the indirect legitimation of good looks, sensuality and extravagant consumption, which supposedly constitutes the "good life" of celebrities. The centrality of celebrities is apparent in "entertainment news," "talk shows," and tabloid magazines about the "lives of the rich and famous." The hosts of these shows become "secondary celebrities," roughly divided between "touts" who sell the celebrity, and gossip columnists who "dish the dirt." This is a variation on the priest and prophet roles. The displacement of more traditional ideological elites by celebrities changes and probably erodes public discourse and debate.

Nor is this trend limited to the entertainment industries. The term "public intellectual" did not come into common usage until the latter third of the twentieth century.[2] It refers to those whose work engages not only other specialists but a broader public by addressing controversial issues. A public intellectual is a particular type of celebrity. They can be priest or prophet, but high social visibility is the sine qua non. More and more economic elites become celebrities. Steve Jobs, Bill Gates, Larry Page, and Mark Zuckerberg are obvious examples. Andrew Carnegie, Henry Ford, and John D. Rockefeller became celebrities, but usually because of later charitable activities. What seems new is the rapidity and intentionality of economic elites seeking visibility and celebrity status.

Politicians also try to become celebrities to gain visibility in the media.[3] They now face instant sound and image recording of virtually all of their public words, which are communicated via around-the-clock news to their whole constituency. The main form of communication becomes brief, generalized sound bites directed to large heterogeneous audiences – even when delivered to a particular specialized audience.[4] This is exemplified by the phrase "staying on message" – now a common part of the cultural vocabulary. Public relations firms specialize in helping politicians, firms, and individuals "stay on message."[5] Being brief, clear, and articulate is a virtue, but often contemporary political discourse involves repeating the same cliché.

Celebrities become politicians: Shirley Temple, Jack Kemp, Ronald Reagan, Sonny Bono, Bill Bradley, John Glenn, Clint Eastwood, Jesse Ventura, and Arnold Schwarzenegger. Inheritance of celebrity status is also important: Joseph Kennedy, Jay Rockefeller, Richard M. Daley, Jessie Jackson, Jr., Mary Bono, Jeb Bush, Al Gore, and George W. Bush. More important, politicians have adopted the tools of the celebrity: the press agent, the publicist, the pollster, and the media coach – who pay as much attention to style, personality, and image as to policy.[6] Being a celebrity politician is a double-edged sword; if visibility and appealing personal qualities become the means to success, competitors have every reason to make visible unappealing qualities. Just as movie stars spawned gossip columnists, celebrity-politicians have led to a press preoccupied with their personal lives – especially scandals. This further contributes to negative campaigning.[7]

The key theoretical point is that the nature of political resources has shifted: visibility through the mass media is increasingly important, especially in democratic regimes. It advantages those already celebrities or those skilled in the ways of the celebrity. This in turn has changed the nature of political organization, including decreasing the significance of political parties, and increasing the importance of fundraising by candidates. In turn, the closest advisors of most politicians are no longer the local and state party activists, but rather the specialists in the media and public relations.

Think tanks

Another important change has been the development of think tanks that conduct and use academic research and theorizing to support particular ideological positions. In many respects these institutions have become the "priests" and the "prophets" of a more secularized society.

Particularly notable has been the development of conservative institutions. In 1971 Lewis F. Powell, a Richmond corporate lawyer who later became an Associate Justice of the Supreme Court, wrote an influential memo to a friend at the U.S. Chamber of Commerce that urged conservatives to establish and fund think tanks that would defend the private enterprise system.[8] Prominent conservative think tanks have included: Heritage Foundation, American Enterprise Institute, Center for Strategic and International Studies, Cato Institute, Hoover Institution, Manhattan Institute, Lexington Institute, Project for the New American Century, Center for Security Policy, Foreign Policy Research Institute, Center for Immigration Studies, Claremont Institute, and Hudson Institute. While some of these organizations had antecedents, many grew significantly in funding and influence during the 1970s and 1980s and moved ideological discourse to the right of what it had been since the New Deal. There were, of course, a number of such institutions that were of a more liberal bent including Center for American Progress and the Economic Policy Institute, as well as less explicitly ideological organizations like the Urban Institute and the Brookings Institution. Celebrity "public intellectuals" frequently have links to think tanks.

A note on traditional status elites

The above discussion focuses on relatively new developments, but this does not mean that more traditional status elites are irrelevant. Clergy, journalists, novelists, and professors all contribute to the discussion of the good and the bad: what persons, organizations, objects, ideas, and types of behaviors should receive expressions of approval and disapproval, and hence have high and low status. Of course, most clergy, professors, and journalists are not elites, but some are: denominational leaders, columnists in the most prestigious papers, and TV commentators for national networks. Along with their more local counterparts, they all play a role in defining the good and the bad. I have focused on celebrities and think tanks because they have become more important and to some degree diminished the influence of more traditional status elites. The latter are, however, still important.

Non-elites

When U.S. politicians and ideologues refer to respectable non-elites they talk about "the middle class." This includes a wide range of occupations and incomes; it typically means those usually employed and not using "welfare." The term "working class" generally referred to those doing manual labor. Its use has declined because much of manual labor has been mechanized or automated, and because much routine work involves manipulating symbols (e.g., data entry, call centers, bookkeeping, and retail sales).

Elites are affected by the exogenous variables, by the actions of other types of elites and by the actions of non-elites. Non-elites are affected by most of the same exogenous variables. They are, however, even more affected by the actions of elites since in most situations elites have substantially more power than non-elites. With this in mind we draw on the general model to identify and analyze some of the key trends and events involving non-elites during the period under study.

Technological and economic changes

During the 1980–2008 period there was modest economic growth. (The downturn of 1982 was an exception.) Compared to Europe unemployment was low, but economic inequality increased substantially. The same technological and economic forces that produced a key cleavage in economic elites also affected non-elites. Non-elites who creatively manipulate symbols (e.g., writers, system analysts, CPAs, and advanced computer programmers) did well. Those with lower skills faced eroding wages and increased job insecurity. This occurred in manufacturing, routine symbolic manipulation (e.g., data entry clerks), low-skilled services (e.g., food and janitorial services), and agriculture workers.[9]

Changes in the distribution of income also polarized. To quote the U.S. Census Bureau (2005):[10]

> Generally, the long-term trend has been toward increasing income inequality. Since 1969, the share of aggregate household income controlled by the lowest income quintile has decreased from 4.1 percent to 3.6 percent in 1997, while the share to the highest quintile increased from 43.0 percent to 49.4 percent. Most noticeably, the share of income controlled by the top 5 percent of households has increased from 16.6 percent to 21.7 percent. Over the same time period, the Gini index rose 17.4 percent to its 1997 level of .459.

Since 1997 the trend toward inequality has accentuated. By 2001 the lowest fifth received 3.5 percent of the total income, while the top fifth received 50.1 percent. The data for 2010 show the top fifth receiving 50.3 percent, but the bottom fifth received 3.3 percent.[11] Stated in other terms, in 1970 the average (mean) income of the households in the top fifth was 10.9 times that of the bottom fifth. By 2010 the top fifth on average made 15.4 times as much as the bottom fifth.[12] When we compare the mean incomes of the bottom fifth with the top five percent, the gap went from $165,112 in 1970 to $290,871 in 2010 (in constant dollars).[13] The result is the top and the bottom increasingly live very different lives. The relative and absolute increases in economic and social distance between the top five percent and the bottom five percent (or the top and bottom one percent) were almost certainly much greater (Johnston 2005). Conversely, the relative position of households in the bottom four-fifths of the population declined, while the top fifth became absolutely and relatively much richer. Those at the bottom are probably worse off not only relatively, but absolutely. Greater income inequality has led to greater residential segregation by class and race (Reardon and Bischoff 2011; Watson 2009).[14] A recent study of nine developed countries found that "The U.S. is the most economically unequal rich nation on Earth and has been so for the last forty years" (Smeeding, Erikson, and Jäntti 2011: 3).[15] There is increasing evidence that increased income inequality is correlated with reduced levels of intergenerational mobility, and that the net effect of educational programs does not increase mobility or equality of opportunity.[16]

Trade unions were largely unsuccessful in protecting the interests of non-elites because of the combination of (1) strong anti-state and pro-business ideology, (2) globalization, and (3) rapidly changing production technology. Membership fell from 33 percent of the non-agricultural workforce in 1955 to about 11.8 percent in 2011. Moreover, public sector workers make up over half of union membership (and most cannot strike), while membership has fallen to 10.7 percent in manufacturing, and to 13.1 percent in construction.[17] Relatively well-paying manufacturing jobs have been replaced with a combination of low-level and high-level service jobs – both more difficult to unionize.[18]

Greater inequality and insecurity have contributed to an alienated, underemployed urban underclass largely composed of minorities.[19] The "dot-com" take-off of the late 1990s and the real estate boom of 2000–5 mitigated this. Nonetheless, many people lost jobs due to technological innovation and moving jobs overseas.[20] While unemployment rates have been lower than in Europe, job creation has barely kept up with population growth. With the downturn of 2008, unemployment became a key economic and political issue. Moreover, many of the jobs created provide low pay and little if any benefits or security.[21] A greater reliance on temporary workers reduced pay increases for regular employees (Houseman, Kalleberg, and Erickcek 2003). Even well-qualified recent college graduates often had to settle for unpaid internships. Fewer constraints on employers lowered costs and contributed to lower unemployment, but this is a source of other critical problems. Real wages have grown only slightly and those of unskilled workers have decreased.[22] Hiring illegal immigrants is often perceived to put a downward pressure on wages (Citrin et al. 1997; Deufel 2003). It can increase ethnic tension – as indicated by the attempts to restrict use of welfare (TANF), Medicaid, and driving licenses (Ellwood and Ku 1998). California's Proposition 187 and Alabama's "Taxpayer and Citizen Protection Act" are examples of efforts to discourage illegal immigration.[23] Despite reducing labor costs, major U.S. corporations went bankrupt or had to be bailed out by the federal government. The airlines, the auto manufacturers, Xerox, and AIG are only the most visible examples. Courts often allowed distressed corporations to cancel pension and healthcare obligations (Barakat 2005; Garmisa 1997).

In 2010, 49.9 million had no health insurance, of whom 7.3 million were children.[24] Even Medicare recipients face out-of-pocket medical expenses averaging 19.0 percent of their total income in 1995. Out-of-pocket costs for those in poor health were 28.5 percent of their income and for the lowest income quintile 31.5 percent (Crystal et al. 2000). To receive long-term care under Medicaid, the elderly must exhaust their assets (including selling their homes), and declare themselves poverty-stricken.[25]

Another effect of the economic decline of non-elites is the neglect of children and public institutions. Income for middle- and lower-class strata declined in real terms until the mid-1990s and has continued to decline in relative terms. Families often attempted to offset this by women entering the labor force.[26] This helped reduce gender inequality, but led to greater commoditization (i.e., having to purchase goods and services formerly produced in the home or by voluntary organizations). Examples include takeout meals, paid childcare, house cleaning services, psychotherapy (rather than pastoral care), and gym fees. Commoditization was both a cause and an effect of the expansion of the service sector, and the transformation of kinship and household patterns.

Many jobs require significant commuting time; in 2009 the average was over fifty minutes a day (McKenzie and Rapino 2011; Wulfhorst 2006). Often jobs require night or on weekend work, complicating families spending time together or sharing meals.[27] "Latchkey children" left at home without adult supervision are becoming common because of a scarcity of affordable daycare.[28] Moreover, some parents try to compensate for their absence by giving children more spending money, which contributes to a whole series of other problems.[29] Finally, this greater labor force participation and complicated work schedules probably contribute to the neglect of public institutions such as local government and voluntary associations and the decline of social capital in general. This is a controversial issue that was the focus of Robert Putnam's *Bowling Alone* (2000). All of this is to say that the changes in the non-elite economic opportunities had important consequences for family structures and civil society.[30] While some evidence suggests that 1990s welfare reform slightly improved the status and wellbeing of single mothers, they are only marginally better off than before.[31] It is by no means clear that the "welfare problem" will not re-emerge (Hays 2003). Extensive homelessness is one indicator that the lowest classes are approaching the state of being outcasts – in fact, if not in ideology.[32]

The "digital divide" has in some respects lessened. Nonetheless, substantial differences exist in people's access to and use of the Internet (Zickuhr and Smith 2012). Moreover, even universal access to the Internet will not produce a socially integrated society, any more than near-universal literacy, telephone access, or automobile use has.

To summarize, those in the top fifth of the population – and especially the top one percent – have become substantially better off economically, while others have made only marginal gains, or have lost ground. A key response to eroding incomes has been increased participation in the labor force: more women working, holding two or three jobs, and teenagers working. This has reduced gender inequality, but has real social costs for families and communities: greater residential segregation, increased suburbanization, and lengthy commuting. The result is different income and ethnic groups have quite different life experiences, and relatively little meaningful contact with one another. Finally, substantial numbers of people – the homeless, drug addicts, illegal immigrants – have in effect become social outcasts.

Political and military changes

As noted in the discussion of political elites, the Democratic Party moved to the right during the Clinton administration and in general supported globalization. This was accompanied by an even more extreme move to the right by elements of the Republican Party. This triggered new forms of resistance among segments of non-elites. This brought a period of political polarization and stalemate during some of George W. Bush's administration and especially Barack Obama's presidency. It was difficult to get any significant legislation passed and implemented. This led to disillusionment with politics among non-elites. In October 2011 approval of Congress reached what was then an all-time low of nine percent. Other measures of confidence in the government, politicians, and politics show similar declines (Zeleny and Thee-Brenan 2011).

A steady decline in voter participation occurred, though this varies depending on whether it is a presidential campaign. In 1964 (Johnson vs. Goldwater) 69.3 percent of the population voted, while in 2008 (Obama vs. McCain) 58.2 percent voted.[33] Starting in 2003, Republicans have attempted to introduce laws in most states requiring elaborate forms of identification in order to vote. Supposedly, this is to reduce voter fraud, though the primary effect is a reduction in voter participation. While the percentage of registered people who vote has increased, the percentage of those who register has been around 60 compared to 70 percent in the 1960s. Moreover, studies suggest the increases in turnout of registered voters since the 2008 election are due to increasing political polarization (Dodson 2010). This has made it more difficult for elected officials to reach compromises and conduct the state's business, which led to more political cynicism among non-elites. Whatever the details of these various trends, they indicate a significant level of indifference, alienation, or cynicism about one of the most fundamental processes in an elective democracy.

More active resistance included the protest against the WTO and the World Bank in Seattle in November 1999, and the 2000 presidential candidacy of Ralph Nader. Libertarianism and even anarchism have been revived as the ideology of several radical groups, including elements of the Green Party. In 2009 the Tea Party movement became important within the Republican Party. While it is a populist, anti-big-government movement, it has received organizing support and large contributions from very wealthy donors including the billionaire brothers David H. Koch and Charles G. Koch. British Ambassador to the U.S. Sir Christopher Meyer characterized the Tea Party movement as a "combination of grassroots populism, professional conservative politics, and big money, floating on a sea of economic distress" (Meyer 2010).

The terrorism of September 11, 2001, the subsequent wars in Iraq and Afghanistan, and the continuing threats of terrorism shifted attention to military and security matters. The model again draws attention to elites using the threat of external and internal enemies to gain the political support of non-elites. Such wars also decrease the non-elites' focus on economic matters. Moreover, wars often provide a major stimulus to capitalist economies that lessen the effects of economic recessions. Failed or extended wars are another matter. By 2005 a majority disapproved of the Bush administration's handling of the economy and the war in Iraq.[34] In the 2006 elections the Democrats gained control of both the House and the Senate.

September 11 and the Iraq war contributed to the creation of several new kinds of reprehensible non-elites. Recent immigrants, especially from Islamic areas, were seen as potential terrorists and economic competitors. As Lipset's notion of American exceptionalism would suggest, the Iraq war and the resulting protests from the majority of governments and people outside of the U.S. made non-elites more nationalistic. Because of France's criticism of U.S. policy in 2003, conservative commentators called for boycotts of French wines. The menu in the U.S. House of Representative's cafeteria relabeled "French fries" as "freedom fries." Protesters against the war in Iraq were often called unpatriotic. Even relatively pro-American elites from abroad were looked upon with suspicion. These new external and internal enemies – real and imagined – gave U.S. elites a new basis of nationalistic solidarity with both respectable and non-respectable non-elites.

In 2006 a controversy arose that illustrated the concern about terrorism and how its impact on nationalism and chauvinism affects politics and vice versa. DP World, owned by the government of Dubai (United Arab Emirates), bought a British company that had been managing several U.S. ports, and many other ports around the world. Both Democratic and Republican politicians criticized the Bush administration for initially approving this arrangement. While most experts claimed that this involved no additional security risks, polls showed that a majority of Americans were opposed. The company was pressured into selling their U.S. operations to an "American company" AIG (Timmons 2006). Their website described the company in the following terms:

> American International Group, Inc. (AIG), world leaders in insurance and financial services, is the leading international insurance organization with operations in more than 130 countries and jurisdictions ... AIG companies are leading providers of retirement services and asset management around the world. AIG's common stock is listed in the U.S. on the New York Stock Exchange [and] the stock exchanges in London, Paris, Switzerland and Tokyo.[35]

Though the "A" in AIG stands for "American," this is a company that had a global rather than an "American" orientation. Ironically, in 2008 the company experienced such large losses that it had to be bailed out by the federal government, and eventually sold its American operations to MetLife.

The Bush administration used the long existing sentiments of patriotism and nationalism to gain support for their policies and intensified these by going to war. They could not always manipulate these sentiments to their advantage – as the controversy over the Dubai company's operation of U.S. ports shows. It was liberal Democratic Senator Charles Schumer who led the fight against DP World, drawing on the same sentiments that the Bush administration had used. Manipulation by elites is neither a necessary nor sufficient condition for creating nationalism. Elites nonetheless frequently used such sentiments for various partisan political ends.[36] Both the initial support for the Iraq war and the protest against DP World are in part rooted in the relatively high levels of patriotism and chauvinism long characteristic of "American exceptionalism."

Though terrorism and wars in Iraq were a key focus of political debates in this period, it cannot be assumed that the public were better informed about what was going on – at least based on the evidence from similar events in the past. A study of the number of people watching the nightly news shows that there was only a very brief increase around the times of the Gulf War and 9/11, and that newspaper readership has continued to decline.[37]

The focus on external enemies and immigrants seems to have played a crucial role in mobilizing non-elite support for the Bush administration and its policies – until it became patently obvious that these had failed to establish a viable democratic and friendly regime in Iraq. Non-elites withdrew their support at the ballot box and their willingness to join the military. Difficulties in recruiting and retaining personnel increased, especially for critical combat positions (U.S. Government Accountability Office 2006), which weakened the military and meant fewer jobs for non-elites. A similar pattern emerged in Afghanistan; a war that President Obama endorsed and which seems to be a stalemate. Again the use of outside enemies to gain non-elite support is not limited to Republicans. On May 2, 2011, President Obama went on national television and radio at 11:35 PM to announce that an American Navy Seal unit had killed Osama bin Laden. His approval ratings increased significantly for several weeks. In subsequent political speeches he has reminded voters of this event.

In short, political elites, especially conservative elites, are frequently successful in securing non-elite political support by identifying or creating internal and external enemies. If, however, wars are lost or persecuting outcasts does not concretely benefit respectable non-elites, then new forms of non-elite resistance, both legal and illegal, tend to emerge. This is what the theoretical model would suggest and is the pattern that is observed in varying combinations in the U.S. during the 1990s and the first years of the twenty-first century.

Status and ideological changes

Non-elites also had significant status and cultural concerns. During the 2004 election a new internal enemy and threat was discovered: the attempt by gays and lesbians to receive equal legal rights. This was not primarily an economic or security matter, but a matter of status and culture. Most threatening was the move to redefine marriage so that it was available to same-sex couples. This was seen to lower the status of the institution of marriage and to provide not only tolerance, but also respectability to gays and lesbians. President Bush and the Republicans proposed constitutional amendments to override judicial decisions that had been sympathetic to the rights of gays and lesbians – even though there was no chance of passing such an amendment. This was a classic case of creating enemies for political purposes. This further de-emphasized economic problems and the difficulties in Iraq, and mobilized conservative non-elites.

While public expressions of racial or gender chauvinism have decreased, actual patterns of behavior still reflected significant biases: lower income of households headed by women and African-Americans, "white flight" to the suburbs, and low rates of cross-race intermarriage.[38] Generally, public figures reject the legitimacy of (status) discrimination based on ethnicity or gender, but avoid policies that would seriously threaten the status, economic, or political interests of the majority of non-elites. As the majority is increasingly composed of minorities, this is becoming a problematic tactic.

The expansion of consumerism is perhaps even more important in influencing the worldview of non-elites.[39] Consumption has become a central measure of individual self-worth and family status. Shopping has been transformed from a largely instrumental activity into an expressive one: instead of attending church, going to the PTA meeting, or heading for the park, a family outing or a vacation destination becomes a trip to the mall.[40] There have long been social and expressive elements to shopping (e.g., rural families "going to town" on Saturday), but shopping and consumption make up a larger part of human experience than in poorer, less developed societies. The abandonment of Sabbath closing laws and stores open 24/7 reveal the increased centrality and legitimacy of consumption.

The increased significance of consumption de-emphasizes political, civic and cultural activities, and reinforces the individual over the collective, the self over the community.[41] Concerns common to many are converted into personal problems to be solved by various forms of therapy or self-help – obscuring the link between the "personal problems," the distribution of power, and the policies pursued by various elites.

Social visibility is a prerequisite to having status – negative or positive. Therefore the increased importance of "celebrityhood," and of being publicly visible, reduces the importance of traditional sources of respect such as being a good spouse, parent, and citizen. Celebrities' association with high consumption accentuates the importance of economic activities, and implicitly decreases the importance of kinship, friendship, community participation, and politics (Putnam 2000). People become admired because they lead a lifestyle that is modeled after "the rich and famous" or because they have become quasi-celebrities.

This was seen in the enormous increase and popularity of "reality" and "discover-the-idol" television. "Ordinary people" subject themselves to stressful situations or try to perform like showbusiness professionals to secure "fame and fortune." These shows became an important ingredient of contemporary popular culture and were a further indicator of the shifting basis of status. Simply being visible in the media, by whatever means, became a mark of individual importance and status.[42]

Another example of the search for visibility is the popularity of historical reenactments. It is a chance to "dress up" as someone else and draw the attention of an audience. Historical reenactments have a long history, but in the past they were often arranged by dominant or ruling groups. In contrast, they now tend to be a part of popular culture rooted primarily in the lower-middle classes. There are many sources and motivations for reenactments, but certainly one of these is people seeking to be mini-celebrities.[43]

The importance of visibility also influenced the criteria of status and what it is important to communicate. Images have increased in importance and pictures of supermodels saturate the mass media and the commercial world.[44] A corollary is that beauty, youth, and sexiness have become more important. People spend significant amounts on exercise, cosmetics, clothes, and plastic surgery to increase their attractiveness for romantic relationships, and to improve their job prospects.[45] Not only movie stars, models, and entertainers need to be good looking; this is also becoming a prerequisite for TV journalists, politicians, authors of mass-audience books, and even many salespersons, waiters, and waitresses. Good looks have always been an asset.[46] It seems to be becoming a near prerequisite for some jobs – often jobs whose ostensible function has little to do with appearance. Politicians and journalists are only the most obvious examples. Conversely, being overweight becomes a social (as well as a physical) handicap, creating yet another way in which inequality is polarized.[47]

The concern with "image" is not restricted to a few professions. A number of firms specialize in "branding" individuals by advising them about how they should present themselves in person, in resumes, in dating service materials, and on their personal websites. The explicit assumption is that the person is a product that must be marketed, and that careful attention should be paid to image and branding. As in the marketing of high-quality products, the image accentuates the positive and downplays the negative, but avoids making false claims. The usual cost is from several hundred to thousands of dollars. Some firms advise about a thousand clients per month. The practice became widespread enough that it was reported and discussed in the mainline public media.[48]

Not only has the criteria for elite status shifted, but also the relationship between elites and non-elites has been transformed. Those of lower status have often attempted to improve their standing by associating with their betters. A version of this is that fans often identify with celebrities, not only because they admire them, but also as a way to increase their own status (Milner 2005, 2010). This has analogues to religious behavior; people seek associations with gods in part to transform their own spiritual status – and sometimes their worldly status too – by being linked to something that is much greater than they are.[49] The more intimate such relationships are, the more the status of the subordinate is improved. Praying daily and worshipping regularly affects people's lives more than attending church a few times a year; marrying a celebrity affects your status more than shaking hands with one. Since few have direct personal contact with celebrities, fans seek intimacy with their "gods" by learning about their "private" lives. Just as the performances in celebrities' public lives are made more visible by the media, so are their backstage behaviors and "private" lives, including embarrassing and deviant behaviors. So the preoccupation with "private lives" and "dirt" is not entirely or even primarily because of the distorted values of contemporary individuals. In contemporary societies people relate to many aspects of the broader world through the mass media, which are inherently impersonal in traditional terms. The media creates various forms of virtual intimacy or imagined intimacy by focusing upon the private lives of celebrities.[50]

An especially striking example of the preoccupation with visibility and intimacy is the proliferation of videos on the Internet that show people having sexual intercourse. Many of these are deliberately created pornography aimed at making money for actors and distributors. Some, however, appear on personal or non-commercial websites. At least some appear to be made by amateurs (though not necessarily posted on the sites by these amateurs). There are undoubtedly varied and multiple motivations for the creation and distribution of such videos, but it seems likely one key reason is the desire for social visibility.[51] Historically, privacy is a relatively modern invention. When many people lived together in small quarters sexual activity was more visible than modern ideals. Moreover, there is a long history of Bacchanalian celebrations and various kinds of orgies. But for these pre-modern examples, social visibility of sexuality was a byproduct, not the goal of the event. In contrast, posting a video of you or friends having sex seems to be in part a near-compulsive striving for social visibility.

To summarize, non-elites have many concerns that are related to, but not reducible to matters of economics and politics. Like economic and political changes, status concerns are shaped by both the emergence of broader social networks, and by relatively unique cultural traditions, and the evolution or transformation of such traditions. These include

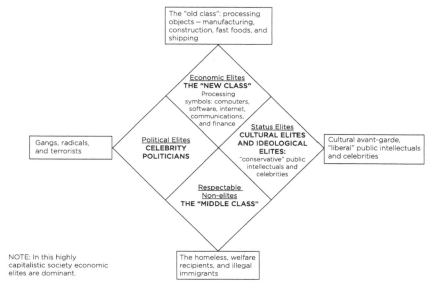

Figure 4: Contemporary United States

the long tradition of emphasizing individual autonomy, high rates of religious participation, the unique history of racism in the U.S., and judging politicians and officials on the basis of their personal sexual behavior. On the other hand, there seems to be a significant change in traditional norms about social visibility and intimacy including sexual relationships.

This concludes the analysis of this period in the U.S. The model is summarized in Figure 4.

Comparison with Other Models

Comparison with Marxism

If one is referring to classical Marxism, then there are relatively few Marxists left. The economic and political inadequacies of twentieth-century Communist regimes, the collapse of the Soviet bloc, and the shift of the remaining Communist regimes to market economies have made this understanding of social change and history implausible in this historical period. Contemporary Marxist sociology ranges from models that continue to emphasize the centrality of the relations of production and class conflict to more cultural models including those inspired by the Frankfurt Institute.[52] In its later versions such neo-Marxism becomes difficult to distinguish from critical theory, postmodernism, and cultural studies.[53] But the most common form of contemporary Marxism seems to focus on the dilemmas and contradictions within capitalism: cutting labor costs versus maintaining consumer demand, reducing government debt versus maintaining infrastructure, schools and welfare systems, and expanding the economy versus minimizing environmental damage.

I would argue that most insights that can be derived from Marxist analyses can be incorporated within the model I have outlined. I agree that the dominant form of power in the U.S. is held by the corporate elite, and that this power needs to be limited and regulated by the state. The proposed model, however, avoids the limitations of most Marxist models. First, it is not wedded to a notion of an expanding and homogeneous proletariat, and the subsidiary argument that an organized proletariat via labor unions and labor parties is the best hope for limiting the corporate elite, and creating a more just society. While not all Marxists have been so wedded, probably the two most prominent Marxist sociologists, Michael Burawoy and Erik Olin Wright, have at points in their career taken this position (Burawoy 2002; Wright and Singelmann 1982). My model does not exclude this possibility, but neither does it assume this is the case. Given the changing nature of work and the labor force, there is good reason to be skeptical that unions can be the primary check on the new forms of capital that are emerging. Second, the most profound reforms in American society during the twentieth and early twenty-first centuries came from social movements that were not primarily based on class or related to conflicts within the production system: the civil rights movement, the women's movement, the anti-nuclear movement, the anti-Vietnam War movement, the animal rights movement, the human rights movement, the environmental movement, and the movement for the rights of gay, lesbian, bisexual, and transgendered people. This is not to say that these movements were not in part motivated by economic and class interests or supported more by some classes than others, but few of these were class-based movements primarily concerned about their economic power vis-à-vis capitalists. While some progressive unions supported these movements, they were resisted by most of the working class and at least implicitly by many of their unions. When histories are written in a hundred years, I suspect that Martin Luther King, Betty Freidan, Gloria Steinem, Rachel Carson, Jane Fonda, and Ralph Nader will be given more attention than most labor leaders of this period. Stated in the terms of the model, status elites will be seen as more important than Marxian analyses would suggest. Marxists also overestimate the power of capital in the political process. Money from rich capitalists and corporations has a disproportionate influence on political processes in general and political elites in particular, and this is probably increasing. Yet, the rise (and to some extent the fall) of the Christian Right, emergence of the Tea Party Movement, or the election of Barack Obama is not primarily due to the support of corporate capitalism. My point is not that Marxists have not or cannot acknowledge the importance of non-class movements, but that their theoretical schemes do not sensitize them to these. Finally, none of this is to rule out the possibility of a more class-based conflict and movements in the future. The increasing income inequality certainly makes this a possibility, but the general model does not assume that this will necessarily be the case.

Comparison with elite theory

Classical elite and contemporary theory tends to neglect the analysis of non-elites. Too often they are characterized as a largely undifferentiated "mass," for example, by comparing opinions of elites with those of everyone else. Thomas Dye and his various colleagues (e.g., Dye 2002; Dye, Zeigler, and Schubert 2012) are probably the best-known and most prolific contemporary exponents of elite theory. If Marxists are overly focused on economic power, elite theorists are primarily focused on political power. Exogenous factors like the effects of TV, the Internet, smart phones, and social media may be discussed, but mainly in terms of how they impact politics by shaping such things as what constitutes "news," the nature of fund raising, and the nature of campaigning. The proposed model recognizes the importance of politics, but also draws attention to the relatively non-political effects of a wide array of social and cultural developments: the increased significance of celebrities and "reality TV," the increase in interaction that is not face-to-face due to the Internet, the proliferation of amateur sex videos, and the increased importance of looks, image, and branding for ordinary people.[54] The model helps us to see that these are in part due to the changing nature of social networks and the increased competition for visibility and status within these broader networks. An important way of conceptualizing such developments is to see them as changes in the nature of the status systems: not just the status of individuals, but the status of activities, ideas, and objects. Having the latest model iPhone may bring more individual status than the latest fashion in jeans; the number of "friends" on Facebook or the number of "hits" on their blog or website may be more important to some people than whom they personally interact with at work. Another important feature of the general model is that it draws systematic theoretical attention to cleavages within non-elites, and particularly that there is often tension and conflict between respectable and unrespectable non-elites – even though the characteristics that define the unrespectable can vary across cultures. Hence, even if one accepts the political analyses of elite theorists, the basic theoretical model from which they work is inadequate in that it under-analyzes non-elites and it pays inadequate attention to status systems that are not primarily political in nature.

Comparison with Weber

The proposed model is strongly influenced by Weber's multidimensional concept of power and group formation. His notion of rationalization helps to identify some of the sources of both increasing commodification and bureaucratization, but it leaves out other sources, for example, the pressures from the market and civic sector for an expansion of state services. Nor does he adequately anticipate or have conceptual tools to deal with the expanded state role in regulating the macro economy. Moreover, he tends to overlook the resistance and counter trends – the Christian Right, the growth of Eastern religious practices such as yoga, and the role of celebrity in marketing, politics, entertainment, and religion. I do not claim that the proposed model by itself explains these phenomena, but with the identification of key exogenous variables it suggests tentative hypotheses. For example, drawing attention to the expansion of social networks and the resulting difficulty in gaining social visibility suggests why celebrities have become more central not only to the realm of status and culture, but also in politics and business. Nor does Weber's discussion of political parties help to understand how and why parties are declining in importance. Similarly, Weber's notion of status groups does not help to understand why status has become less stable and more fluid – even most celebrities are only famous for "fifteen minutes" – even though social visibility and celebrity status have increased in importance.[55]

Outlining these problems is not to be unappreciative or dismissive of Weber's seminal contributions, but rather to argue that the proposed general model can incorporate many of his insights, and in some respects synthesize these with the other traditions discussed. Weber argues that cultural factors can be important in understanding economic outcome – for example the Protestant ethic effect on the development of early capitalism and Judaism's legitimation of charging interest as a crucial factor to the role of Jews in banking and finance. In a similar fashion the increasing significance of shopping as an expressive activity and the abandonment of limitations, such as restricted store hours and Sabbath laws, can be conceptualized in the general model as not simply an economic change, but a change in the content of the status structure of postmodern societies. Stated in other terms, the general model sensitizes the analyst to look for parallels to the specific historical cases that are characteristic of Weber's analyses.

Comparison with Bourdieu

As noted in the chapter on India, Bourdieu's work offers no systematic insights into the forms of differentiation and conflict that are likely to emerge within each type of elite and non-elite. Drawing primarily from the French and Algerian experience, he tends to overstate the degree and form of reproduction that has and is likely to occur within the U.S. Children of the affluent and well educated likely have a significant advantage over those from lower socioeconomic backgrounds – and that this tendency is probably increasing. Nonetheless, the vast majority of current elites are not children of earlier elites. With respect to differentiation within elites and non-elites, there is nothing in Bourdieu's theoretical scheme that suggests: that when elites have fewer external enemies the unrespectable non-elites are likely to become targets of derision, that social visibility and celebrities will become more important, that the distinction between prophets and priests will be accentuated and politics and culture will become more polarized, or that even though the scope of the state expands, its power to control a society's destiny will decline. The claim is not that the proposed general model predicts and explains these occurrences, but it does sensitize analysts to this possibility and makes it possible to see these as an example of patterns that have occurred in other societies and times. Of course, to point out these limitations is not to be dismissive of Bourdieu's important contributions.

Conclusion

These two chapters have covered a wide array of issues and it is appropriate to summarize what has been considered. In the case of the U.S. c. 1980–2008, the model helps to sensitize us to how and why:

1. New modes of production rooted in the manipulation of symbols create new economic elites. The top economic elites, however, must

acquire not only human capital to create these new modes, but also enormous amounts of private property, which significantly qualifies notions of a "new class" based on advanced knowledge.

2. New forms of communication have
    a. increased the value of visibility in the mass media and have greatly accentuated the importance of the status elites known as celebrities;
    b. decreased at least the proportion (and probably) the absolute amount of communication that is carried on face-to-face;
    c. made both elites and non-elites more dependent upon digital technology for both information and status.

3. The increased centrality of celebrities has transformed
    a. politics by increasing the centrality of celebrity politicians and political assistants oriented to the mass media and decreased the importance of political parties;
    b. patterns of marketing and consumption by encouraging non-elites to follow the styles of the "rich and famous" – this is in contrast to earlier periods when non-elites were prevented from doing so by closed status groups or sumptuary laws;
    c. the status concerns of non-elites toward visibility in mass media, personal "image," and association with celebrities – and demoted their concern about the approval of neighbors.

4. The wars in Iraq and Afghanistan (and the execution of Osama bin Laden) are not solely due to international considerations, but are linked to the concerns of political elites to maintain the support of respectable non-elites.

5. Conflicts over gay marriage have as much to do with the status concerns of non-elites and the electoral strategies of political elites as they do with morality.

6. The locus of power has increasingly shifted from local to national and international elites.

7. Non-elites are increasingly differentiated into those with high and low skills and this has led to:
    a. greater economic inequality (and probably reduced mobility);
    b. residential segregation;
    c. longer commuting times and less "family time";
    d. decreased community solidarity.

8. These economic and cultural changes produced an increasing cultural and political polarization, especially among political elites. This has
    a. resulted from and stimulated a parallel polarization among at least a significant sector of non-elites;
    b. led to political stalemates and ineffective governance;

   c. greatly lowered the public's approval of the government, especially of Congress;

   d. lowered the political participation of many non-elites;

   e. polarized those who do participate.

What the model helps to do is to see these as a set of interrelated phenomena, many of which have parallels in other quite different societies and other historical periods.

The 2007–2009
Financial Crisis

In the previous chapter the unit of analysis was a near thirty-year period. Here I focus on a shorter time period and one relatively specific event, the 2007–2009 financial crisis. In many respects this chapter is a post-script to the previous one, but it focuses not on general trends, but on one specific event: the near collapse of the financial system. The focus is even more specific in that I am primarily concerned with the technological, structural, and cultural context that made the crisis possible. While I briefly summarize the sequence of events that led to the crisis, I do not try to provide an exhaustive description of these, nor do I try to cover the consequences of the crisis including the severe economic recession that followed.

What Happened?

There are many accounts of the events that led to the financial crisis of 2007–2009.[1] The basic story is that there was a market bubble in housing prices. Demand for housing was greater than the number of houses available and prices went up. Because of the rising prices investors started speculating by buying houses and then reselling them at a higher price.

Construction companies started building more houses in anticipation that they could be sold at a sizeable profit. Since the value of people's houses was increasing, many borrowed against their equity to meet expenses or increase their standard of living (Redmond 2007). Eventually the supply of houses became too great for the demand, prices dropped, and the bubble burst. Speculators and home builders began lowering their prices to get rid of houses before prices declined further. The value of family-owned residences also declined to the point where the market value of a house was often less than the mortgage that was owed. Such bubbles are not uncommon and perhaps inherent in market economies (Minsky 1986). What made this particular case different and why did it affect the whole economy?

As is often noted, concrete historical events are usually "overdetermined." That is, they have many complex causes and in most cases even good and useful analyses only identify some of these. Hence the task here is not to definitively explain the financial crisis of 2007–2009, but rather to demonstrate that the model, in conjunction with key exogenous variables, helps to understand this event and place it in a broader historical and comparative context.

I have argued that three exogenous variables are especially significant for understanding the contemporary U.S. These are: (1) the increasing importance of processing symbols relative to processing objects and substances, (2) the broader, more complex social networks that have emerged, in part, as a consequence of our greater ability to process symbols, and (3) American exceptionalism that refers to long and deeply held values and assumptions about how the world works and how it should work. Now we take up how these variables shaped the relationship between various types of elites and between elites and non-elites in ways that led to the crisis.

Economic Elites

The general model suggests new means and modes of production tend to arise and serve as the base for a new group of economic elites. Economic elites who make technology to process symbols (e.g., Microsoft and Apple) or who primarily process symbols (e.g., Google and Facebook) have gained in power and importance relative to those who process objects and substances. A special category of the symbol processing elites are financial elites. They process and exchange money, ownership, capital, and risks, usually as various kinds of financial instruments.

The increased capacity to process symbols and the expansion of social networks made possible modern markets and many of the new types of financial instruments. The sheer number of calculations that some of the new financial instruments require would be impractical without modern computers and communication technologies.[2] The speed with which money and capital is moved between accounts has vastly increased.[3] Finally, the Internet has made it practical for people in virtually any location to trade on the major world exchanges, and to vastly increase the number of over-the-counter and privately arranged trades via various electronic bulletin boards. Between 1990 and 2008 the value of equities, options, and securities futures jumped from $2.2 trillion to $82.0 trillion.[4] The number of shares traded on the New York Stock Exchange went from $40 trillion to $800 trillion. The average daily share volume on one of the over-the-counter trading sites went from $41.0 million in 1995 to $1.9 trillion in 2008.[5] Financial activities also became more profitable, moving from about 15 percent of all profits in 1950 to approximately 30 percent of all profits just before the financial crisis (Tomaskovic-Devey and Lin 2011: Table 1). Financial power has also become increasingly concentrated (Johnson and Kwak 2010). A relatively small number of large bank chains have been created that have thousands of branches, tens of thousands of employees, and offer multiple services from checking accounts to investment banking. This has resulted in banks that are "too big to fail" and are more difficult for both senior managers and regulatory agencies to supervise.[6] At the same time the investment bank branches of these institutions operate in a fairly small community of similar people who have a proclivity to "herding behavior," all pursing whatever form of investment seems hot at the time (Carruthers 2009); in this respect they are similar to teenagers trying to keep up with the latest fashions – until the point where what is hot becomes so common that its value collapses.

The increased volume and variety of financial instruments made rating more difficult and complex. Investors relied heavily on the traditional bond rating agencies such as Standard and Poor's, and Fitch and Moody's to judge the risks associated with a particular financial instrument. These agencies, however, used methods that were developed in the older, less complex markets, and these often underestimated the risks associated with the new more complex instruments and markets. To make matters worse, the rating agencies, which were private profit-making companies, made their money from fees that were paid by companies they were rating. Unsurprisingly, they were reluctant to give low ratings; companies issuing the securities might take their business elsewhere.

In sum, this new elite created new financial instruments and a financial system of unprecedented complexity and interdependence. In principle this increased the efficiency with which resources were utilized; "idle" money was "put to work." It undoubtedly contributed to the profits, wealth, and political influence of elites in the financial industry. Unfortunately, there were additional consequences. First, the complexity reduced visibility and transparency, and hence risky and even illegal behavior became more difficult to detect. Second, the high profits of both financial institutions and rating agencies reduced the motivation to find malfeasance and detect risks. Third, it reduced the slack, backup, or reserves in the financial system, so if anything went wrong it was more likely to affect the broader system. These developments were necessary conditions for the 2007–2009 financial crisis and the recession that followed.

Of course, this more complex financial system involved many non-elites, but it was the top financial elites that allowed and encouraged these changes.

Status and Ideological Elites

In most historical settings conservatives who defend the existing system are the priests and liberals are the prophets who criticize it. From the New Deal on, there was a steady (but by international standards relatively modest) expansion of the welfare state under both Democratic and Republican administrations. Eventually conservatives, critical of this trend, became the prophets, berating big government and the erosion of personal responsibility. America was "exceptional" in the degree to which certain tenets were widely accepted and even taken for granted. First, businesspeople had unusually high levels of legitimacy and respect, and politicians and government officials were held in relatively low esteem. Second, market competition was nearly always considered preferable to government rules as a means of disciplining economic activities. Third, when the distribution of income by markets results in some people being unable to meet their basic needs, this should be addressed by non-government charitable organizations. These are some of the common assumptions of American exceptionalism.

Mizruchi (2010) has argued that prior to the 1970s, elites were relatively moderate and made largely pragmatic decisions about the appropriate mix of markets and government regulation. In the 1970s the economic thought of conservative and libertarian thinkers such as Ludwig von Mises, Friedrich von Hayek, and Milton Friedman became increasingly influential and government regulations were increasingly suspect. It was argued that personal and political freedom were dependent upon economic freedom rooted in private property. The new, more active ideological elites associated with such institutions as the American Enterprise Institute, Heritage Foundation, and the Cato Institute went to great efforts to articulate and inculcate this ideology. The Heritage Foundation ranked countries on an "Index of Economic Freedom," in which how well the state protected property rights was an important component.[7] Beginning in the 1960s and 1970s a neo-conservative movement became increasingly active and articulate. Conservative notions became prominent in the 1980s during the Ronald Reagan administration. As the Soviet Union was collapsing, the then neo-conservative Francis Fukuyama (1989) wrote an influential, if controversial, essay that suggested that liberalism in the form of democratic political institutions and market economies may be the final form of social evolution – "the end of history"; supposedly these institutions would eventually be adopted by virtually all societies.[8] Government was increasingly seen as the cause of economic and social problems rather than the primary means to their solution. This is not to say that all ideological elites were conservatives, but certainly conservative voices became more prominent and in many respects dominant.

Political Elites

Political elites increasingly leaned toward putting this more conservative ideology into practice. For example, in 1987 Reagan appointed Alan Greenspan, a self-proclaimed friend and disciple of Ayn Rand's libertarian "objectivism," as chairman of the Federal Reserve System; he continued in this office until 2006 (Greenspan 2007). Some suggested his successor Ben Bernanke also has strong libertarian leanings, though this is debated (Bullock 2009). While they varied in the details, both liberals and conservatives tended to support various forms of deregulation. Airlines, railways, and trucking were largely deregulated. Laws prohibiting branch banks and the separation of banking and more speculative kinds of investing were largely repealed. Even farm subsidies came under increasing criticism and have been reduced if not eliminated. As noted earlier, Bill Clinton and "New Democrats" strongly supported welfare reform and law and order, and many forms of deregulation. "The government" and its programs were looked upon with a jaundiced eye. Government regulatory agencies were often lax in forcing financial institutions to desist from risky, shoddy, and deceptive lending practices. The conservative ideological ambiance and a "revolving door" of personnel between financial institutions and regulatory agencies contributed to a bureaucratic culture that was overly deferential to those being regulated. This was exacerbated by the small size and budgets of the regulatory agencies – compared to the enormous expansion of financial instruments and the size and complexity of the financial industry.

If politicians and bureaucrats were reticent to intervene in market processes, they made an exception with respect to encouraging home ownership. To quote the rhetoric of the Census Bureau, "Owning one's home has long been considered a part of the "American Dream" (U.S. Census Bureau 2011). Democratic and Republican administrations have supported government programs that encourage home ownership. This is rooted in Americans' strong cultural and ideological commitment to the rights associated with owning private property. While most societies have some notion of private property, there are significant variations concerning exactly what this constitutes.[9] For example, Scotland has much less restricted laws against entering or crossing private open land than is the case in England or the U.S.[10] Even within the U.S., there have been variations and changes in the extent to which property owners can restrict the rights of others.[11] The degree to which non-owners have access to streams and beaches has been an ongoing debate. Nonetheless, the rights of ownership are especially strong and are a central element of U.S. culture.

I want to suggest that the strong commitment to the notion of private property is one of the reasons that government encouragement toward home ownership has a long history and broad support. Homeowners have long been allowed to reduce their taxable income by the amount of their interest payments on their home mortgages. This amounts to a very sizeable reduction in taxes and subsidy for homeowners.

In the Eisenhower administration, programs were undertaken to expand home ownership. This is seen in the 1953 report of the President's Advisory Committee on Government Housing Policies and Programs, in President Eisenhower's Message to Congress on Housing in January 1954, and the revisions to the Federal Housing Act that same year (President's Advisory Committee on Government Housing Policies and Programs 1953). For example, the report of the Advisory Committee included such recommendations as: (1) the "Extension of long-term FHA mortgage insurance into designated older areas of our communities so that liberal financing will be available to build and to rehabilitate dwelling units for sale and rent" (p. 2), and (2) "[A] privately financed secondary market facility should be established to level out the peaks and valleys in the flow of funds for mortgage investment, particularly in the smaller communities and those areas chronically short of investment capital" (p. 3).

Similar views were voiced by other Republican administrations. While the 1968 Fair Housing Law was proposed and passed during the Lyndon Johnson administration, it was the support of Republican Senate Leader Everett Dirksen and a number of his Republican colleagues that enabled the Senate to shut off a southern filibuster and pass this landmark housing legislation. The bill outlawed discrimination in renting, selling, and financing housing. It was eventual Republican presidential candidate George Romney, appointed by Richard Nixon as Secretary of Housing and Urban Development, who played a key role in implementing the law. It was during the Nixon admiration that Freddie Mac was created to expand the secondary loan market and encourage relatively low cost home mortgages. President George W. Bush said in a 2003 speech, "This Administration will constantly strive to promote an ownership society in America. We want more people owning their own home. It is in our national interest that more people own their own home. After all, if you own your own home, you have a vital stake in the future of our country." During the 2004 election campaign he said, "We're creating ... an ownership society in this country, where more Americans than ever will be able to open up their door where they live and say, welcome to my house, welcome to my piece of property."[12] The Democratic Party has been even more committed to expanding home ownership. This is not to say that the actual policies and programs of the two parties have been identical. It is to say that a core part of American ideology – as articulated by both ideological and political elites – has been an expansive concept of private property and home ownership.

The conservative support for home ownership was in part a way to gain non-elite support for notions of a limited government and an expansive private sector regulated by markets – and undergirded by a deep commitment to private property. Conservatives opposed most efforts to reduce the unequal distribution of property, but favored assisting non-elites in becoming homeowners in order to reinforce the legitimacy of private property. This also helped gain the political support of most of the existing and potential homeowners who were the core of respectable non-elites. Moreover, it garnered political backing from the construction industry and financial institutions since both gained economically from having an expansive housing sector. The tax deduction for interest on home mortgages also fostered the loyalty of the rich since the largest benefits went to those buying expensive homes (Schwartz 2006: 5).

Non-elites

If a fundamental distinction is between the "respectable" and "unrespectable," this raises the question of what the markers of respectability are. In his survey of U.S. housing policy, Schwartz (2006: 2) says, "Housing is far more than shelter from the elements ... It is also loaded with symbolic value, as a marker of status and an expression of style." Conversely, it is not accidental that homelessness nearly always results in a loss of respectability. Hence, an especially strong symbol of respectability has been home ownership. A report by the Pew Research Center says, "In a 1991 nationwide Time/CNN/Yankelovich survey, seven-in-ten respondents said homeownership was essential to being in the middle class, while just one-third said the same about having 'a white collar job'" (Wang 2012).[13]

Fair housing laws were intended to improve the physical and social setting of minority families *and* to change the way these families are perceived and labeled – moving them into the "respectable" category. A third goal was changing their behavior. Home ownership is correlated with political participation, community involvement, good childrearing practices, self-esteem, and more regular patterns of employment. It is not clear, however, to what extent home ownership causes any of these.[14] Nonetheless, whatever the positive and negative consequences actually are, it is clear that U.S. ideology and policy have encouraged home ownership, and that most non-elites aspire to owning their own home.

Conclusion

I will begin with brief note on alternative models: Marxian models that focus on the contradictions within capitalism or models that focus on the policies and machinations of elites – as important as these may be – are inadequate. They largely ignore the cultural context and how it shaped non-elites, and hence cannot explain why this crisis originated in the U.S. at the time that it did, and why this occurred in the housing sector.

Now I will summarize the argument. Obviously the financial crisis of 2007–2009 had many causes. What does the general model contribute to our understanding? How is it that a market bubble, which has occurred many times in capitalist societies, became so extensive that it threatened the entire financial structure, and why did this happen in the housing sector? Let us summarize the sources of this event.

1. The increasing power and centrality of the financial elite is seen as an example of the rise of new economic elites who gain power by creating new means and modes of production via the increased ability to process symbols and the expansion of social networks.
2. By taking seriously the power of status and ideological elites and Americans' "exceptional" commitment to private property and markets – as well as the presumption that business is inherently more efficient than government – the model helps to pinpoint the cultural factors that contributed to multiple kinds of deregulation.

3. The greed of brokers and investors may well have played a crucial role both in ignoring the risk involved and in deliberate deceptions to hide this risk, but ample amounts of greed are nearly always present. It is variations in the technological and cultural context that explain why greed was allowed to run rampant.

4. Highlighting this "exceptional" legitimacy of private property helps to understand why conservative political elites have generally supported housing subsidies and fair housing laws – even though they generally oppose "the welfare state" and "big government." This is a key reason loans in the housing sector became such an extensive part of the financial system.

5. It was a combination of the expansive scope of this sector and the lax regulation of this market that brought on the crisis. In addition to (1) complexity and opaqueness, and (2) an ideology of deregulation, there was another reason financial systems largely escaped regulation and social criticism. Home ownership was the symbol of respectability and multiple government programs made ownership easier. Hence, non-elites were largely uncritical of banks and other financial institutions. Later non-elites tended to blame the government for bailing out failing banks and businesses rather than condemning the financial industry per se – even though ordinary people's financial pain would have been much worse if the government had allowed the banks, AIG, and the auto industry to collapse. If the new economic elites were rapacious, and if the regulators were lax, respectable non-elites (and non-elites who sought respectability through home ownership) were in a sense "bought off" by subsidies and increasing home values that seemed too good to be true. As is usually the case, they were not true and many paid a terrible price.

A caveat is required. I have argued that home ownership in the U.S. is an especially strong symbol of respectability and that this played a role in public and business policies that encouraged home ownership – even to those who could not afford it. I know of no study that compares the ideology about home ownership across countries, but it is clear that the U.S. is by no means the only country that encourages people to own their own homes. In nearly all developed countries home ownership is encouraged and subsidized in various ways. Given this, it is striking and perhaps ironic that the U.S. has relatively low rates of home ownership among the developed countries. In the U.S. 65% of families are homeowners, while the percentages in other countries are Norway 84%, Spain 83%, Italy 73%, Canada 69%, Australia 69%, and the U.K. 68%. On the other hand, some developed countries have lower percentages: France

63%, Japan 60%, and Germany 53% (DeSilver 2013). So the U.S. is not unique in policies that are friendly to ownership.

My argument is not that the U.S. is "exceptional" in encouraging home ownership, but rather that, relative to other government programs, subsidies to home ownership have had exceptionally high levels of support from both conservatives and liberals, which in turn further legitimizes private property. This, along with the ideology of deregulation and the increasing complexity and opaqueness of financing, was the context that both contributed to a housing bubble and allowed it to spiral out of control and nearly bring about the collapse of the entire financial system.

8

Conclusions

Many of the phenomena discussed in chapters 3–7 have been described before. They have not, however, been framed within a model of elites and non-elites that is potentially applicable to all complex societies, and that provides a paradigm and "checklist" of actors, relationships, and typical patterns of conflict and cooperation. Obviously, it is impossible to capture all of the complexities of traditional India, Classical Athens, contemporary American society, or even the relatively brief financial crisis of 2007–2009 in a few pages. Nonetheless, the model has helped to systematically inventory, organize, and relate a wide array of phenomena that can be observed in these three quite different periods and cultures and for the more specific event of the U.S. financial crisis.

How the Model is Different

How does this model differ from most previous models? First, it subsumes class analysis within an elite–non-elite model. This is not to reject Marxian insights, but rather to specify the conditions under which they might be most useful. Stated slightly differently, the model certainly recognizes the possibility that control of property and the means of production may be the dominant forms of power, but it does not assume that this is always the case. There are situations in which political elites or status elites may be the dominant actors. In India status elites, especially Brahmins, have sustained their dominance in a way that economic or political elites were not able to. In Classical Athens political elites were in many respects more powerful than those who were simply rich or those who were primarily status elites (e.g., dramatists, winning athletes, and religious leaders).

Second, while the model fully recognizes the importance of economic and political elites, it pays more systematic attention to status/cultural/ ideological elites than previous theoretical schemes. To attempt to understand traditional India without considering the importance of Brahmins and their ideology, or to reduce these to disguised economic interests, is to miss a central feature of that society and culture. Similarly, to attempt to understand the contemporary U.S. without paying serious attention to celebrities is likely to lead to an incomplete, distorted analysis. A further indication of the importance of culture and ideology is the behavior of contemporary authoritarian regimes. They have long attempted to control the press. It is not accidental that they have become very concerned to limit the impact of the Internet by editing the content that is available to their citizens. These regimes sometimes seem to be more aware of the power of ideology than social scientists and the models these scholars use to analyze such regimes.

Third, the model also systematically includes the analysis of non-elites as well as elites. While by definition elites on average have much more power than non-elites, this does not mean that history is made only by the decisions and actions of elites. The American Civil Rights Movement and the Arab Spring clearly negate that assumption. In contrast, the European Union and its predecessor organizations have been the project of elites; it certainly did not begin because of popular demand for a unified Europe. With the European economic and debt crises and the elite-imposed austerity measures of 2011–12, non-elites rose up in protest and at least slowed this process. The model not only includes an analysis of non-elites, but also does not reduce non-elites to a homogeneous "mass." Rather, it identifies a key fissure – the respectable vs. the non-respectable – that again and again plays a crucial role in the politics of a wide variety of societies. It also makes room to identify additional ways in which non-elites are differentiated, such as the distinction between clean and unclean Shudra castes in India, *metics* and slaves in Classical Greece, or the distinction between those with high-skill levels and those who do more routine work in the American middle class.

Fourth, the model attempts to avoid two pitfalls. One is assuming that all social change and power dynamics are fundamentally reducible to a small number of factors and that the course of history is essentially determined. This is the weakness of most forms of Marxism and of classical elite theory. The other pitfall is to lapse into a historicism that eschews the possibility of seeing common patterns across time and cultures. The more sophisticated versions of this tendency emphasize the importance of historical and cultural context, which I have also tried to do, but this too can lapse into a form of historicism.[1] Hence, the broader strategy, of which the model is a part, calls for the identification of crucial exogenous variables that are relevant to the particular time and place under analysis. Often these are technological developments that affect the means of production or coercion. They can also be ideologies that reshape economic and political institutions. The Protestant ethic, constitutional electoral democracy, women's movements, human rights, and Islamic fundamentalism are obvious examples.

To elaborate on this point, the proposed model is not a general theory of social change that largely denies the significance of human agency and historical uniqueness. It does not assume there is a limited and theoretically predetermined set of exogenous variables such as changing means of production, the iron law of oligarchy, or the gradual predominance of one type of psychological disposition or "residue" among elites. On the other hand, it identifies the key forms of power and power relationships that are important in most complex societies and points to tensions, conflicts, and relationships that are extremely common across societies and historical periods. It provides a framework of analysis that may be useful for a variety of social settings and historical contexts.

Fifth, the model's usefulness is not dependent upon how much is known about the action of particular individuals. Of course, all social phenomena result from the past and present actions of particular historical actors. Sometimes historians and social scientists can identify the actions of particular individuals. Other times they cannot. Sometimes the actions of unknown individuals become deeply institutionalized patterns that can shape subsequent behavior for centuries. In the Indian case, we do not know who the specific actors were who made religious status and notions of purity and impurity so central to that society. But we do know that the centrality and inalienability of status helps us understand the stability of the Varna scheme, and the model also points to important categories of actors (e.g., bandits, holy men, and Untouchables) that the Varna scheme ignores and obscures. The model, in conjunction with the theory of status relations, helps us understand the long ideological dominance of Brahmins, and the persistence of various forms of the caste system for approximately 3,000 years. This relative cultural stability persisted in spite of the rise and fall of numerous regimes, and the attempts of other ideologies such as Buddhism, Jainism, Sikhism, and

Islam to replace Hinduism and its Brahmins. This is not to embrace a cultural essentialism that sees change as impossible. With the rapidly changing modes of production, the introduction of democratic politics, and the prominence of egalitarian ideologies in modern media, the legitimacy of Brahmin cultural dominance is fast eroding.

In contrast to the Indian case, in Classical Greece the relatively unique innovations of particular individuals whose names and actions are known played a crucial role in shaping the future. Arguably, Cleisthenes' leadership in a time of crisis introduced innovations that led to the radical form of democracy which was sustained in Athens for nearly two centuries. The Athenian model has not been copied in detail, but it has served as an inspiration for many subsequent forms of democracy.

Similarly, the American Revolution and U.S. Constitution, which was largely the work of a relatively small number of well-identified political elites, have certainly affected much of modern political history. Very few contemporary elites around the world openly deny the legitimacy of democracy. Yet, as the experience of numerous developing nations has shown, the transition to democratic institutions is not easy or certain. This point was driven home yet again following the American-led invasion of Iraq, which was the project of specific neo-conservative individuals who were part of the George W. Bush administration. A similar point can be made about the expansion of U.S. presence in Afghanistan by the Obama administration and the subsequent difficulties in exiting. The model points to categories of people, but does not deny the importance of identifying the role of individual actors. Hence, the model can be useful in organizing cases in which much is known about particular individuals and in cases where the concrete actors are unknown.

Comparisons across Time and Space

I am agnostic about whether a general theory of social change is possible. Earlier models (e.g., Marx and Pareto) have often clouded our understanding as much as they have enhanced it. Consequently, I have proposed a more restricted theoretical strategy that leaves open the factors that are likely to increase the relative power and impact of various elites and non-elites in particular historical settings. Nonetheless, the model offers guidance about what to look for.

Let me give a few examples. In each of the three very different societies considered, elites often attempt to gain the *support of respectable non-elites by criticizing and even demonizing the lowest strata* of that society. There were significant historical differences in the nature of the lowest strata and in the rationales given for considering them reprehensible. Untouchables differ from Greek slaves or *metics* and these differ from the American underclass. All of these are quite different from the "counter revolutionaries" and political prisoners of the Soviet Union, or the Jews in Hitler's Germany. Yet in all of these cases internal enemies played an important role in legitimizing the dominant elites, even though each society was dominated by a different kind of elite.

Similarly, in all three societies, and in most other historical settings, *political elites seek legitimation by associating themselves with status elites.* This may involve associations with: well-known cultural elites such as Nobel Prize winners, little-known heroes such as ordinary soldiers killed in war, movies stars, Hindu gurus, or ideological elites such as the king's Brahmin priests, the priestesses of Athena (the "official" goddess of Classical Athens), TV evangelists, partisan newspaper columnists, and "public intellectuals." Conversely, it can involve disassociation and rejection of critics, whether these are Socratic-like philosophers, the prophets of Israel, or the political dissidents in Communist countries.

A third example is the frequent *tension between those who control old and new modes of production.* This is seen in the tensions between land controlling castes and merchant or artisan castes in traditional India, the landed aristocracy and the new mining and shipping magnates of Athens, the nineteenth-century U.S. ranchers who wanted open ranges and the farmers who wanted to fence their land, or the manufacturing industrial elites and digital post-industrial elites of the contemporary U.S. Sometimes these relationships involve cooperation, but they nearly always involve divergent interests that frequently lead to conflict.

These examples do not exhaust the possible comparisons, but hopefully they illustrate the relevance of the model for comparisons across time and space.

Future Research

How might the model guide future research? Obviously, there are many additional societies that could be analyzed. I have considered no societies from Latin America or Africa. While I have focused upon cultures, societies, and a particular event as the unit of analysis, in principle the model could be used to analyze local communities, regional subunits of a nation-state (e.g., U.S. states), or global networks. Such analyses are beyond the scope of this book.

Instead, I will suggest the potential for additional research by proposing some hypotheses about a few aspects of one society. Obviously, contemporary China is an increasingly important actor in a globalized world. I have never been to China nor studied China other than through a few novels, newspapers and other press reports. In 2012 some of the questions raised in the headlines included:

1. Why did the Christian groups and the Falun Gong become so popular and why has the government systematically persecuted the latter, but largely ignored the former?
2. Why did the rise and fall of the politician Bo Xilai, his former police chief, and his wife receive so much attention both inside and outside of China?
3. Why has China seemed to go out of its way to become involved in disputes with several of its neighbors (e.g., Japan and Philippines) over uninhabited islands or sparsely inhabited mountainous regions (e.g., India) when these have little immediate economic or strategic value?
4. Why is there rising tension between rural and urban populations?

Let us consider these questions in the order listed above.

It is obvious that China has de facto abandoned Marxism and Maoism. This raises the question of what is going to be the *ideology* that individuals will use to make sense of their lives and that will be used by elites to legitimize the contemporary society and the regime that governs it. It seems likely that the emergence of Christian groups and the Falun Gong, as well as an adamant form of nationalism, are a largely non-elite search for a meaningful ideological foundation. There are also both scholarly and government efforts to revitalize Confucianism (Bell 2008, Fan 2011). These developments raise the question of who will be the new ideological elites.

The history of Christianity in China is long and complex. By "Christian groups," I refer to both registered churches, recognized by the Chinese government, and unregistered groups. The first are primarily members of the [Protestant] China Christian Council or the Chinese Patriotic Catholic Association, which officially does not recognize the authority of the Pope. While many of these churches have historic ties to Western missionary movements of the nineteenth and twentieth centuries, most are locally governed and supported. Unregistered groups include numerous "house churches" and evangelical prayer groups that have no legitimate standing with the government. There is considerable overlap between the registered churches and house churches, but many of the latter have been started by relatively conservative Evangelical groups. The fact that a church is "registered" means among other things that it is visible and subject to government surveillance. Christians tend to be seen by many non-Christians as espousing a foreign ideology. Hence, they apparently are seen as less of a threat by the government and their persecution would almost certainly bring criticism from other countries.[2]

Falun Gong centers on a set of meditation techniques. Perhaps the government is so negative about Falun Gong precisely because it is a diffuse, clearly indigenous, highly moralistic, non-hierarchical, and widespread popular movement. Hence it cannot be easily controlled or shaped by government or party officials. This positions Falun Gong to become a credible prophetic voice or at least an implicit form of criticism and resistance to the materialism that is still a key assumption of the regime. It is probably more likely to become a threat to the party and the regime than Christian groups. The model suggests that credible ideologies with recognized and respected elites are important to legitimization, especially if these elites are "priests" with whom political and economic elites can create mutually beneficial relationships. With a diffuse social movement like Falun Gong, such cooptation seems problematic. The model also suggests that where a regime's legitimation and a society's solidarity become problematic, there is a strong tendency for elites to find reprehensible *internal enemies* – and this is the way in which Falun Gong is treated by the Chinese government.

The case of Bo Xilai may well be an example of both the tendency of elites to become *robbers rather than cops* and the tendency to create *internal enemies*, and how these two tendencies can interact. Bo Xilai was a rising Chinese politician with charismatic populist inclinations. He led campaigns against corruption, and was not especially deferential to his superiors. Like many populist politicians (e.g., Louisiana's Huey Long, Argentina's Juan Peron, and Venezuela's Hugo Chavez), Bo Xilai was not very concerned about the niceties of rules and laws; he wiretapped other government officials, used questionable means to expand his power, and may have used government resources for private gain. In 2012 he was removed from office, expelled from the party, and subjected to criminal investigation. He was further stigmatized when his wife was charged with poisoning British businessman Neil Heywood. This event is complex and many of the details are unknown, but, at least in part, Bo Xilai appears to be an example of the tendency of cops to become robbers.[3] It may also be an example of established elites turning internal critics or competitors into "an enemy of the people." (This is a phrase coined not by Lenin, Stalin or Mao Tse Tung but by Norwegian playwright Henrik Ibsen as the title of his 1882 play about a doctor who is persecuted for showing that the hot wells of his resort spa community are contaminated.) Converting critics into internal enemies has happened in many societies.

China has been engaged in territorial disputes with a number of countries in its region including Japan, Korea, India, Pakistan, Vietnam, Philippines, and Malaysia. In many cases it is doubtful that any significant economic or military resources are at stake. Rather, it is often a matter of status and honor. For example, in September of 2012 a dispute between China and Japan arose over the Senkaku/Diaoyu islands, which are barren and uninhabited (Perlez 2012). This dispute has a fairly long history, but it seems clear that China has deliberately intensified the conflict in the last couple of years. (The salience of the dispute is probably exacerbated by the fact that the Japanese government in this period was relatively conservative and nationalistic.) While there may be undersea oil reserves in the area, the islands themselves seem to be of little value. Not only did the dispute involve government actions, but it sparked apparently spontaneous popular protest in both China and Japan. As the model points out, the creation of *external enemies* can also be useful for domestic politics. This may be one of the reasons both governments seem willing to risk limited amounts of international conflict in part to increase their own legitimacy at home.

There have been rising tensions in rural China over low incomes and appropriation of land for roads, factories, and various development projects – with the officials often enriching themselves in the process (e.g., Kahn 2006). These are probably an example of conflict between those associated with *old and new modes of production*. In 2012 agriculture was still China's largest economic sector, comprising about 37 percent of the labor force, but it produced only 10 percent of the GDP. Income of rural families is about one-third of that of urban families. On the other hand, industrial production has been expanding rapidly, including high-tech items such as wind and solar power generators. Tensions and disturbances in rural areas have been frequent, and, as the model would suggest, there is likely to be even more conflict between those tied to old and new means of production.

I want to stress that these comments about China are simply a set of hypotheses developed from information in widely available press reports – and seen through the lens of the model. They certainly require testing with more systematic evidence. Nonetheless, the model has been a useful way to begin to ask questions about the four events that have been described. It is not accidental that such issues are central to the novel *POW!* by the Chinese Nobel Prize-winning writer Mo Yan (Mo 2012).[4]

Three additional caveats are needed. First, there are obviously many other things that are important about China. Second, it would be possible to suggest these hypotheses without using the model, but the virtue of the model is that it *systematically* suggests important patterns and connections that have been important in many times and places. A third caveat is that any model simplifies and can cause the analyst to overlook important features of the data that are not included in the model. Hence, empirical analyses should not be restricted to the categories of the model.

As I said at the beginning of this book, the model is a way to begin analysis, not to end it.

Appendix: Some Implications and Elaborations of the Model

In chapter 2, I outlined the basic model and its purpose; here I want to spell out certain elaborations and implications that will be of special concern to scholars and specialists.

Interdependence and Restructuring of Social Categories

There is typically a high level of *interdependence between important social categories*; changes in one category usually affect people in other categories. For example, where Communist parties came to power, the status and power of the old economic and political elite declined precipitously; many were imprisoned or killed. The economic security of non-elites generally improved; most had their basic physical needs met. With respect to status, old honorific titles were abolished and everyone formally became a "comrade." The political power and rights of non-elites did not increase, and in some respects decreased. Conversely, when Communist regimes collapsed, the power of political elites declined, political freedoms of non-elites increased, but their economic security declined and dramatic differences in wealth and status emerged. Similarly, shifts within a given type of elite usually have implications for non-elites. For example, the coming to power of conservative political elites usually benefits the upper strata of non-elites at the expense of the lower strata; the rise of new economic elites who invest in new forms of production usually disadvantages the non-elites who are part of the old forms. Power is not simply a zero sum resource, but shifts in the nature, function, and relative power of different social categories usually affect the other categories and vice versa.

Dominant Elites and Degraded Non-elites

The relative importance and legitimacy of different resources and different types of elites and non-elites vary in different historical circumstances. The centrality of status as a form of power in India meant Brahmins were uniquely important compared to other elites, and Untouchables were especially demeaned and ill-treated. In Classical Athens orator-politicians were the key movers of the society. In the Soviet Union, party and government officials were at the top and political dissidents were at the bottom.

In contrast, the heavy ideological commitment to capitalism characteristic of the U.S. suggests that the economic resources and elites are especially prominent and legitimate. A number of concrete examples of this dominance are identified in chapter 5. (This form of dominance is an example of what I referred to as a deep structure on the cultural level.) In short, in adamantly capitalist U.S. society, the possession of economic capital is especially commendable and, if you do not possess such wealth, a failure to labor is especially blameworthy.

The broader point is that societies and historical periods vary in the level of legitimacy they attribute to a particular kind of power. This in turn affects which elites have special rights to deference and dominance, and which non-elites deserve derision and degradation.[1]

The Scope and Depth of Elite Power

Elites vary in the size of the arena within which their power is relevant and the degree of their control within particular arenas. Alexander the Great operated in a wider arena than George Washington, Pope John XXIII than the Rev. Jerry Falwell, and Bill Gates than Henry Ford. Hitler operated in a wider arena than Fidel Castro, but Castro impacted almost every aspect of the lives of the residents of Cuba.

Different types of elites in the "same society" often operate in different size arenas.[2] In medieval Europe effective political power was usually exercised over relatively small areas; Europe was divided into numerous small princedoms and dukedoms. In contrast, the Catholic Church and especially monastic orders had an ideological impact on most parts of Europe. At the beginning of the twenty-first century economic power and institutions are becoming global in scope at a much faster rate than political power and institutions. On the other hand, NGOs are playing an increasing role in creating international norms and values, such as the expansion of human rights.

Variations in the scope and depth of different forms of power need to be kept in mind when analyzing relationships between different types of elites and between elites and non-elites.

Defining and Operationalizing the Categories

The primary purpose of the proposed model is to help identify, organize, and interpret the common social categories and patterns of cooperation and conflict, and how these shape social stability or change. Just as Marx never fully defined and operationalized his concept of class and Pareto was generally cryptic about how to identify elites, I shall not deal with methodological issues at any length. Nonetheless, a few words about the method for deciding who is a member of the elite are appropriate. There are two broad approaches to this issue. The positional approach usually defines what social positions allow their occupants to exercise the greatest influence/power over others. Such definitions usually focus on the chief officers or board members of corporations, the top government officials, and perhaps the top officials of the largest NGOs, such as the Red Cross, political parties, religious denominations, the NAACP, etc. If a local community or region rather than an entire society is being studied, owners of the largest businesses, local government officials, and voluntary agencies can be selected. The other approach that has been largely restricted to local studies is the reputational approach. This involves asking a panel of knowledgeable people to identify the most influential member of the community.

Another approach uses an indirect reputational method. There is not a formal position called "richest individual," "top celebrity," "most influential intellectual," or "most revered religious leader." However, it is possible to identify the individuals who are estimated to be the top wealth holders by various business publications, Academy Award winners of the last five years, the most cited scientists, and the most quoted journalists. At the societal level an obvious strategy would be to draw on a combination of the positional and the indirect reputational approach.

Another question is how to define and operationalize the dividing line between different types of elites and between elites and non-elites. There will always be some ambiguity about the placement of some individuals. A few will be both status elites and political elites (Václav Havel, Ronald Reagan, Nelson Mandela), both economic elites and political elites (Ross Perot, Mitt Romney, Michael Bloomberg), both status elites and economic elites (Oprah Winfrey, Warren Buffett). Few CEOs of major corporations ever hold a political office; they may attempt to exercise political influence, but this does not make them a member of the political elite – any more than Paul Newman or Robert Redford's political activities made them political elites. Any operationalization of a concept will produce some measurement of error, but that does not mean the concepts or their operationalization are not useful.

Where to draw the line between elites and non-elites depends on the unit of analysis and the particular focus of the analysis. Studies of village elites will usually include a higher percentage of the population than studies of large nation-states. If you are interested in who influences tax policy you will probably want to consider a smaller number of elites than if you are interested in who sets fashion trends; the decisions about the former are usually more explicit and identifiable than the latter.

Since my purpose here is primarily to suggest the utility of a particular theoretical model rather than an empirical study per se, I shall not elaborate further on these methodological issues.

Exogenous and Intervening Variables

For Marx class and class conflict are at the center of the story of social transformation, but antecedent or exogenous factors shaped the concrete nature of class relations. One does not have to reduce Marx to a "vulgar" technological determinist to recognize that he thought major changes in the means of production usually produced substantial changes in the way work was organized and in many other aspects of society – including the structure of class relations. Similarly, while elites and non-elites are at the center of my story, their composition and relationships in a given historical context are affected by exogenous factors. These factors are exogenous in a formal sense: they are not variables in the model of elites and non-elites per se. Rather they tend to impact relationships between elites and non-elites, which in turn have effects on other aspects of society. This is not to deny that in the empirical world the actions of elites and non-elites may affect these exogenous factors, but rather that the primary effects on which I will focus flow in the other direction.

I will illustrate this with a historical example. When effective firearms were developed, they eventually spread to most groups of warriors. In the fifteenth and sixteenth centuries came the "gunpowder revolution" and the development of effective siege canons. These made the old forms of city walls and fortresses an ineffective defense, though new, relatively effective defensive structures were soon developed (McNeill 1982: 79–95). In the seventeenth and eighteenth centuries mobile field artillery and effective small arms were developed, such as various forms of the musket. The development and spread of such weapons in turn usually contributed to the reorganization of fighting units and changed relationships between military elites and non-elites (McNeill 1982: chap. 4; Dupuy and Dupuy 1993, esp. 575–9). For example, armies became more bureaucratic, weapons became more expensive and complex, and political elites who were not in the military tended to have more responsibility for supplying the arms needed to fight battles, usually by establishing various kinds of taxes. Tactics also changed; virtually no modern army expects soldiers to march in formation toward a heavily armed enemy position.[3] Pointing out such trends is not to embrace any simple technological determinism, nor to suggest that elites and non-elites have no agency. The inclinations and actions of elites may affect whether particular weapons or tactics are developed, adopted, or eschewed. For example, King Gustavus Aldolphus (1594–1632) of Sweden was famous for his innovations in weaponry, tactics, and logistics – and these were widely copied (Dupuy and Dupuy 1993: 575ff). The traditions, experiences, and economic resources of particular cultures also shape the proclivity to adopt weapons. This was apparent in the tendency of Muscovite, Mogul, and Chinese empires of the sixteenth century to rest content with large siege guns. Many Western European rulers, however, eagerly looked for and adopted new military innovations and the military superiority of these regimes was soon made evident, for example, in the wars with the Ottomans (1593–1606) and in the various wars that created Western colonialism (McNeill 1982: 97–8). We see such cultural variations in the contemporary period in the reluctance of post-World War II Japan to arm itself with nuclear weapons and the determination of the much less developed countries to do so (e.g., China, India, Pakistan – and apparently Iran and North Korea). Moreover, countries can band together to outlaw the use of some weapons as was done for chemical weapons and soft nose bullets in the Hague Conventions and subsequent protocols. Recognizing that there are complex interactions between technological innovations and other social and cultural factors does not mean that it is not useful to treat some variables as relatively exogenous when attempting to analyze long-term historical trends.

The key point is that the arguments presented about the relationship between exogenous variables and the typology of elites and non-elites focus on the usual and predominant sequences of causation, but do not deny the possibility of other sequences.

Not all of the factors that are exogenous *directly* impinge upon or interact with the structure of elites and non-elites. Often there are intermediary structures and processes that are *intervening variables*. For example, the invention and adaptation of power looms did not directly affect public sanitation. Rather it was the use of such looms that encouraged the organization of factories, which contributed to urbanization and higher population densities. This in turn concentrated waste and pollution, which affected public health – conditions described in such classic sources as Fredrick Engel's *The Condition of the Working Class in England* and Charles Dickens's novels such as *Our Mutual Friend*. That is to say, the organization of factories and urbanization were intervening variables that linked the use of power looms and levels of public sanitation.

Reporting Results

Since the purpose of this book is to introduce a new model, I have used the categories of the model to organize the materials about each case considered. That is, I discuss each type of elite and non-elites in turn, the internal differentiation within each category and the patterns of conflict and cooperation that are relevant. The order in which I take up these categories varies for different cases since the prominence and relevance of these categories varies for different historical settings.

This format certainly does not mean that I think this is the only appropriate way to organize the results of research that might draw on this model. How much attention will be devoted to each category and relationship suggested by the model will certainly depend upon the historical circumstances and the interests of the analyst. As I said above, the model is a checklist of actors and relationships that need to be considered, not a straightjacket for reporting results of research.

Notes

Chapter 1 Introduction

1 Pareto argued that there were six classes of residues, but most of his analysis focuses on the first two: (1) the "instinct for combinations" that looks for relationships between value, ideas, and things, and attempts to relate them to some more general theories, and (2) the "persistence of aggregates" that seeks stability and the maintenance of "social aggregates." Actually the exact meaning Pareto attributed to "residues" is problematic. In general, "residues" refers to deeply held, largely often non-rational, inclinations that lay behind the various rationalizations (in the Freudian sense) that are offered to explain them. The meaning and effect of residues is not relevant to this analysis, and as Pareto himself recognizes, it is difficult to sort out the causal connections between residues and behaviors. Hence, I will not elaborate on this issue. For his discussion of the relationship between residues, derivations, and derivatives, see Pareto (1935: 876–86).

2 The Protestant ethic was only one of a number of attributes that he saw as contributing to the emergence of bourgeois capitalism in the West, in contrast to China and India. For a useful summary of these developments, see Anthony Giddens' introduction to *The Protestant Ethic and the Spirit of Capitalism* (Weber 1976b: 7–8).

3 For example, the distinction in structural linguistics between *language* (referring to the abstract patterns of grammar and syntax) and *speech* (referring

149

to the actual practices of people in talking with one another) can distort our understanding of human action. No one learns their first language in the abstract; rather they learn to speak. The language of structural linguistics is a set of abstractions from the actual speaking practices. There is a parallel in the relationship between social structure and everyday practices. See Bourdieu (1990, pp. 31–4). To quote Bourdieu: "Thus the dualistic vision that recognizes only the self-transparent act of consciousness or the externally determined thing has to give way to the real logic of action, which brings together two objectifications of history, objectification in bodies and objectification in institutions or, which amounts to the same thing, two states of capital, objectified and incorporated, through which a distance is set up from necessity and its urgencies" (1990: 56–7).

4   Of course previous social theorists have also pointed out the power and significance of habit; see, e.g., Weber 1968: 25).

5   I am sympathetic to his critique of an overly optimistic view of the leveling effects of education, but he overstates a good argument. The title of my first solo book was *The Illusion of Equality: The Effect of Education on Opportunity, Inequality, and Social Conflict*. It argued that attempts to reduce the relationship between family background and later socioeconomic status by expanding enrollments and years of schooling are seldom effective. Stated another way it was largely illusory that expanding education would equalize opportunity, much less reduce inequality of income and wealth. This theme has run through much of my work (e.g., Milner 2004). Hence, I am not unsympathetic to many of Bourdieu's analytical and political concerns. It is rather that both his empirical analyses and his theoretical scheme overstate the degree of social reproduction and come close to lapsing into a kind of tragic determinism – though in principle he rejects this conclusion. For a summary of the research and data that calls such reproduction into question, including the case of France, see Kingston (2000), especially pp. 192–3.

Chapter 2   The General Model

1   Previous works of relevance include Weber's (1968: 926–40) notions of class, status, and party, Etzioni's (1975: 96–126) typology of organizational elites, Runciman's (1966: chap. 3) discussion of three dimensions of stratification, Béteille's (1965) analysis of caste, class and power, and Poggi's discussions of power (especially 1978 and 2001).

2   Milner (1994, 2004). I realize that "inexpansibility" does not appear in dictionaries, but its meaning is relatively obvious and it phonetically parallels "inalienability."

3   See Scott (2001) for a useful discussion of this point.

4   Economic or political power may give one status, but status can also be a source of other kinds of power, e.g., Ronald Reagan, Oprah Winfrey, and Martin Luther King. Knowledge is also a source of power, but it is not a sanction per se. Knowledge is in certain respects expansible and alienable,

but I will not discuss these issues here. See Milner (1994: 24–26) for an elaboration of this point.

Different discussions of the three types of power tend to emphasize different elements within these types of power. Poggi provides a useful review of these discussions (2001: 16–20). Poggi's own primary usage – custom, exchange, and command – draws attention to the typical type of social relationship correlated with each type of power. My discussion focuses on the type of sanction, in part, because I think this helps to relate the types of power to specific concrete actions and the nature of a relationship is largely derived from the typical type of sanction.

5   In most constitutional monarchies people are both citizens and subjects, but the latter is largely a matter of maintaining a kind of symbolic continuity over time rather than a power relationship. In the U.K., the queen may read a speech to her subjects outlining the government's policies, but the speech is written by the citizen prime minister and addressed to the citizen-voters of this particular nation-state. For many years U.K. passports used the term 'subject of her Majesty' to refer to the holder; now the language refers to "British citizen."

6   For a description of the ideal-typical patterns of deference in eighteenth-century Britain and the U.S. and a critique of this model, see Pocock (1976) and Phillips (1989); for a description of deference and paternalism in nineteenth-century Britain, see Russell (1987) and Read (1981). For more recent trends in Canada, see Nevitte (1996, 2001). For more popular accounts of changes in contemporary Britain, see Dalrymple (1999) and Clayton (2010). There is considerable debate about to what degree social inferiors actually respected superiors in earlier periods, but there is little doubt that the symbols and rituals of deference have declined over time. Of course, sometimes the symbols of equality, such as blue jeans and use of first names, become a kind of "required uniform," as in various companies in Silicon Valley, California, and other more subtle forms of deference emerge such as the lower probability that superiors' opinions and proposals will be questioned or criticized.

7   Transience is related to inalienability, but one is not reducible to the other. Physical goods may be alienable and easily appropriated, but they are not necessarily transient – as the economic term "durable goods" indicates. Status is inalienable, but it can be transitory. On the other hand, well-institutionalized status tends to be both inalienable and intransitory.

8   See Lukes (2004) for an influential conceptualization of power that expands its scope beyond the analysis of particular decisions.

9   For additional discussions of the concept of legitimacy and its relationship to the notions of status and authority, see my *Status and Sacredness*, pp. 11–12, 66, 81–3, 231–2. For a survey of the literature on legitimacy, see Smelser and Balfas (2001), esp. the articles by Stryker, Ansell, and Badie.

10   Gifts and prestations are important in a number of societies including the *kula* ring in the Trobriand Islands, the notion of *dan* in India, and *moka* exchange in Papua New Guinea. The precise definition and nature of such non-market exchanges has been extensively debated by anthropologists. For

an overview of these debates, see Parry (1986). The degree to which gifts carry an obligation to reciprocate is certainly variable in different social contexts and for different relationships, and this interacts with the extent to which any exchange is explicit. In the contemporary U.S., sending someone a bouquet of flowers may make them more amenable to one's romantic overtures; offering them cash is likely to have the opposite effect. In contrast, a prostitute is unlikely to accept flowers in lieu of money.

11 Poggi (2001) refers to "ideological/normative," perhaps drawing on Etzioni's (1975) use of the latter term. I will discuss the relationship between ideological elites and other types of status and cultural elites shortly.

12 Roth (1968) notes in his introduction to Max Weber's *Economy and Society*, "As the greatest force of legitimation in history, the priesthood is ceaselessly struggling for power with secular rulership (ch. XV); their relationship is one of mutual antagonism as well as dependence."

13 For example, Burton and Higley (2001: 189) say, "researchers have estimated that political elites in large and institutionally complex Western countries such as the USA number roughly 7,500 people (Dye 2002: 11), closer to 5,000 in middle-sized countries like Australia (Higley et al., 1979), France (Dogan, 1994), and the former West Germany (Hoffman-Lange, 1993) and between 1,000 and 2,000 persons in small countries like Denmark and Norway (Higley et al., 1976; Pedersen, 1976). This last estimate of 1,000 or 2,000 elite persons is probably the most accurate for all countries during the early modern historical period and it probably holds, too, for all but the most populous non-Western countries today."

14 Obviously slave societies are the exception, especially those of early capitalism. For example, in the sugar plantations in the British Caribbean in the early nineteenth century, slaves made up 70–95 percent of the population (Higman 1984, esp. Table 4.2). In the U.S. South between 1790 and 1850, blacks represented 35–38 percent of the population and 92–95 percent of these were slaves (Gibson and Jung 2002).

15 According to Skrentny (2002), the black civil rights movement led to a broader "minority rights revolution" which substantially changed American politics, even though the details of how different minorities were treated and how successful their efforts were often depended upon highly contingent factors including the cultural entrepreneurship of the leaders of different groups.

16 For a very useful survey of the images and ideologies used to describe these groups and how the interplay between these generally negative images and the notion of citizenship led to various social policies, see Morris (1994).

17 For example, at its founding the NAACP was initially the project of white educated liberals. It is important, however, to remember that elites in the sense that the term is used in this work and most elite theory is a relatively small group – for example, political elites are restricted to about 7,500 people in the contemporary U.S. Martin Luther King, John Lewis, Jessie Jackson, Gloria Steinem, Betty Friedan, and Caesar Chavez were certainly not elites in the early days of the movements that they led. This is not to deny that established elites do sometimes mobilize the unrespectable, but

the much larger category of educated and the respectable should not be confused with elites.

18 To state the matter more precisely, most of the time rulers use force-backed orders, that is the threat of force rather than force per se. In situations other than those of arbitrary despotism, the orders are usually in the form of laws. The degree to which laws and legal procedures limit and guide *both* the elites and non-elites is historically variable. For example, do political elites respect the laws of due process in arresting and trying those accused as criminals? Arbitrarily created and applied "laws" can, of course, be primarily a disguise for despotism.

19 For Poggi's very thoughtful review of this dilemma, related issues and their relationships to previous theory, see his *The Development of the Modern State* (1978), "Introduction," pp. 1–15.

20 In some periods conservatives may consider the best defense to be isolationism – having as little to do as possible with other societies – and liberals may think the best way to maintain good relations with others is to support them in conflicts with their enemies; World Wars I and II are examples of this.

21 I want to stress that the terminology is very historically conditioned. Some "conservatives," for example Bismarck and the British Tories, were often concerned with limiting economic exploitation of workers by "liberals" associated with ascendant commercial classes. The meanings of the terms "right" and "left" are even more historically variable. Whatever the labels, however, political conflict within elites often revolve around relative emphases on external and internal security and whether these are obtained by a carrot or a stick. The concepts of "conservative," "liberal," "right," and "left," and terms like "arms race," "law and order," "defense," and "good relations," are examples of contemporary phrases that have analogs that are relevant in most historical situations.

22 http://en.wikipedia.org/wiki/Gilded_Age (accessed May 8, 2012). Editors and reviewers complain that one should never cite Wikipedia; I disagree. In my experience, articles in Wikipedia about frequently researched and discussed topics usually have no more inaccuracies and biases than articles in many other surveys and encyclopedias – and if they do these are quickly corrected or contested. More esoteric topics that only a few scholars or groups care about are another matter.

23 Mann (1986) has drawn a definite distinction between military and political elites. For a critique of Mann's four types of power and elites and a defense of the "Trinitarian" model, see Poggi (2006).

24 There has been much discussion and some research about the Napster case. The following articles point to the key issues and a range of perspectives: Wayne (2004), Rojek (2005), and Spitz and Hunter (2005).

25 It is noteworthy that it is much harder to identify contemporary status elites who are not cultural or ideological elites. For example, when people are asked to name contemporary heroes they usually mention categories, such as the firefighters who responded on 9/11, or "our soldiers" rather than individuals. Individuals tend to be heroes of the moment such as U.S. airline

pilot Captain Chesley Sullenberger, who, in 2009, made an emergency landing in the Hudson River, saving the lives of all the passengers on board.

26   Frank Sinatra had interpersonal connections with figures in the Kennedy administration and Walter Cronkite after his retirement became associated with several organizations supporting freedom of the press and the separation of state and church, but neither of these individuals were perceived as ideological elites.

27   This is not to deny that any given pattern of expression, such as a form and style of cultural performance, excludes other possibilities. Hence a form that is "non-ideological" can be a way of discouraging criticism of existing social and political patterns. Nonetheless, there are patterns of cultural performance that are much more explicitly ideological than others and that is the focus of my term "ideological elites."

28   For an extensive elaboration of this theory see my *Status and Sacredness* (1994), especially chapter 3, and *Freaks, Geeks, and Cool Kids* (2004: 30–4).

29   The long-term maintenance of high status requires the careful management of visibility; being too visible or accessible can lower one's status. The point here, however, is that a prerequisite to status is a significant level of social visibility. This may not require personal visibility, but rather visibility for one's work or specialized activities. Famous writers, for example, may be personally reclusive.

30   A word of clarification is required about two forms of devaluing conventional worldly structures. Those I have called renouncers devalue the conventional life, and usually abandon it in favor of some form of asceticism, often joining various kinds of monastic group or alternative communities. Another approach is to devalue worldly structures, but to continue to live conventional lives for the present rather than trying to devalue or transform them; what should be of concern is a life that will gain entrance to the world to come. Hence existing structures are legitimate in the present world, but ultimately irrelevant. Following Martin Luther's notion of the two kingdoms, this has been characteristic of many Lutheran churches (see Milner 1994: 218–20). This is in contrast to groups that not only devalue present structures but demand their transformation.

31   Not surprisingly intellectuals, including sociologists, have written about their role in society. See, for example, Shils (1972). See Lipset and Basu (1975) for a useful fourfold typology that suggests alternative roles. One dimension of this typology is very similar to my prophet–priest distinction, but their distinctions can be subsumed within my typology as subcategories of status elites. More recent writings on intellectual elites include Cummings (2005) and Etzioni and Bowditch (2006).

32   Of course, even "general theories" only apply to some units of analysis. As I have pointed out before, Newton's theory of falling bodies is fully adequate only in a vacuum; psychoanalytic theory is not relevant to understanding the behavior of bugs; and the "general" model of elites is only relevant to complex societies that have differentiated elites.

Chapter 3   Traditional India: the Varna Scheme

1   This chapter is a revision of my discussion of the Varna scheme in Milner (1994: 67–78).

2   The renowned Marxian scholar Irfan Habib (1995: 161) says, "Caste is the most characteristic – and, many would say, unique – social institution of India. No interpretation of our history and culture can demand a hearing unless it encompasses the caste system."

3   Perhaps they were actual social groups initially, but that certainly has not been the case for 2,500 years.

4   See Fairbank and Goldman (1998: 108) for the "four occupations," Ratz (1983) for the notion of estates, and Burgess (1992) on the Divine Right of Kings.

5   It is noteworthy that the concept of equality of opportunity is often defined in contrast to caste; see, for example, Arneson (2008). The notion of the "American dream" has many sources, but was popularized by James Truslow Adams in his 1931 book *Epic of America*.

6   In the 1990s some relatively authoritarian regimes in South East Asia argued that there were a distinctive set of "Asian Values," which supposedly drew on Confucian notions of hard work, loyalty to the family and the nation, and place less of an emphasis on personal freedom. The key point, however, is that they did not publicly reject the basic concept of human rights.

7   The original Aryan invaders and early Vedic groups were probably herders, but certainly by the middle of the first millennium B.C.E. India was primarily a plow-based agrarian society.

8   Often each group's way of life is conceptualized by the notion of *varnasrama-dharma*, which combines the varna scheme with the idealized stages of life (*asrama*) and the notion of law (*dharma*).

9   For a classic discussion of the varna system, including its relationship to the way Indian society has actually been organized over its long history, see Kane (1973).

10 There were, of course, exceptions. Brahmins were rulers and land controllers in a few areas such as Mithila, and there were non-Brahmin kings who played a significant role in shaping the culture and ideology of their time (e.g., Ashoka and Akbar). Some kings were also considered the incarnation of Visnu and in some circumstances were a religious symbol. Nonetheless, typically Brahmins, gurus, and sadhus were religious elites, not kings, and most kings were not ideological elites.

11 At times Kshatriyas were replaced by outside conquerors or those of another religion, e.g. Muslims, but rulers usually had to work out some kind of *modus vivendi* with Hindu culture in general and Brahmins in particular.

12 See Thapar (1966: 38–9), who outlines this argument. For classic discussions of the origin, activities, and disabilities of Shudras, see Kane (1973, vol. 2, part 2, chap. 3, 120–2, 154–64) and Sharma (1980).

13 Ancient Sanskrit texts such as *The Laws of Manu* frequently use the term *chandala* to refer to outcast groups.

14 For a survey of the discussions of theft and especially *sashasi*, see Kane (1973, vol. 3, pp. 519–37).

15 Some examples include: In the late seventeenth and eighteenth centuries, groups known as *Pindaris* were irregular and unpaid troops attached to Marathi and Mogul armies who made their living by plunder. At the end of the nineteenth century the British promulgated the Criminal Tribes Act, which "denotified" certain castes and tribes as "addicted to the systematic commission of non-bailable offences" (Yang 1985). This included the famous Thugs who strangled and robbed travelers, supposedly to honor the goddess Kali. Mayaram (2003) provides a very useful analysis of the political role and implications of bandits under colonialism by focusing on the Muslim community of the Meos and especially their myths and stories. In modern India groups of robbers known as *dacoits* are widely dispersed and have become almost a stock character in Bollywood movies.

16 "I think you'll find, among ancient texts, richer materials on this in the early Buddhist and Jain canons than you will in Vedic sources. The Buddhist arhat Angulimaala comes immediately to mind as an ideal typical proto-thug." Private communication (via my University of Virginia colleague Robert A. Hueckstedt) from Matthew Kapstein, Directeur d'études, Ecole Pratique des Hautes Etudes, Numata Visiting Professor of Buddhist Studies, The University of Chicago, June 6, 2013.

17 Holy women have also played a role, but a much less common and visible one.

18 Bourdieu's work has been used by scholars of India but mostly to analyze colonial and post-independence India dealing with such subjects as social reproduction of inequalities through education, family structures, gender, etc. See Lardinois and Thapan (2006: 18–46) for a review of the way Bourdieu has been used in the analysis of India.

19 See Calhoun (1993) for a discussion of the problems of using "capital" as a trans-historical concept. This is not to argue that analytic concepts should not be applied to social phenomena that predated them, but only that I think that capital is not the best theoretical concept to understand early Indian culture.

Chapter 4 Athens in the Classical Period

1 The contrast between East and West goes back at least to the "first historian," Herodotus (1923: e.g., vol 2, 94–106), c. 484–425 B.C.; some of his accounts specifically contrast the Greeks and Persians with parts of India. It was India that Rudyard Kipling had in mind when he proclaimed that "Oh, East is East and West is West and never the twain shall meet," 1989). Kipling is often accused of being a cultural essentialist, imperialist, racist,

or worse. Whatever the merits of such critiques, it needs to be kept in mind that other lines and a key theme of the poem is to emphasize the possibilities of respect between individuals, and even enemies, from different cultures.

2   Bracketing events of the period are the victories of the Greeks over the Persians (especially Marathon 490 B.C. and Plataea 479 B.C., though intermittent conflicts continued until the Peace of Callias in 449 B.C.), and the defeat of the Greeks by Philip II of Macedonia, first at the Battle of Chaeronea in 338 B.C., and the Macedonian defeat of the Athenian-led rebels at Cannon in 322 B.C. These ended Athenian independence and seriously compromised its democracy. The other crucial events of the period are the First Peloponnesian War (460 B.C.–c. 445 B.C.) and Second Peloponnesian War (431–404 B.C.) with Sparta, and Athens' attempt to invade Syracuse (c. 414–415 B.C.), which ended in disaster for the Athenians.

3   As Finley (1963: 61) notes: "One could easily compile a catalogue of the cases of repression, sycophancy, irrational behavior, and outright brutality in the nearly two centuries that Athens was governed as a democracy. Yet they remain no more than so many single incidents in this long stretch of time when Athens was remarkably free from the universal Greek malady of sedition and civil war."

Even after this 186-year period most of the formal institutions of Athenian democracy continued. In this later period, however, democracy was compromised by oligarchic tendencies from both within and without. At some periods there were virtual puppet rulers appointed by outside powers. Moreover, power tended to shift from the Assembly to the courts. For an overview of the complex events following the Battle of Crannon and the emergence of Macedonian hegemony, see Ellis (1994). The last vestiges of democracy ended when Athens was incorporated into the Roman Empire by Augustus (63 B.C.– A.D. 14).

4   The sources I have found especially useful for this purpose are Ober (1989), Sinclair (1988), Osborne (2010), and the various essays in Samons II (2007).

5   Finley (1963) estimates that, at its zenith, the total population was 250,000. Samons II (2007: 5) says, "it cannot have been less than 100,000 souls and may have been as great as 400,000 or more." Ober (1989: 128) puts the total at 150,000–250,000. Scholars disagree about the estimated numbers. I have relied most heavily on Ober's evaluations of these figures.

6   As Finley (1985: 31) says, "The Mediterranean constitutes a single 'climatic region' marked by winter rains, and long summer droughts, by light soils, and dry farming … in contrast to the irrigation farming on which most of the ancient Near Eastern economy is based."

7   To do this, I will in large measure summarize Josiah Ober's (1989) version of these developments. My account also draws on the useful essays in Samons II's *The Age of Pericles* (2007), Stockton's (1990) very useful overview in *The Classical Athenian Democracy*, and D. M. Lewis et al. (1992), *The Cambridge Ancient History*, 2nd edn, especially J. K. Davies, "Society and Economy," vol. V, and P. J. Rhodes, "The Polis and the Alternatives," vol. VI.

8 Also see Frederiksen (1975), Greene (2000), and Nafissi (2004) for useful discussions of these issues and as examples of the debate. See also Patterson (1992) for a critical review of Finley.

9 The word "*idiotai*" meant ignorant or layman and is one of the etymological roots of the modern word "idiot."

10 I think it is accurate to say that this is the "standard" view, probably articulated most extensively in Ober (1989). For a dissenting view that places greater emphasis on the power of the wealthy, see Kallet-Marx (1994).

11 This is from chapter 2 of Thucydides' *History of the Peloponnesian War*, chapter 2; http://en.wikisource.org/wiki/History_of_the_Peloponnesian_War/Book_1#Causes_of_the_War_-_The_Affair_of_Epidamnus_-_The_Affair_of_Potidaea (accessed June 13, 2012).

12 Osborne (2010) places special stress on the relative homogeneity and solidarity of Athenian citizens and the role that the exclusion of women and slaves played in producing citizen solidarity. He says, "The thesis advanced in this paper, that the success of Athenian democracy depended … upon … a high degree of common experience enhanced by the exclusion of women and slaves is one by which I stand … " (p. 38). While he does not explicitly mention the significance of the exclusion of metics, this certainly is congruent with his general argument.

13 See Bugh (1988) for a lengthy discussion of the origin, makeup, and role of the cavalry in Athens and its impact on Athenian politics.

14 For an understanding of Greek religious life I have found Mikalson (2010), Boedeker (2007), and Garland (1990) especially helpful.

15 For a survey of some of these complications, see Horster (2011: 161–208), though much of her discussion focuses on the Hellenistic and Roman Imperial periods, rather than the earlier Classical period.

16 For an overview of Athens' cultural life – in the sense of art, literature, etc. – see Ostwald (1992), though I do not try to deal with all of the realms that he surveys.

17 Dithyrambs were enthusiastic and even frenzied events involving singing and dancing usually dedicated to Dionysus.

18 This modern usage of "philosophy" is anachronistic since many ancient philosophers were students and teachers of subjects that would now be called the natural sciences. I have found Wallace (2007) and Oswald (1992) useful in portraying the political and social role of philosophy.

19 It is highly questionable, however, whether his characterization of this category, or those to whom he assigned to the category, is historically accurate.

20 Winters's book on oligarchy (2011), which focuses on a variety of modern and historical societies, discusses Classical Greece. He rightfully emphasizes the repressive nature of Athenian slavery, and how the threat of a slave rebellion contributed to solidarity among Athenian citizens and oligarchs. He does not, however, place this in the context of the surrounding and succeeding regimes, noting that Athenian forms of social control of slaves were probably less repressive than most and that the power of non-elites was certainly greater on the whole. Hence in emphasizing the dominance exer-

cised by oligarchs, he screens out the features of Athenian democracy that made it seem so distinctive for its period. Moreover, Winters has virtually no discussion of status and cultural elites, referring only to the political writings of Plato and Aristotle, and making no mention of Greek playwrights, Olympic heroes, or Greek religion. Hence, his theoretical framework screens out much that is important in understanding the power dynamics and the broader features of Athenian social and cultural life.

21 This is not, of course, to claim that these indigenous categories were completely unique to Athens or that the analysis captures all of the variations in the meaning of these categories that occurred over time and space.

22 That is, from Cleisthenean reforms in 507 B.C. to Athens' defeat by the Macedonians in 322 B.C.

Chapter 5   The U.S. 1980–2008: Economics and Politics

1 The "small world" research, testing how many intermediaries are required for one random person to contact another random person, touches upon what I am calling the increasing span of networks. This research has not, however, been going on long enough to provide significant data about long-term trends over time. For an illustration of such small world research, see http://smallworld.columbia.edu/ (accessed November 30, 2006).

2 There is considerable skepticism about the extent to which values shape behavior as contrasted to being after-the-fact rationalizations used to justify the behavior. Much of this discussion focuses on the level of the individual rather than on macro outcomes, which is the focus here. For an overview of these debates by sociologists, see Vaisey (2008a, 2008b) and Swidler (2008). One link between the analysis of elites and the effect of core values is the work of Higley and Burton (1989, 2006). They show considerable skepticism about being able to quickly introduce viable democracies in societies that have a history of violent internal conflicts, more authoritarian traditions, and strongly held cultural differences, e.g., Iraq and Afghanistan. While they do not specifically address the issue of American exceptionalism, their findings and arguments suggest that societies have deeply rooted values and traditions that will limit the kinds of institutions and policies that are likely to be viable, at least in the short run. John Torpey (2009) has provided a useful review of the origins and uses of the notion of American exceptionalism. A primary thrust of his argument is the need to avoid a cultural essentialism that sees the historical values of a society as a kind of "cultural genetic code" that makes significant changes nearly impossible. He also argues against thinking of such values as "deviant" because this would suggest that there is a norm against which to judge a particular society's values. On this point, I would simply point out that "deviant" and "deviation" can be used in a statistical sense as well as a moral sense. Moreover, there are emerging global norms that do in fact lead to moral judgments

about the values and behavior of societies. The emergence of human rights norms is an obvious example; societies may fail to live up to such norms or offer alternative interpretations of their content, but no modern nation-state openly denies the legitimacy of some notion of human rights. While it is certainly the case that clusters of core values and symbols do not make future changes impossible, they may very well bias the probabilities of alternative outcomes. In my opinion if it is detached from triumphalism and self-congratulation, exceptionalism is still a useful analytic concept.

3   This is not to suggest that discrimination against women has been eliminated. At least one study (Bertrand and Hallock 2001) found that the unexplained gap between the compensation for men and women CEOs was less than five percent when controls for size of company, age, and seniority were introduced. Of course, the percentage of CEOs who are women is still quite low. The point here is not that there is gender equity, but that the shift from processing material substances to symbols has made women more competitive in the labor market.

4   In Bourdieu's terminology this primacy of a particular kind of power is referred to as the "dominant principle of domination."

5   See Poggi (2001: 156) for a description of how and why economic elites perceive their moral superiority. In other historical settings such as European feudalism, commercial groups had at best an ambiguous moral status (see Tawney 1962 [1926]) and were looked down upon by warrior-aristocrats as "mere merchants." In India, Brahmins, holy men, and Untouchables were prominent social categories. Socialist regimes gave first importance to party and government officials.

6   Nearly all college and university websites have pages dealing with the rules and procedures and the forms and reports that are required.

7   For a description of these procedures and techniques and how they are used, see Marwick (2014). Just as this was going to press the Federal Trade Commission released a report urging new legislation to require greater transparency in the way data was collected and used for commercial purposes (Lohr 2014). It remains to be seen whether Congress will actually enact any of the recommended reforms.

8   See Mazzucato (2011, 2013) for an elaboration and defense of this argument.

9   This is, of course, an example of what some would call structural power. I have already discussed why I think this conceptualization is misleading and detrimental.

10   There are many articles in the opinion and news media about this, including some by respected economists, for example, Borjas (2004), Martinez (2013), and Hobson (2013).

11   For a useful non-technical description of this process, see Yang (2013).

12   See Forbes (2006); the exception is the Walton family that owns Wal-Mart.

13   Calculated from earnings reports for these companies; http://investor.google.com/pdf/2012Q4_google_earnings_slides.pdf; http://media.gm.com/content/dam/Media/gmcom/investor/2013/q4/2012-Q4-Financial-

Highlights.pdf;   http://www.citigroup.com/citi/investor/data/qer412.pdf?
ieNocache=428 (all accessed December 8, 2013).

14 Chrysler merged with German-based Daimler-Benz in 1998 and eventually
    became part of Italian-based Fiat in 2009.

15 See www.weforum.org for the "official" view of the World Economic Forum
    (accessed December 2, 2013).

16 For a journalistic account of this broader elite of "cosmocrats" and globali-
    zation in general, see Micklethwait and Wooldridge (2000: esp. chap. 12).

17 These figures are derived from Bureau of the Census Historical Table, No.
    HS-49. Federal Government – Outlays and Debt: 1940 to 2003, http://
    www.census.gov/statab/hist/HS-49.pdf (accessed July 19, 2013); Depart-
    ment of the Treasury, Historical Debt Outstanding – Annual 2000–2012,
    http://www.treasurydirect.gov/govt/reports/pd/histdebt/histdebt_histo5.htm
    (accessed July 19, 2013).

18 For a more elaborate description and discussion of this process, see Milner
    (1980: 150–4).

19 The amount that federal, state, and local governments spend to assist those
    in need is a complex question and the answers given are highly contested.
    It is clear, however, that government "welfare expenditures" (in the broadest
    sense of that phrase) have increased over time. For example, government
    transfer payments to individuals increased from $566 billion in 1990 to
    $2.1 trillion in 2009. This included retirement and disability insurance
    benefits, medical payments, income maintenance benefits, unemployment
    insurance benefits, and federal education and training assistance payments
    (U.S. Census Bureau 2012a).

20 Naím (2013) argues organizational and political elites have less and less
    power. Others have argued that the power of the executive branch to shape
    policies has increased not decreased (see Skrentny 2002: 346–7 for a useful
    summary of the arguments and data). Even if the latter is the case, the ability
    of the executive branch to shape policy is not the same as the overall ability
    of the state to actually shape events and trends that are often affected by
    factors beyond the control of any one state.

21 See Bauman (2014) for an essay that discusses how this dilemma affects the
    members of the European Union.

22 There is, of course, a vast literature on the effects of international financial
    institutions such as the IMF and the World Bank, various trade agreements
    such as the WTO, the expansion of human rights, and the development of
    international courts. Some useful examples include Bacchetta and Drabek
    (2002) on the effects of the WTO on policy making in sovereign states,
    Blaser (1992) on the role of non-governmental tribunals on the development
    of human rights, Born (2012) on international adjudication, Stuckler and
    Basu (2009) on the effect of the IMF on health policy, and Mulcahy (2004)
    on the development of a world labor regime. The collapse of a Bangladesh
    factory building on April 23, 2013 that killed over 1,000 people resulted in
    intense international pressure on the Bangladesh garment industry, the inter-
    national garment companies, and the Bangladesh government for labor and
    safety reforms. At least two factory owners were indicted, wages were

increased, and safety reforms were supposedly implemented. The revelations of the U.S. National Security Agency's interception of phone calls have led to both domestic and international pressure to limit such activities. The point is that nation-states and their governments are increasingly limited by emerging domestic and international norms and institutions.

23   A recent report on youth in India illustrates the universality of jeans: "The uncertainty about how to report the findings began with the selection of the cover design. A strong candidate for visually representing the new world of youth in India was the idea of a pair of jeans: blue jeans, black jeans, studded jeans, jeans with patch pockets, jeans with messages, jeans, jeans, jeans. They have become the ubiquitous symbol of youth in India, from the large village, to the small town to the big city" (DeSouza, Kumar, and Shastri 2009: xix). For a discussion of McDonaldization, see Ritzer (2008).

24   For an early analysis of the Arab Spring focusing on the effect of technology, see Howard and Hussain (2011). For analysis that stresses the potential longer-term effects of social media on creating and sustaining civil society and its effects on politics, see Shirky (2012).

25   Some examples of this debate include from the popular press Samuelson (2012) and Rosser (2012), and from the more scholarly literature Jacobs (2000), Manza and Cook (2002), and Jones and McDermott (2009).

26   See Nagourney (2006); see McKibben (2006) for a view that sees these developments as a fundamental rebalancing of political power in the U.S. See Institute for Politics, Democracy, and the Internet (2006) for an analysis of the 2004 election.

27   *Citizens United vs. Federal Election Commission.*

28   For contemporary versions of this argument, see Hunter and Wolfe (2006: especially 53–5, 68–71, and 92).

29   See Higgs (1987) for a discussion of how both defense spending and welfare state expenditures increased during the period of the Cold War. Higgs is a "classical" liberal so his primary concern is with what he sees as the growth and invasiveness of the federal government and the attenuation of individual liberty. His work, however, documents the expansion of both defense and non-defense government expenditures and emphasizes that elites often exaggerate external threats to increase taxes.

30   See, for example, Boushey (2004) and Katz (1996). Katz's important history of welfare in America indicates that "wars" against the poor have occurred a number of times. He specifically labels the 1980s as "the war on welfare" (1996: chap. 10). It is clear that most Americans have a negative view of welfare recipients (Gilens 1999). This has probably been accentuated by portrayals in the mass media. See Bullock, Wyche, and Williams (2001) for a survey of the literature on the images of the poor in the press that led up to welfare reform (Personal Responsibility and Work Opportunity Reconciliation Act of 1996). They report: "During the 1980s and early 1990s considerable attention focused on the depiction of poor, inner-city African Americans. The image of urban Black men as members of a threatening and violent underclass prevailed both in the news media (Gans 1995) and in popular films, ... single Black mothers were, and continue to be vilified as

'lazy welfare queens' using the system to avoid work or as ignorant, pro-miscuous women caught in a self-perpetuating 'cycle of dependency'" (p. 236).

31 See, for example, Perea (1997).
32 For discussions of gangs, see Attinger (1990) and Miller (2001). For com-parative data that describe urban gangs in India, see Mehta (2004).
33 Attinger's (1990) description of life in New York City exemplifies the nega-tive, if not slanted, view of problems created by primarily the lower strata of society: *Time*, Sep. 17, 1990:

> Until recently, the negative aspects of New York living were more than com-pensated by the exhilaration of simply being there. [...]
> But that balance has now begun to shift. Reason: a surge of drugs and violent crime that government officials seem utterly unable to combat. [...] Last year 1,905 people were murdered in New York, more than twice as many as in Los Angeles. [...]
> This summer, in one eight-day period, four children were killed by stray gunshots as they played on the sidewalks, toddled in their grandmother's kitchens or slept soundly in their own beds. Six others have been wounded since late June. So many have died that a new slang term has been coined to describe them: "mushrooms," as vulnerable as tiny plants that spring up underfoot.
> [...] "Crime is tearing at the vitals of this city and has completely altered ordinary life," says Thomas Reppetto, president of the Citizens Crime Com-mission." [...]
> "New Yorkers can put up with dirty streets, poor schools and broken subways," warns Mitchell Moss, director of the urban research center at New York University. "But [they] cannot take uncertainty – risks, yes, but not uncertainty."
> At times the city has seemed so consumed with crime that it was incapable of thinking about anything else. Nursery-school teachers in some of the city's tougher neighborhoods train children barely old enough to talk to hit the floor at the sound of gunshots. They call them "firecrackers" and reward the swift with a lollipop.

34 For an analysis that disputes the accuracy of the data used to describe the problems with drugs, see Robinson and Scherlen (2007).
35 This report, published by the Department of Justice, provides an overview of the expansion of gang activity in the U.S. from 1970 to 1998, the chang-ing nature and location of such activities, and a survey of the purported causes of gang activity.
36 See Freilich (2001) and Crothers (2002).
37 Kaste (2006): "The radical environmentalists of Eugene, Ore., have disap-peared or gone quiet. Some say it's because of a government crackdown that includes stiff fines and harsh prison sentences. The sentences have been so harsh, in fact, that even a victim of one arson attack isn't sure it was fair." One eco-radical received a 22-year sentence for burning three SUVs in a dealer's lot. (Presumably this refers to the sentencing of Kevin Tubbs

who was charged with a number of other crimes as well.) Also see Janofsky (2006).

38   For a striking example of gangs both exploiting and protecting in India's largest city, see Mehta (2004). The situation in U.S. cities is by no means as extreme, but Mehta describes well the general logic of how criminal groups provide both threats and dangers when the state is not effective in maintaining social order. As Mehta makes clear, such criminal gangs vary in the degree to which they consider themselves loyal citizens of the state or the protectors of certain ethnic or religious groups, or sometimes both.

39   There is no clear consensus about either the definition or the causes of terrorism or the extent to which contemporary terrorism is distinct from earlier historical examples. Most definitions, however, emphasize attacks on noncombatants. When I suggest that contemporary terrorists can be seen as a particular kind of guerrilla, and hence a subtype of "bandit," I do not mean to suggest that this is the only type of terrorism or that the state or other established political authorities do not engage in terrorism. For an array of recent sociological perspectives on these issues, see the symposium organized by Senechal de la Roche (2004).

40   See *The New York Times*, "The Wealthiest Benefit More From the Recent Tax Cuts," June 5, 2005. The more technical literature on which the article is based is cited at the end of this article.

41   See Coryn, Beale, and Myers (2004) for a brief summary of the relevant polling data following 9/11 and a more theoretical microanalysis of the social psychological processes of chauvinism and patriotism. See Erenberg and Hirsch (1996), especially Gerstle, "The Working Class Goes to War" (pp. 105–27), for a variety of historical analyses of the waxing and waning of American patriotism and chauvinism.

42   For a very useful account of the actions of the elites associated with the George W. Bush administration, see Higley and Burton (2006: 197–201).

43   There are many news articles to this effect, for example, Constable (2013).

44   Of course, corporations have long had an influence on local communities (see, e.g., Pellegrin and Coates 1956), and there were, of course, relatively small "company towns" that were virtually run by the company, but the phenomenon I am referring to is now affecting areas that in the past had largely locally owned businesses.

45   For an excellent review article on urban politics in a globalizing world, see Reichl (2005).

46   http://www.clearchannel.com/Corporate/ (accessed September 13, 2012). For a more general discussion of concentration of media ownership, see McQuail and Siune (1998).

Chapter 6   The U.S. 1980–2008: Other Actors

1   Part of this is, of course, due to the enormous increase in the size of the world population and the percentage of that population that is exposed to

the mass media. The absolute size of the audience that is familiar with any one celebrity is not necessarily smaller than in earlier periods.

2   The first example of its use in the etymology of the *Oxford English Dictionary* is in 1967.

3   While the Internet, cable channels, and low-power radio outlets have increased the variety of voices available, nonetheless since the Telecommunications Act of 1996 the ownership of media outlets is more concentrated and the content of the news tends to be from a few national media companies (Compaine and Gomery 2000). For an overview of where Americans get their news, and how their ideologies are related to their news sources, see The Pew Research Center for the People and the Press (2004).

4   See Scheuer (1999) for an analysis of the effects of the simplification of communication via sound bites.

5   One such firm, "Consensus Communications," explains their philosophy of "Strategic Public Relations" in the following terms: "**Your Message.** It's not something you leave on voicemail. Your message is the concise story that communicates the essence of your business to potential clients and investors. Your message is the straightforward … and doesn't succumb to misinformation that could tarnish your image … In today's fast-paced world, you sometimes get just one chance to communicate your message – so every word counts – and so does every opportunity. **Our Job.** Our job is to help you develop, communicate and manage your message – so that when the stakes are their highest – you are on message. **Our Approach.** We develop creative communication strategies by analyzing your situation, conducting sophisticated market research, and taking it to the streets and actually shaping public opinion." http://www.onmessage.com/philosophy.htm (accessed December 21, 2006).

A Google search for "on message" produced 538,000 hits and "staying on message" produced 10,000 hits, showing that these phrases are a common and frequent notion in public discourse.

6   For an analysis of the use and importance of pictorial images for the 2000 presidential campaign between George W. Bush and Al Gore, see Verser and Wicks (2006).

7   This is not, of course, a totally new phenomenon. Thomas Jefferson was (apparently rightly) accused of having a black mistress. Andrew Jackson and Alexander Hamilton fought duels over things political opponents said. Nonetheless, the frequency and intensity of negative campaigning is generally perceived to have increased.

8   http://law.wlu.edu/deptimages/Powell%20Archives/PowellMemorandum Printed.pdf (accessed December 8, 2013). The initial significance of this memo has been disputed (Schmitt 2005), but it seems clear that it has become an important ideological document in the struggles between right and left.

9   See Reich (1989) for a brief non-technical summary and Perrucci and Wysong (2003) for a useful textbook overview. For a detailed analysis of this issue, see Kalleberg (2011). For a market oriented explanation of why the polarization occurred, see Autor and Dorn (2013). See Sassen (2001)

for an influential statement about polarization in global cities, Hamnett (1994, 2002) for discussions that qualify this argument, and Walks (2001) for a detailed analysis of the polarization in Toronto. See Nightingale and Fix (2004) for a more U.S.-oriented analysis that focuses on the interaction between the changing mode of production and immigration from low wage areas.

10   This is not to argue that the changing distribution of income is simply the result of changes in the occupational structure. Changes in the family structure and probably in the tax structure have also contributed to greater income inequality.

11   Table H-2. Share of Aggregate Income Received by Each Fifth and Top 5 Percent of Households, All Races: 1967–2012; http://www.census.gov/hhes/www/income/data/historical/inequality/index.html (accessed May 30, 2014).

12   Table H-3. Mean Income Received by Each Fifth and Top 5 Percent of Households, All Races: 1967 to 2012, http://www.census.gov/hhes/www/income/data/historical/inequality/index.html (accessed May 30, 2014).

13   Ibid.

14   While more people live in racially and ethnically integrated neighborhoods, the percentage of minorities living in highly segregated or decaying neighborhoods has increased. See the essays in Frankenberg and Orfield (2012) for an overview of changing residential patterns and the policy implications for school desegregation.

15   After this book was finished the English translation of Thomas Piketty's *Capital in the Twenty-First Century* became available (Piketty 2014). It provides data about the distribution of wealth and income over a longer period of time than has previously been available. While many of its recommendations are controversial, it adds both further evidence and an explanation of why economic inequality has been increasing.

16   A comparative study of ten developed nations addresses this question (Ermisch, Jäntti, and Smeeding 2012, esp. chaps. 2 and 19). "The most important motivation for the [study] … is the concern that rising income inequality will have the long-run effect of reducing intergenerational mobility" (p. 463). While the study does not definitively answer this question, it does provide strong evidence that the effect of parents' socioeconomic status (SES) in their children's SES is substantial in most countries and that it is strongest in the U.S. This latter finding is, of course, the opposite of the usual notion that there is more equality of opportunity in the U.S. than in Europe. Moreover, overall education systems did not reduce the extent of intergenerational transmission of privilege, that is, schools did not increase equality of opportunity. "Education systems matter, but the evidence indicates that their net effect is not to reduce the relationship between parental SES and child achievement, but to maintain or strengthen the patterns of differences in outcomes already evident at younger ages" (p. 472); on this latter point also see Roksa and Potter (2011, 2013) for analyses of the complex details of the way family background differences increase the gap

in academic achievement over time. While these studies provide more data and more sophisticated analyses, the failure of expanding schooling to reduce class inequality is not a new finding. Over 40 years ago I argued that expansion of higher education was unlikely to increase equality of opportunity for social classes unless the degree of inequality was limited (Milner 1972).

17   U.S. Bureau of Labor Statistics (2014a); rate of union membership for 1955 is from U.S. Census Bureau (1975).

18   For a review of the state and trends for labor unions through the 1990s, see Clawson and Clawson (1999) and Katz and Autor (1999) about wage structure. Most analysts agree there is increasing inequality, and a greater premium for having a college degree. There is no clear consensus about the source of these changes.

19   The issues and the evidence are complex. Social distance and suspicion often exist between blacks and whites (Hacker 1992: 23ff) and for the very poor and others. A debate over the existence and extent of the underclass is ongoing. Movement in and out of officially defined poverty is relatively high, but the evidence about the poorest of the poor is more ambiguous, and those who leave ghettos often return later. See Quillian (2003) for evidence that most blacks live in poor urban neighborhoods for ten years or longer while only ten percent of whites do. "Further, most of this racial difference cannot be accounted for by differences in poverty status or household structure … the measure of immobility and total exposure … do indeed suggest that to be 'trapped' is a meaningful descriptive term for a substantial share of the black residents of poor neighborhoods" (pp. 243–4). See also Pattillo (1999) and Cashin (2004). Crowder, South, and Chavez (2006), however, report the retarded movement of minorities into Anglo neighborhoods is not primarily due to differences in wealth. Fernandez and Fernandez-Mateo (2006) report that for the factory they studied, the differences in access to networks did not explain differences in employment. While most second generation immigrants learn English, many assimilate into an underclass and this status seems to be transmitted to the next generation (Portes and Rumbaut 2005). See Lichter (1988) for an analysis and discussion of the "mismatch" between where the poor lived and where the jobs were during the 1972–82 period. For an even stronger statement of the tendencies toward "apartheid," see Massey (1990) and Massey and Denton (1993); for an analysis of the relatively recent experiences and costs of being immigrant to the U.S., see Massey and Sánchez (2010). See Fainstein (1994) about the negative effects of residential segregation. Such complex findings fuel ongoing debate over whether an underclass is due primarily to low pay and scarce jobs, or to a "culture of poverty" and behaviors that cause people to fail economically. See Jencks (1992: chap. 4) for a fair, but dated summary of the complexities. For a survey of this issue that argues the elimination of an underclass requires both better economic opportunities and changes in the culture and behaviors of the poor, see Sawhill (2003).

20   It is hotly debated whether increases in international trade and firms moving jobs overseas affects wages and job security for American workers – and inequality within the U.S. The economists generally agree that outsourcing tends to increase labor market volatility, increases average labor productivity (by replacing less productive labor), lowers the costs of products, increases the variety of products available, and weakens labor unions – though the strength and persistence of these relationships is less clear. There is less agreement about the whether it increases domestic unemployment, reduces wages, increases the cost of transfer payments (e.g., unemployment benefits), and increases domestic income inequality. The tendency seems to be to increase the wages of high-skilled employees and reduce the wages of low-skilled employees. Some of the relevant literature includes Katz and Autor (1999), Biscourp and Kramarz (2007), Autor and Dorn (2013), Feenstra (2008), Grossman and Rossi-Hansberg (2006), and McLaren and Hakobyan (2010).

21   Houseman (1995) notes, "Although job growth was high, many argued that the quality of American jobs – as measured by wages, benefits and job security – deteriorated. The decline of jobs in the high-paying manufacturing sector and the growth of jobs in the low-paying service sector, the growth in part-time and temporary employment, and the general decline in real wages among less-educated, less-skilled workers have been presented as evidence of erosion in job quality." See Nightingale and Fix (2004) for a view that links recent immigrants and dual job structure. For a more positive view, but one that focuses on the nature of jobs that will make up the occupation structure without directly addressing the issue of wages and benefits, see Bailey (1999).

22   According to a paper published by the International Monetary Fund: "At the same time, the average real wage in the United States (that is ... adjusted for inflation) has grown only slowly since the early 1970s and the real wage for unskilled workers has actually fallen. It has been estimated that male high school dropouts have suffered a 20 percent decline in real wages since the early 1970s" (Slaughter and Swagel 1997). Moretti (2011) suggests that part of the wage gap between high school graduates and college graduates is because the latter live in more expensive urban areas. Whatever the reason, the social distance between these two groups increased.

23   See Martin (1995) for an overview of its content, who supported the measure, and the initial effects.

24   U.S. Census Bureau, Table HIB-1, "Health Insurance Coverage Status and Type of Coverage by Sex, Race and Hispanic Origin"; and Table HIB-3, "Health Insurance Coverage Status and Type of Coverage – Children Under 18 by Age: 1999 to 2010," http://www.census.gov/hhes/www/hlthins/data/historical/HIB_tables.html (accessed March 7, 2012).

25   See Pear (2002), Kassner (2006), Mullen (1996), and Centers for Medicare & Medicaid Services (CMS) (2004).

26   The percentage of women over 16 participating in the labor force increased from 33 percent in 1950 to 52 percent in 1980 to 60 percent in 2008 (U.S. Bureau of Labor Statistics 2014b).

27   According to studies reported by the U.S. Center for Disease Control (CDC), the most recent studies based on large data sets such as the Current Population Survey (CPS) and National Survey of Families and Households (NSFH) show that the total hours worked by parents and the high probability that many will work different shifts tend to decrease marital satisfaction and quality family time and increase the probability of conflict and divorce. See Presser (n.d.). A smaller study using earlier time series data found relatively little effect of the total family work hours (TFWH) in dual-earner couples. See Barnett (2004).

28   In 1997 children ages 5–11 spent an average of 6.4 hours per week in self-care, while those ages 12–14 spent 9.2 hours per week in self-care. See Smith (2002: Table 6).

29   See Milner (2004) for a discussion of teenagers, consumerism, and some of the effects on family life.

30   This is not, of course, to suggest that it is the fault of women that children or public institutions are neglected or that the solution is for women to return to their "traditional" roles. Rather it is to suggest more resources need to be devoted to family and community institutions – especially by men.

31   For an overview of the effects of welfare reform, see Jencks (2005).

32   See Jencks (1994) for a thoughtful, but dated analysis of the issues surrounding homelessness up to the early 1990s. The data on the number, composition, and sources of homelessness are complex and problematic. Most of the data suggest that the numbers of homeless are increasing rather than decreasing. The commonly cited source for "point in time" estimates is the National Survey of Homelessness Providers and Clients conducted in 1996, which estimated that on a given night in October 444,000 people were homeless. A source for studies of extensiveness or "prevalence" is the National Law Center's estimate that about one percent of the population experience homelessness during the course of a year (National Law Center on Homelessness and Poverty 2004). For a useful summary of what is known, see National Coalition for the Homeless (2002).

33   U.S. Census Bureau, Voting and Registration, Historical Time Series Tables, Table A-1. "Reported Voting and Registration by Race, Hispanic Origin, Sex and Age Groups: November 1964 to 2010," http://www.census.gov/hhes/www/socdemo/voting/publications/historical/index.html   (accessed March 7, 2012).

34   USA Today/CNN/Gallup Poll (2005) compared with earlier polls, http://www.usatoday.com/news/polls/tables/live/2005-05-23-poll.htm   (accessed July 10, 2005).

35   http://www.aig.com/gateway/aboutaig/1-70-0-0-5-index.htm   (accessed December 13, 2006).

36   See Whitmeyer (2002) for a useful discussion of the role of elites in creating popular nationalism that comes to this conclusion.

37   See Althaus (2002): "If 9/11 has founded a new era of civic-mindedness in the U.S., it seems to have left Americans' collective appetite for news largely undisturbed. The size of the network television news audience grew only

slightly, and newspaper readership continued to decline after 9/11. While the average size of the cable-news audience has doubled, it remains a small fraction of American adults, and the audiences for both network and cable news have diminished with each passing month" (p. 520).

38 "White flight" is an especially complex phenomenon that not only reflects personal attitudes about race, but the perceived effects of the composition of one's neighborhood and the surrounding neighborhoods (Crowder and South 2008; Crowder, South, and Chavez 2006).

With respect to interracial marriages, in 1980 there were 167,000 white/black marriages out of 49,714,000, which was .34 of one percent of marriages. By 2008 there were 481,000 white/black marriages out of 60,129,000 which was .79 of one percent of marriages. Obviously there has been an increase, but interracial marriages are still quite rare (U.S. Census Bureau 2010b).

39 In 1970, 62 percent of the GDP was personal consumption expenditures, while in 2010 personal consumption expenditures were 71 percent of the GDP (calculated from U.S. Census Bureau 2012b).

40 For example, the Mall of America outside of Minneapolis urges people to: "Think Mall of America for group tours, birthday parties, corporate events, conventions, field trips, reunions, senior outings, weddings, receptions and more!" It also offers a "Free Visitors Kit," and "Group Travel Planner" and visitor guides in Chinese, Japanese, and Spanish; http://www.mallofamerica.com/visit/visitor-information (accessed January 3, 2014); see Graham, Graham and MacLean (1991) for a scholarly article about malls as a recreational activity for the elderly.

41 Skocpol and Fiorina (1999) observe that "Americans of many persuasions agree that troubles for our democracy may lie in a loss of social ties or in the changing universe of voluntary associations. Observers suspect that solutions to current ills may involve rebuilding group life beyond as well as within formal politics." They survey the research, the issues, theoretical approaches and the findings at the end of the twentieth century. More recently Kidd (2011: 12–23) surveys the trend data on voting, associational membership, church membership and attendance, and non-voting political activities and concludes: "In sum, the last half century appears to be a period of general retrenchment in traditional forms of civic and political participation" (2011: 23). It is unclear whether newer forms of participation (e.g., via the Internet) will be an adequate substitute.

42 To give a rough approximation of the scope of this genre, I counted the number of reality shows listed by Wikipedia (approximately 525) and by Reality TV World (approximately 1,100) that have been produced worldwide. Little of the sizeable literature on reality television focuses on what motivates people to participate. It is taken for granted that people want to be "famous," even if portrayed as bad parents, drug addicts, and adulators. As Graeme Turner (2006: 157) says, "Much of the participation in reality TV is aimed at a certain kind of recognition of the self." My point is that many people seem to be willing to undergo stress and humiliation (e.g.,

Serpe 2013) in order not to be invisible in the arenas/fields that are increasingly central.

43   The literature on the sources of reenactments (e.g., Gapps 2009; Manning 2012) tends to focus on the concern to create pseudo authenticity rather than explanations of who participates and why.

44   Research shows the effect of media images on women's self-evaluations (Henderson-King, Henderson-King, and Hoffmann 2001). While this study shows that some women resist the legitimacy of model-like images, it is based on studies of undergraduate women where feminist attitudes are likely to be more prevalent than in the general population.

45   According to the American Society for Aesthetic Plastic Surgery [composed of more than 100 board certified plastic surgeons]: "The demand for plastic surgery procedures increased almost 9% last year ... [The society] has collected multi-specialty procedural statistics since 1997 [and] the overall number of cosmetic procedures has increased 155 percent since the tracking of the statistics first began. Almost 9.5 million cosmetic surgical and nonsurgical procedures were performed in the United States in 2010. The most frequently performed surgical procedure was breast augmentation and the most popular nonsurgical procedure was injections of Botulinum Toxin Type A (including Botox and Dysport) ... The top five surgical procedures were: Breast Augmentation (318,123), Liposuction (289,016), Eyelid Surgery (152,123), Abdominoplasty (144,929), Breast Reduction (138,152) ... Americans spent nearly $10.7 billion on cosmetic procedures in 2010. Of that total almost $6.6 billion was spent on surgical procedures; $1.9 billion was spent on injectable procedures; $1.8 billion was spent on skin rejuvenation procedures; and almost $500 million was spent on other nonsurgical procedures including laser hair removal and laser treatment of leg veins" [dated April 4, 2011]; http://www.cosmeticplasticsurgerystatistics.com/statistics.html#2010-NEWS (accessed March 8, 2012).

46   There is a long line of research that documents this (e.g., Adams 1977); for some relatively recent examples, see Mazur, Mazur, and Keating (1984), Frieze, Olson, and Russell (1991), Jackson, Hunter, and Hodge (1995), Biddle and Hamermesh (1999), Jæger (2011), and Williams (2011).

47   For an analysis that questions the extent to which being overweight is an actual health problem rather than a socially constructed norm, see Saguy (2013).

48   See, for example, Lee-St. John (2006) and Langfitt (2006). I recently received the following message from my own university's Director for Graduate Student Development Programs – Office of the VP for Research. "Branding: Branding is important not only for products and services but also for you as a graduate student! Your 'brand', made up of your online presence, application materials, and personal interactions, is what future employers (academic and beyond) will use to decide if you are the right candidate for the job. We will discuss how to enhance your 'brand' during this interactive seminar. All graduate students are strongly encouraged to attend, even those no longer in coursework, and especially those going on the job market."

49 See Milner (1993, 1994) for a discussion of the relationship between sacred-ness and status and for the parallels between religious behavior and doc-trines and more mundane status systems.

50 See, for example, Greenwood and Long (2011).

51 The literature about sex on the Internet is substantial, but I have been unable to find analyses of why amateurs are motivated to make and post these. The closest I have found is a short essay by Marche (2008) and an essay that indirectly deals with this by Benedict (2007).

52 The most influential discussion of the Frankfurt Institute for Social Research is Jay (1973). For a useful and thoughtful sociological perspective on critical theory, see Calhoun (1995). For my own view on the relationship between sociology and postmodernism, see Milner (2014).

53 For useful overviews of the range of concepts and arguments that make up contemporary Marxist sociology, see Burawoy et al. (2006), Burawoy and Wright (2002), and Ellerman (2010).

54 Of course, if the notion of "political" is expanded to include every kind of conflict and struggle, rather than efforts to control the state, then by defini-tion everything becomes "political," but this handicaps rather than aids our efforts to understand the contemporary social world.

55 Fifteen minutes of fame refers to Andy Warhol's 1968 quip: "In the future, everyone will be world-famous for 15 minutes."

Chapter 7 The 2007–2009 Financial Crisis

1 For example, Havemann (2008), Johnson and Kwak (2010), Federal Reserve Bank of St. Louis (2010), Mizruchi (2010: 106–10), U.S. Senate (2011), U.S. Financial Crisis Inquiry Commission (2011), and Binder (2013). Perhaps the most detailed accessible account is Binder (2013: chaps 2–3). The U.S. Senate report is especially helpful in identifying inadequate, ques-tionable, and duplicitous practices by financial institutions, ratings agencies, and government regulators. This report has, however, been criticized for not giving more attention to the largest financial institutions that are still in business and continue to be key actors in both business and politics, e.g., JP Morgan Chase, Bank of America, Wells Fargo, and Citibank. See, for example, Mintz (2011). Also important is the U.S. Financial Crisis Inquiry Commission (2011) appointed by the leaders of the House and Senate. (The Democrats were then in the majority in both houses. Three each were chosen by the Speaker of the House and by the Senate Majority Leader and two each by the two Republican Minority Leaders.) Judge Rakoff (2014) makes useful comments about the probable intentional fraud committed by many in the financial industry, the government's failure to prosecute these individuals, and some of the possible reasons for this. He also provides a useful summary of the government's role in creating the crisis.

2 As Carruthers (2009: 24) notes, "Wall Street firms hired lots of physicists and mathematicians to do their numbers ... "

3   Especially important is the development of The Society for Worldwide Interbank Financial Telecommunication (SWIFT). This has made it possible for banks and other financial institutions throughout the world to communicate with each other and conduct transactions on a secure system.

4   U.S. Census Bureau. 2012. U.S. Statistical Abstract of the United States: 2012, Tables 1209 and 1210. During the 2008–2010 economic recession trades declined about 20–25 percent from their 2008 high.

5   OTC Bulletin Board, December 2, 2013; http://www.otcbb.com/TradingData/HistAnnualStats.stm (accessed February 23, 2014).

6   For example, Rakoff (2014: 6) reports: "[B]efore 2001, the FBI had more than one thousand agents assigned to investigating financial frauds, but after September 11 many of these agents were shifted to antiterrorism work ... [T]he result was that by 2007 or so there were only 120 agents reviewing more than 50,000 reports of mortgage fraud filed by banks." Rakoff notes that the FBI "is not the primary investigator of fraud in the sale of mortgage-backed securities; that responsibility lies mostly with the SEC. But at the very time the financial crisis was breaking, the SEC was trying to deflect criticism from its failure to detect the Madoff fraud and this led it to concentrate on Ponzi like schemes ... More recently the SEC has been hard hit by budget limitations ... "

7   http://www.heritage.org/index/book/chapter-7#fn-1 (accessed December 10, 2013).

8   "Have we in fact reached the end of history? Are there, in other words, any fundamental 'contradictions' in human life that cannot be resolved in the context of modern liberalism that would be resolvable by an alternative political-economic structure?" (1989). Fukuyama has since broken with the neo-conservative movement (Fukuyama 2006).

9   There are claims that private property is rooted in certain biologically based inclinations that are seen in many animals as well as humans (Gintis 2007). While this may well be the case, this does not mean that there are not significant cultural variations in how this basic inclination is channeled and organized.

10 Contrary to some "urban myths," it is certainly not the case that there are no laws against trespassing in Scotland. It is true that owners are much less able to restrict non-owners from entering or crossing open land than is the case in many regions – though those entering can certainly be prosecuted for damaging the property or causing other forms of harm. See Land Reform (Scotland) Act of 2003; http://www.legislation.gov.uk/asp/2003/2/section/1 (accessed December 9, 2013).

11 For a useful nontechnical overview of the history of property rights in the U.S., see "Introduction to Property Rights: A Historical Perspective," http://urbanext.illinois.edu/lcr/propertyrights.cfm (accessed December 9, 2013).

12 http://georgewbush-whitehouse.archives.gov/infocus/achievement/chap7.html (accessed December 9, 2013).

13 It is telling, however, that in the 2012 poll, having a secure job was the top indicator of middle-class status followed by having health insurance, with

homeownership in third place. This is almost certainly related to the high level of unemployment in 2008–13 and the increasing cost of health care. It seems likely if the economy picks up and if the Affordable Care Act actually works that homeownership will again increase in importance as an indicator of middle-class status. Obviously, one can be a respectable member of society without being middle class or owning one's home, but home ownership has long been a key and powerful symbol of respectability.

14   This is a complex literature with mixed findings. While earlier research made strong claims for the contribution of home ownership to good citizenship, much recent research calls this into question. Some representative articles on this topic include Coulson and Li (2013), DiPasquale and Glaeser (1999), Engelhardt et al. (2010), Grinstein-Weiss et al. (2010), Harkness and Newman (2003), Holupka and Newman 2012, and Rohe and Stegman (1994).

Chapter 8   Conclusions

1   For thoughtful articles that recognize the importance of context and particularity, especially in the interpretation of text and intellectual history, but also point out the dangers of an overemphasis on these notions, see Jay (2011) and Holsinger (2011).

2   I am indebted to Ray Whitehead for information and guidance about the nature of Christian movements in contemporary China.

3   There were many accounts in standard news sources. See, for example, Wong and Ansfield (2013).

4   These include: old and new means of production, old and new forms of ideology, rural–urban conflicts of interest, cops who are robbers, and characters who either move from being respectable to unrespectable or vice versa.

Appendix: Some Implications and Elaborations of the Model

1   As indicated earlier, this is what Bourdieu refers to as the "dominant principle of domination."

2   See Tilly (1984: 20–6) for a discussion of the problems of comparing whole societies. Mann (1986) makes a similar point and argues that we should talk about networks of power rather than societies. While I agree that the scope of different forms of power vary, I do not think doing away with the notion of societies is going to solve that problem.

3   Some brief quotes from Dupuy and Dupuy (1993) illustrate the point: "Thanks to increased firepower and rate of fire, [Aldolphus] arranged his musketeers and his reduced number of pikemen in relatively thin lines … This was the genesis of modern linear tactics which remained basically unchanged – though constantly modified – until World War I … [E]ven

today ... [the] linear concept remains the modern infantry doctrine" (p. 575). And, "This century also saw the real beginning of the militarization of the supporting arms and services ... a natural concomitant of the emergence of the standing army ... to militarization of artillery personnel was later added the militarization of the teamsters who hauled the army's supplies" (p. 577). "The enormous advantage which [these innovations] provided in battle was soon imitated in other armies" (p. 579).

References

Adams, Gerald R. 1977. "Physical Attractiveness Research: Toward a Developmental Social Psychology of Beauty," *Human Development*, 20: 217–39.

Adams, James Truslow. 1931. *The Epic of America*. Boston: Little, Brown, and Company.

Althaus, Scott L. 2002. "American News Consumption during Times of National Crisis," *PS: Political Science and Politics*, 35: 517–21.

American Community Survey. 2003. "Average Travel Time to Work of Workers 16 Years and Over Who Did Not Work at Home (Minutes)." Washington, D.C.: U.S. Census Bureau.

Ansell, C. K. 2001. "Legitimacy: Political," in *International Encyclopedia of the Social and Behavioral Sciences*, eds. Neil Smelser and Paul B. Balfas. Amsterdam: Elsevier, pp. 8704–6.

Arneson, Richard. 2008. "Equality of Opportunity," *The Stanford Encyclopedia of Philosophy* (Fall 2008 Edition), ed. Edward N. Zalta; http://plato.stanford.edu/archives/fall2008/entries/equal-opportunity/ (accessed May 29, 2013).

Attinger, Joelle. 1990. "The Decline of New York," *Time*, September 17, 36–44.

Autor, David H. and David Dorn. 2013. "The Growth of Low-Skill Service Jobs and the Polarization of the US Labor Market," *The American Economic Review*, 103 (5): 1553–97.

Bacchetta, Mark and Zdenek Drabek. 2002. "Effects of WTO Accession on Policy-Making in Sovereign States," Staff Working Paper DERD-2002-02.

Geneva: World Trade Organization, Development and Economic Research Division.

Badie, B. 2001. "Legitimacy: Sociology," in *International Encyclopedia of the Social and Behavioral Sciences*, eds. Neil Smelser and Paul B. Balfas. Amsterdam: Elsevier, pp. 8706–9.

Bailey, Michael. 2004. "Money and the Possibility of Democratic Governance," in *Is This Any Way to Run a Democratic Government?*, ed. Stephen J. Wayne. Washington, D.C.: Georgetown University Press.

Bailey, Thomas. 1999. *The Changing Occupational Structure, Conservation of Human Resources*. Institute on Education and the Economy (Document No. B-7). New York: Columbia University.

Baker, James A., III, Lee H. Hamilton, Lawrence S. Eagleburger, Vernon E. Jordan, Jr., Edwin Meese, III, Sandra Day O'Connor, Leon E. Panetta, William J. Perry, Charles S. Robb, and Alan K. Simpson. 2006. *Iraq Study Group Report*. New York: Vintage Books.

Barakat, Mathew. 2005. "Judge Cancels Machinists' Contract, Pension Plans with US Airways," *Associated Press*, January 7.

Barnett, Rosalind Chait. 2004. "Work Schedules: Shift Work and Long Work Hours as a Predictor of Stress Outcomes." Atlanta, GA: Center for Disease Control, National Institute for Occupational Safety and Health; http://www.cdc.gov/niosh/topics/workschedules/abstracts/barnett.html (accessed March 10, 2010).

Bauman, Zygmunt. 2014. "The European Experiment," *The Hedgehog Review*, 16 (1): 18–25.

Becker, Gary S. 1964. *Human Capital*. Chicago: University of Chicago Press.

Bell, Daniel A. 2008. *China's New Confucianism: Politics and Everyday Life in a Changing Society*. Princeton: Princeton University Press.

Bell, Kim. 1993. "Gang 'Summit' Mostly Secret; Press Barred from Meetings; No St. Louis Gangs Attending," *St. Louis Post-Dispatch*, May 2, 1A.

Benedict, Elizabeth. 2007. "What I Learned about Sex on the Internet," *Daedalus*, 136 (2): 58–65.

Bertrand, Marianne and Kevin F. Hallock. 2001. "The Gender Gap in Top Corporate Jobs," *Industrial and Labor Relations Review*, 55 (1): 3–21.

Béteille, André. 1965. *Caste, Class, and Power: Changing Patterns of Stratification in a Tanjore Village*. Berkeley: University of California Press.

Biddle, Jeff E. and Daniel S. Hamermesh. 1999. "Beauty, Productivity, and Discrimination: Lawyers' Looks and Lucre," *Journal of Labor Economics*, 16 (1): 172–201.

Binder, Alan S. 2013. *After the Music Stopped: The Financial Crisis, the Response, and the Work Ahead*. New York: The Penguin Press.

Biscourp, Pierre and Francis Kramarz. 2007. "Employment, Skill Structure and International Trade," *Journal of International Economics*, 72 (1): 22–51.

Blaser, Arthur W. 1992. "How to Advance Human Rights without Really Trying: An Analysis of Nongovernmental Tribunals," *Human Rights Quarterly*, 14 (3): 339–70.

Block, Fred L. 1987. *Revising State Theory: Essays in Politics and Post-industrialism*. Philadelphia: Temple University Press.

Boedeker, Deborah. 2007. "Athenian Religion in the Age of Pericles," in *The Age of Pericles*, ed. Loren J. Samons II. Cambridge: Cambridge University Press.

Boli, John and George M. Thomas. 1999. *Constructing World Culture*. Stanford: University of Stanford Press.

Borjas, George J. 2004. "Making It Worse: President Bush Has Tackled the Immigration Problem – Wrongly," *National Review*, February 9: 24–26.

Born, Gary. 2012. "A New Generation of International Adjudication," *Duke Law Journal*, 61 (4): 775–878.

Bourdieu, Pierre. 1977. *Outline of a Theory of Practice*. Cambridge: Cambridge University Press.

Bourdieu, Pierre. 1984. *Distinction: A Social Critique of the Judgement of Taste*. Cambridge: Harvard University Press.

Bourdieu, Pierre. 1986. "The Forms of Capital," in *Handbook of Theory and Research for the Sociology of Education*, ed. John G. Richardson. Westport: Greenwood Press.

Bourdieu, Pierre. 1990. *The Logic of Practice*. Stanford: Stanford University Press.

Bourdieu, Pierre. 1996. *The State Nobility: Elite Schools in the Field of Power*. Stanford: Stanford University Press.

Bourdieu, Pierre. 1998. *Practical Reason: On the Theory of Action*. Stanford: Stanford University Press.

Bourdieu, Pierre, et al. 1999. *The Weight of the World: Social Suffering in Contemporary Society*. Cambridge: Polity Press.

Bourdieu, Pierre and Jean-Claude Passeron. 1977. *Reproduction in Education, Society, and Culture*. London and Beverly Hills: Sage Publications.

Boushey, Heather. 2004. "The Enigma of Working-Class Conservatism, A House Divided: How Welfare Reform Pits Working Families Against the Nonworking Poor," *New Labor Forum*, 13 (3): 27–35.

Brint, Steven G. 1994. *In an Age of Experts: The Changing Role of Professionals in Politics and Public Life*. Princeton: Princeton University Press.

Bryant, Joseph M. 1986. "Intellectuals and Religion in Ancient Greece: Notes on a Weberian Theme," *The British Journal of Sociology*, XXXVII (2): 269–96.

Bugh, Glenn Richard. 1988. *The Horsemen of Athens*. Princeton: Princeton University Press.

Bullock, Heather E., Fraser Wyche, and Wendy R. Williams. 2001. "Media Images of the Poor," *Journal of Social Issues*, 57 (2): 229–46.

Bullock, Penn. 2009. "Bernanke's Philosophy," *Reason: Free Minds and Free Markets*, November 17.

Burawoy, Michael. 2002. "What Happened to the Working Class? Errors of an Unrepentant Marxist," *The Future of Market Transition*, 19: 69–76.

Burawoy, M., P. Evans, A. Harris, D. Moon, and E. O. Wright. 2006. "Roundtable Discussion: Possibilities for Socialism in the Twenty-First Century," *Berkeley Journal of Sociology*, 50 (2006): 168–82.

Burawoy, Michael and Erik Olin Wright. 2002. "Sociological Marxism," in *Handbook of Sociological Theory*, ed. Jonathan H. Turner. New York: Kluwer Academic/Plenum Publisher, chap. 22.

Burgess, Glenn. 1992. "The Divine Right of Kings Reconsidered," *The English Historical Review*, 107 (425): 837–61.

Burton, Michael G. and John Higley. 1987. "Invitation to Elite Theory," in *Power Elites and Organizations*, eds. G. William Domhoff and Thomas R. Dye. Newbury Park: Sage Publications.

Burton, Michael G. and John Higley. 2001. "The Study of Political Elite Transformations," *International Review of Sociology*, 11 (2): 181–99.

Calhoun, Craig. 1993. "Habitus, Field, and Capital: Questions of Historical Specificity," in *Bourdieu: Critical Perspectives*, eds. Craig Calhoun, Edward LiPuma, and Moishe Postone. Cambridge: Polity Press.

Calhoun, Craig. 1995. *Critical Social Theory*. Oxford: Blackwell.

Carruthers, Bruce G. 2009. "A Sociology of Bubbles," *Contexts*, 8: 22–26.

Cashin, Sheryll. 2004. *The Failures of Integration: How Race and Class Are Undermining the American Dream*. New York: Public Affairs.

Centers for Medicare & Medicaid Services (CMS). 2004. "National Health Accounts, 2004, 2004 Medicare & Medicaid Statistical Supplement." Washington, D.C.: Department of Health and Human Services.

Chernoff, Fred. 1991. "Ending the Cold War: The Soviet Retreat and the US Military Buildup," *International Affairs*, 67 (1): 111–26.

Citrin, Jack, Donald Green, Christopher Muste, and Cara Wong. 1997. "Public Opinion Toward Immigration Reform: The Role of Economic Motivations," *The Journal of Politics*, 59 (3): 858–81.

Clawson, Dan and Mary Ann Clawson. 1999. "What Has Happened to the US Labor Movement? Union Decline and Renewal," *Annual Review of Sociology*, 25: 95–119.

Clayton, Stuart. 2010. "Television and the Decline of Deference," *History Review*, 68: 39–44; http://www.historytoday.com/stuart-clayton/television-and-decline-deference (accessed May 22, 2013).

Clinton, William. 1996. "The Era of Big Government is Over: CNN Transcript of President Clinton's Weekly Radio Address," *Cable News Network*, January 27; http://www.cnn.com/US/9601/budget/01-27/clinton_radio/index.html (accessed February 20, 2008).

Cloud, David S. and Eric Schmitt. 2006. "More Retired Generals Call for Rumsfeld's Resignation," *The New York Times*, April 14; http://www.nytimes.com/2006/04/14/washington/14military.html?hp&ex=1144987200&en=155d5469db2762de&ei=5094&partner=homepage (accessed February 20, 2008).

Coleman, James S. 1990. *The Foundations of Social Theory*. Cambridge: Harvard University Press.

Compaine, Benjamin M. and Douglas Gomery. 2000. *Who Owns the Media? Competition and Concentration in the Mass Media Industry*. Mahwah, NJ: Lawrence Erlbaum Associates.

Constable, Pamela. 2013. "Virginia Latinos, Courted by Democrats, Plunge into State Political Activism," *The Washington Post*, October 28.

Cooley, Alexander and James Ron. 2002. "The NGO Scramble: Organizational Insecurity and the Political Economy of Transnational Action," *International Security*, 27 (1): 5–39.

Coryn, Chris L., James M. Beale, and Krista M. Myers. 2004. "Response to September 11: Anxiety, Patriotism, and Prejudice in the Aftermath of Terror." *Current Research in Social Psychology*, 9 (12): 166–84.

Coulson, N. Edward and Herman Li. 2013. "Measuring the External Benefits of Homeownership," *Journal of Urban Economics*, 77: 57–67.

Crothers, Lane. 2002. "The Cultural Foundations of the Modern Militia Movement," *New Political Science*, 24 (2): 221–34.

Crowder, Kyle and Scott J. South. 2008. "Spatial Dynamics of White Flight: The Effects of Local and Extralocal Racial Conditions on Neighborhood Out-Migration," *American Sociological Review*, 73: 792–812.

Crowder, Kyle, Scott J. South and Erick Chavez. 2006. "Wealth, Race, and Inter-Neighborhood Migration," *American Sociological Review*, 71: 72–94.

Crystal, Stephen, Richard W. Johnson, Jeffrey Harman, Usha Sambamoorthi, and Rizie Kumar. 2000. "Out-of-Pocket Health Care Costs Among Older Americans," *Journal of Gerontology: Social Sciences*, 55B (1): S51–S62.

Cummings, Dolan, ed. 2005. *The Changing Role of the Public Intellectual*. London: Routledge.

Dahl, Robert. 1961. *Who Governs?* New Haven: Yale University Press.

Dalrymple, Theodore. 1999. "No One Tips Their Cap Anymore," *New Statesman*, December 20, 1999–January 3, 2000, 66–67.

Das, Sukla. 1977. *Crime and Punishment in Ancient India*. New Delhi: Abhinav Publications.

Davies, J. K. 1992. "Society and Economy," in *The Cambridge Ancient History*, ed. David M. Lewis, John Boardman, J. K. Davies, and M. Ostwald, vol. V, chap. 8g, pp. 287–305. Cambridge: Cambridge University Press.

Davis, Gerald. 2009. *Managed by the Markets: How Finance Reshaped America*. New York: Oxford University Press.

DeSilver, Drew. 2013. "Around the World, Governments Promote Home Ownership," Fact Tank: News in Numbers, Pew Research Center, August 6; http://www.pewresearch.org/fact-tank/2013/08/06/around-the-world-governments-promote-home-ownership/ (accessed December 15, 2013).

DeSouza, Peter Ronald, Sanjay Kumar, and Sandeep Shastri. 2009. *Indian Youth in a Transforming World*. New Delhi: Sage Publications.

De Ste. Croix, G. E. M. 1981. *The Class Struggle in the Ancient Greek World*. Ithaca: Cornell University Press.

Deufel, Benjamin. 2003. "A Working Town Welcome: Economic Context and Local Receptivity Toward Latino Immigrants." Workshop on Immigrant Incorporation. Maxwell School of Syracuse University: Campbell Public Affairs Institute, April 18.

DiPasquale, D. and E. Glaeser. 1999. "Incentives and Social Capital: Are Homeowners Better Citizens?" *Journal of Urban Economics*, 45: 354–84.

Dodson, Kyle. 2010. "The Return of the American Voter? Party Polarization and Voting Behavior, 1988 to 2004," *Sociological Perspectives*, 53 (3): 443–9.

Domhoff, G. William. 1967. *Who Rules America?* Englewood Cliffs: Prentice-Hall.

Domhoff, G. William. 1998. *Who Rules America? Power and Politics in the Year 2000*. Mountain View: Mayfield Publishing.

Domhoff, G. William. 2013. *Who Rules America? The Triumph of the Corporate Rich*, 7th edn. New York: McGraw-Hill.

Dumont, Louis. 1980. *Homo Hierarchicus: The Caste Systems and Its Implications*, enlarged edition. Chicago: University of Chicago Press.

Dupuy, R. Ernest and Trevor N. Dupuy. 1993. *The Harper Encyclopedia of Military History*. New York: HarperCollins.

Dye, Jane Lawler. 2005. "Fertility of American Women: June 2004," Current Population Reports, P20-555. Washington, D.C.: U.S. Census Bureau; http://www.census.gov/prod/2005pubs/p20-555.pdf (accessed March 6, 2006).

Dye, Thomas R. 2002. *Who's Running America? The Bush Restoration*, 7th edn. Upper Saddle River, NJ: Prentice Hall.

Dye, Thomas R., Harmon Zeigler, and Louis Schubert. 2012. *The Irony of Democracy: An Uncommon Introduction to American Politics*. Boston: Wadsworth.

Ellerman, David. 2010. "Marxism as a Capitalist Tool," *The Journal of Socio-Economics*, 39 (6): 696–700.

Ellis, J. R. 1994. "Macedonian Hegemony Created," in *The Cambridge Ancient History*, ed. David M. Lewis, John Boardman, J. K. Davies, and M. Ostwald, vol. VI, chap. 15, pp. 723–90. Cambridge: Cambridge University Press.

Ellwood, Marilyn R. and Leighton Ku. 1998. "Welfare and Immigration Reforms: Unintended Side Effects for Medicaid," *Health Affairs*, 17 (3): 137–51.

Engelhardt, Gary V., Michael D. Eriksen, William G. Gale, and Gregory B. Mills. 2010. "What Are the Social Benefits of Homeownership? Experimental Evidence for Low-Income Households," *Journal of Urban Economics*, 67: 249–58.

Erenberg, Lewis A. and Susan A. Hirsch, eds. 1996. *The War in American Culture*. Chicago: University of Chicago Press.

Ermisch, John, Markus Jäntti, and Timothy M. Smeeding, eds. 2012. *Inequality in Achievements during Adolescence*. New York: Russell Sage Foundation.

Etzioni, Amitai. 1975. *A Comparative Analysis of Complex Organizations*, revised and enlarged edition. New York: Free Press.

Etzioni, Amitai and Alyssa Bowditch, eds. 2006. *Public Intellectuals: An Endangered Species?* Lanham: Rowman & Littlefield.

Fainstein, Susan S. 1994. *The City Builders: Property, Politics, and Planning in London and New York*. Cambridge: Blackwell.

Fairbank, John King and Merle Goldman. 1998. *China: A New History*. Cambridge: The Belknap Press of Harvard University Press.

Fan, Ruiping. 2011. *The Renaissance of Confucianism in Contemporary China*. Philosophical Studies in Contemporary Culture 20. Dordrecht and New York: Springer.

Federal Reserve Bank of St. Louis. 2010. "The Financial Crisis: A Timeline of Events and Policy Actions," http://timeline.stlouisfed.org/index.cfm?p=articles&ct_id=7 (accessed May 23, 2014).

Feenstra, Robert C. 2008. "Offshoring in the Global Economy," The Ohlin Lectures, Stockholm School of Economics, September; http://cid.econ.ucdavis.edu/Papers/pdf/Feenstra_Ohlin_Lecture_2008.pdfhttp://cid.econ.ucdavis.edu/Papers/pdf/Feenstra_Ohlin_Lecture_2008.pdf (accessed January 25, 2014).

Fernandez, Roberto M. and Isabel Fernandez-Mateo. 2006. "Networks, Race, and Hiring," *American Sociological Review*, 71 (1): 42–71.

Finley, M. I. 1963. *The Ancient Greeks*. New York: The Viking Press.

Finley, M. I. 1985. *The Ancient Economy*, 2nd edn. Berkeley: University of California Press.

Forbes. 2006. "The 400 Richest Americans," http://www.forbes.com/lists/2005/54/Rank_1.html (accessed November 13, 2006).

Foucault, M. 1995 [1977]. *Discipline and Punish: the Birth of the Prison, 2nd Vintage Books edn*. New York: Vintage Books.

Frankenberg, Erica and Gary Orfield. 2012. *The Resegregation of Suburban Schools: a Hidden Crisis in American Education*. Cambridge: Harvard Education Press.

Frederiksen, M. W. 1975. "Theory, Evidence and the Ancient Economy," *Journal of Roman Studies*, 65: 164–71.

Freilich, Joshua David. 2001. "Mobilizing Militias: Examining State-Level Correlates of Militia Organizations and Activities," Ph.D. dissertation, The Humanities and Social Sciences, State University of New York, Albany.

Frieze, Irene Hanson, Olson, Josephine E., and June Russell. 1991. "Attractiveness and Income for Men and Women in Management," *Journal of Applied Social Psychology*, 21 (13): 1039–57.

Froud, Julie, Adam Leaver, Gindo Tampubolon and Karel Williams. 2008. "Everything for Sale: How Non-Executive Directors Make a Difference," in *Remembering Elites*, eds. Mike Savage and Karel Williams. Malden: Blackwell/Sociological Review, pp. 162–86.

Fukuyama, Francis. 1989. "The End of History?" *The National Interest*, 16: 3–18.

Fukuyama, Francis. 2006. "After Neoconservatism," *The New York Times Magazine*, February 19.

Gabel, Medard and Henry Bruner. 2003. *Global Inc.: An Atlas of the Multinational Corporation*. New York: The New Press.

Gans, Herbert. 1995. *The War Against the Poor: the Underclass and Antipoverty Policy*. New York: Basic Books.

Gapps, S. 2009. "Mobile monuments: A View of Historical Reenactment and Authenticity from Inside the Costume Cupboard of History," *Rethinking History*, 13 (3): 395–409.

Garland, Robert. 1990. "Priests and Power in Classical Athens," in *Pagan Priests*, eds. Mary Beard and John North. London: Duckworth.

Garmisa, Steven P. 1997. "Small Print Gutting Lifetime Benefits," *Chicago Sun-Times*, August 2.

Gerstle, Gary. 1996. "The Working Class Goes to War," in *The War in American Culture*, eds. Lewis A. Erenberg and Susan A. Hirsch. Chicago: University of Chicago Press, pp. 105–27.

Gibson, Campbell, and Kay Jung. 2002. "Historical Census Statistics on Population, Totals By Race, 1790 to 1990, and by Hispanic Origin, 1970 to 1990, for the United States, Regions, Divisions, and States," Working Paper Series No. 56. Washington, D.C.: U.S. Census Bureau.

Giddens, Anthony. 1984. *The Constitution of Society*. Los Angeles: University of California Press.

Gilens, Martin. 1999. *Why Americans Hate Welfare: Race, Media, and the Politics of Antipoverty Policy*. Chicago: University of Chicago Press.

Gintis, Herbert. 2007. "The Evolution of Private Property," *Journal of Economic Behavior and Organization*, 64 (1): 1–16.

Goffman, Erving. 1974. *Frame Analysis: An Essay on the Organization of Experience*. Cambridge: Harvard University Press.

Gouldner, Alvin W. 1965. *Enter Plato: Classical Greece and the Origins of Social Theory*. New York: Basic Books.

Graham, Dawn Fowler, Ian Graham, and Michael MacLean. 1991. "Going to the Mall: A Leisure Activity of Urban Elderly People," *Canadian Journal on Aging/La Revue Canadienne du Vieillissement*, 10 (4): 345–58

Gray, Andrew and Kristin Roberts. 2007. "Petraeus Grilled over Bush's Iraq Strategy," *The Washington Post*, September 11.

Greene, Kevin. 2000. "Technological Innovation and Economic Progress in the Ancient World: M. I. Finley Re-Considered," *The Economic History Review*, New Series, 53 (1), 29–59.

Greenspan, Alan. 2007. *The Age of Turbulence: Adventures in a New World*. New York: Penguin Books.

Greenwood, Dara N. and Christopher R. Long. 2011. "Attachment, Belongingness Needs, and Relationship Status Predict Imagined Intimacy with Media Figures," *Communication Research*, 38 (2): 278–97.

Grinstein-Weiss Michal, Trina R. Williams Shanks, Kim R. Manturuk, Clinton C. Key, Jong-Gyu Paik, and Johann K. P. Greeson. 2010. "Homeownership and Parenting Practices: Evidence from the Community Advantage Panel," *Children and Youth Services Review*, 32: 774–82.

Grossman, Gene M. and Esteban Rossi-Hansberg. 2006. "Trading Tasks: A Simple Theory of Offshoring," *American Economic Review*, 98 (5): 1978–97.

Habib, Irfan. 1995. "Caste in Indian History," in *Essays in Indian History: Toward a Marxist Perception*. New Delhi: Tulika.

Hacker, Andrew. 1992. *Two Nations: Black and White, Separate, Hostile, Unequal*. New York: Scribner's.

Hamnett, Chris. 1994. "Social Polarization in Global Cities: Theory and Evidence," *Urban Studies*, 31 (3): 401–24.

Hamnett, Chris. 2002. "Social Polarization in London: The Income Evidence, 1979–93," in *Globalization and the New City: Migrants, Minorities and Urban Transformations in Comparative Perspective*, eds. Malcolm Cross and Robert Moore. Basingstoke: Palgrave, pp. 168–99.

Harker, Richard, Cheleen Mahar, and Chris Wilkes, eds. 1990. *An Introduction to the Work of Pierre Bourdieu: the Practice of Theory*. Basingstoke: Macmillan.

Harkness, Joseph M. and Sandra J. Newman. 2003. "Effects of Homeownership on Children: the Role of Neighborhood Characteristics and Family Income," *Economic Policy Review* [of the Federal Reserve Board of New York], June: 87–107.

Havemann, Joel. 2008. "The Financial Crisis of 2008: Year in Review 2008," in *Britannica Book of the Year, 2009*; http://www.britannica.com/EBchecked/topic/1484264/Financial-Crisis-of-2008-The (accessed December 20, 2013).

Hays, Sharon. 2003. *Flat Broke with Children: Women in the Age of Welfare Reform*. New York: Oxford University Press.

Hemingway, Colette and Seán Hemingway. 2002. "Athletics in Ancient Greece," in *Heilbrunn Timeline of Art History*. New York: The Metropolitan Museum of Art; http://www.metmuseum.org/toah/hd/athl/hd_athl.htm (accessed June 12, 2012).

Henderson, Jeffrey. 2007. "Drama and Democracy," in *The Age of Pericles*, ed. Loren J. Samons II. Cambridge: Cambridge University Press.

Henderson-King, Donna, Eaaron Henderson-King, and Lisa Hoffmann. 2001. "Media Images and Women's Self-Evaluations: Social Context and Importance of Attractiveness as Moderators," *Personality and Social Psychology Bulletin*, 27: 1407–61.

Herodotus. 1923. *Herodotus, with an English Translation by A.D. Godley*. London: William Heinemann.

Higgs, Robert. 1987. *Crisis and Leviathan: Critical Episodes in the Growth of American Government*. New York: Oxford University Press.

Higley, John and Michael G. Burton. 1989. "The Elite Variable in Democratic Transitions and Breakdowns," *American Sociological Review*, 54: 17–32.

Higley, John and Michael G. Burton. 2006. *Elite Foundations of Liberal Democracy*. Lanham: Rowman & Littlefield.

Higley, John and Gwen Moore. 2001. "Political Elite Studies at the Year 2000: Introduction," *International Review of Sociology/Revue Internationale de Sociologie*, 11 (21): 175–80.

Higley, John, G. Lowell Field, and Knut Grøholt. 1976. *Elite Structure and Ideology: A Theory with Applications to Norway*. New York: Columbia University Press.

Higley, John, Desley Deacon, and Don Smart. 1979. *Elites in Australia*. Boston: Routledge & Kegan Paul.

Higman, Barry W. 1984. *Slave Populations of the British Caribbean, 1807–1834*. Baltimore: Johns Hopkins University Press.

Hobsbawm, E. J. 1959. *Social Bandits and Primitive Rebels: Studies in Archaic Forms of Social Movement in the 19th and 20th Centuries*. Glencoe: Free Press.

Hobson, Jeremy. 2013. "What's at Stake for Farmers in the Immigration Debate," NPR Marketplace Morning Report for Thursday, February 7.

Holsinger, Bruce. 2011. " 'Historical Context' in Historical Context: Surface, Depth, and the Making of the Text," *New Literary History*, 42 (4): 593–614.

Holupka, Scott and Sandra J. Newman. 2012. "The Effects of Homeownership on Children's Outcomes: Real Effects or Self-Selection?" *Real Estate Economics*, 40 (3): 566–602.

Horster, Marietta. 2011. "The Tenure, Appointment and Eponymy of Priesthoods and their (Debatable) Ideological and Political Implications," in *Civic Priests*, eds. Marietta Horster and Anja Klöckner. Berlin: DeGruyter.

Houseman, Susan N. 1995. "Job Growth and the Quality of Jobs in the U.S. Economy," *Labor*, Special Issue: 93–124.

Houseman, Susan N., Arne L. Kalleberg, and George A. Erickcek. 2003. "The Role of Temporary Agency Employment in Tight Labor Markets," *Industrial and Labor Relations Review*, 57 (1): 105–27.

Howard, Philip N. and Muzammil M. Hussain. 2011. "The Role of Digital Media," *Journal of Democracy*, 22 (3): 35–48.

Hunter, James Davidson and Alan Wolfe. 2006. *Is There a Culture War? A Dialogue on Values and American Public Life*. Washington, D.C.: Brookings Institution Press.

Institute for Politics, Democracy, and the Internet. 2006. "Small Donors and Online Giving: A Study of Donors to the 2004 Presidential Campaigns," The Graduate School of Political Management. Washington, D.C.: The George Washington University.

Jackson, L. A., J. E. Hunter, and C. N. Hodge. 1995. "Physical Attractiveness and Intellectual Competence: A Meta-Analytic Review," *Social Psychology Quarterly*, 58 (2): 108–22.

Jacobs, Lawrence R. 2000. *Politicians Don't Pander*. Chicago: University of Chicago Press.

Jæger, Mads Meier. 2011. "'A Thing of Beauty is a Joy Forever'? Returns to Physical Attractiveness over the Life Course," *Social Forces*, 89 (3): 983–1003.

Janofsky, Michael. 2006. "11 Indicted in 17 Cases of Sabotage in West," *The New York Times*, January 21, A9.

Jay, Martin. 1973. *The Dialectical Imagination: a History of the Frankfurt School and the Institute of Social Research, 1923–1950*. Boston: Little, Brown.

Jay, Martin. 2011. "Historical Explanation and the Event: Reflections on the Limits of Contextualization," *New Literary History*, 42 (4): 557–71.

Jencks, Christopher. 1992. *Rethinking Social Policy: Race, Poverty, and the Underclass*. Cambridge: Harvard University Press.

Jencks, Christopher. 1994. *The Homeless*. Cambridge: Harvard University Press.

Jencks, Christopher. 2005. "What Happened to Welfare?" *The New York Review of Books*, 52 (20): 76–86.

Johnson, Simon and James Kwak. 2010. *13 Bankers: The Wall Street Takeover and the Next Financial Meltdown*. New York: Pantheon.

Johnston, David Cay. 2005. "Richest Are Leaving Even the Rich Far Behind," *The New York Times*, June 5.

Jones, David R. and Monika McDermott. 2009. *Americans, Congress, and Democratic Responsiveness*. Ann Arbor: University of Michigan Press.

Jütte, Robert. 1994. *Poverty and Deviance in Early Modern Europe*. Cambridge: Cambridge University Press.

Kahn, Joseph. 2006. "Chinese Premier Says Seizing Peasants' Land Provokes Unrest," *The New York Times*, January 21.

Kalleberg, Arne L. 2011. *Good Jobs, Bad Jobs: The Rise of Polarized and Precarious Employment Systems in the United States, 1970s–2000s*. New York: Russell Sage Foundation.

Kallet, Lisa. 2007. "The Athenian Economy," in *The Age of Pericles*, ed. Loren J. Samons II. Cambridge: Cambridge University Press.

Kallet-Marx, Lisa. 1994. "Money Talks: Rhetor, Demos, and the Resources of the Athenian Empire," in *Ritual, Finance, Politics: Athenian Democratic Accounts Presented to David Lewis*, eds. Robin Osborne and Simon Hornblower. Oxford: Clarendon Press.

Kane, P. V. 1973. *History of Dharmasastra*, vol. 2, part 2, chap. 2, pp. 19–104. Poona, India: Bhandakar Oriental Research Institute.

Kassner, Enid. 2006. "Medicaid and Long-Term Services and Supports for Older People," Washington, D.C.: AARP Public Policy Institute; http://www.aarp.org/research/assistance/medicaid/fs18r_medicaid_06.html (accessed February 24, 2006).

Kaste, Martin. 2006. "Harsh Sentences Silence Radical Environmentalists," *All Things Considered*. National Public Radio, March 8; http://www.npr.org/templates/story/story.php?storyId=5252269 (accessed March 9, 2006).

Katz, Lawrence F. and David Autor. 1999. "Changes in the Wage Structure and Earnings Inequality," in *Handbook of Labor Economics*, vol. 3A, pp. 1463–555, ed. Orley C. Ashenfelter and David Card. Amsterdam: Elsevier.

Katz, Michael. 1996. *In the Shadow of the Poorhouse: A Social History of Welfare in America*. New York: Basic Books.

Khan, Shamus. 2012. "Sociology of Elites," *Annual Review of Sociology*, 38: 361–77.

Kidd, Quentin. 2011. *Civic Participation in America*. New York: Palgrave Macmillan.

Kingston, Paul W. 2000. *The Classless Society*. Stanford: Stanford University Press.

Kipling, Rudyard. 1989. "The Ballad of East and West," *Barrack-Room Ballads and Other Verses*. London: Methuen.

Krippner, Greta. 2011. *Capitalizing on Crisis: The Political Origins of the Rise of Finance*. Cambridge: Harvard University Press.

Lamy, Philip. 1996. *Millennium Rage: Survivalists, White Supremacists and the Doomsday Prophecy*. New York: Plenum.

Langfitt, Frank. 2006. "Startups Help Clean Up Online Reputations," *Morning Edition*. National Public Radio, November 15.

Lardinois, Roland L. and Meenakshi Thapan, eds. 2006. *Reading Pierre Bourdieu in a Dual Context: Essays from India and France*. London: Routledge.

Lee-St. John, Jeninne. 2006. "It's a Brand You-World," *Time*, October 30.

Lenski, Gerhard. 1970. *Human Societies: a Macrolevel Introduction to Sociology*. New York: McGraw-Hill.

Levi-Strauss, Claude. 1963. *Structural Anthropology*. New York: Basic Books.

Levi-Strauss, Claude. 1975. *The Raw and the Cooked*. New York: Harper and Row.

Lewis, David M., John Boardman, J. K. Davies, and M. Ostwald, eds. 1992. *The Cambridge Ancient History, Volume 5: The Fifth Century BC*, 2nd edn. Cambridge: Cambridge University Press.

Lewis, David M., John Boardman, Simon Hornblower, and M. Ostwald, eds. 1992. *The Cambridge Ancient History, Volume 6: The Fourth Century BC*, 2nd edn. Cambridge: Cambridge University Press.

Lewis, Michael. 2010. *The Big Short: Inside the Doomsday Machine*. New York: Norton.

Lichter, Daniel. 1988. "Racial Differences in Unemployment in American Cities," *American Journal of Sociology*, 93 (4): 771–92.

Lindblom, Charles E. 1965. *The Intelligence of Democracy: Decision Making through Mutual Adjustment*. New York: Free Press.

Lipset, Seymour Martin. 1963. *The First New Nation: the United States in Historical and Comparative Perspective*. New York: Basic Books.

Lipset, Seymour Martin. 1996. *American Exceptionalism: A Double-edged Sword*. New York: W.W. Norton.

Lipset, Seymour Martin. 2000. "Still the Exceptional Nation?" *The Wilson Quarterly*, Winter, 24 (1): 31–45.

Lipset, Seymour Martin and Asoke Basu. 1975. "Intellectual Types and Political Roles," in *The Idea of Social Structure: Papers in Honor of Robert K. Merton*, ed. Lewis A. Coser. New York: Harcourt Brace Jovanovich.

Lohr, Steve. 2014. "F.T.C. Urges Legislation to Shed More Light on Data Collection," *New York Times*, May 27; http://www.nytimes.com/2014/05/28/technology/ftc-urges-legislation-to-shed-more-light-on-data-collection.html?hp&_r=0 (accessed May 27, 2014).

Lounsbury, Michael. 2001. "Institutional Investors," in *International Encyclopedia of the Social and Behavioral Sciences*, eds. Neil Smelser and Paul B. Balfas. Amsterdam: Elsevier, pp. 7750–4.

Lukes, Steven. 2004. *Power: A Radical View*, rev. edn. New York: Palgrave Macmillan.

Mann, Michael. 1986. *The Sources of Social Power*, vols. 1 and 2. New York: Cambridge University Press.

Manning, Chandra. 2012. "All for the Union … and Emancipation, Too: What the Civil War Was About," *Dissent*, 59 (1): 91–5.

Manza, Jeff and Fay Lomax Cook. 2002. "A Democratic Polity? Three Views of Policy Responsiveness to Public Opinion in the United States," *American Politics Research*, 30: 630–66.

Marche, Stephen. 2008. "What's with All the Ugly People Having Sex?" *Esquire*, 150 (6): 50–6.

Martin, Philip. 1995. "Proposition 187 in California," *International Migration Review*, 29 (1): 255–63.

Martinez, Jennifer. 2013. "Tech and Agriculture Industries Team up to Lobby for Immigration Reform," *The Hill*, August 1, 2013; http://thehill.com/blogs/hillicon-valley/technology/315077-tech-and-agriculture-industries-team-up-to-lobby-for-immigration-reform (accessed December 8, 2013).

Marwick, Alice E. 2014. "How Your Data Are Being Deeply Mined," *The New York Review of Books*, 61 (1): 22–25.

Marx, Karl. 1852. *The Eighteenth Brumaire of Louis Bonaparte*. http://www.marxists.org/archive/marx/works/1852/18th-brumaire/ch05.htm (accessed November 12, 2013).

Massey, Douglas S. 1990. "American Apartheid: Segregation and the Making of the Underclass," *The American Journal of Sociology*, 96 (2): 329–57.

Massey, Douglas S. and Nancy A. Denton. 1993. *American Apartheid: Segregation and the Making of the Underclass*. Cambridge: Harvard University Press.

Massey, Douglas S. and Magaly Sánchez R. 2010. *Brokered Boundaries: Creating Immigrant Identity in Anti-Immigrant Times*. New York: Russell Sage Foundation.

Mataloni, Raymond J. 2005. "U.S. Multinational Companies: Operations in 2003," *Survey of Current Business*, July: 9–29.

Mayaram, Shail. 2003. "Kings versus Bandits: Anticolonialism in a Bandit Narrative," *Journal of the Royal Asiatic Society of Great Britain & Ireland*, 13: 315–38.

Mazur, Allan, Julie Mazur, and Caroline Keating. 1984. "Military Rank Attainment of West Point Class: Effects of Cadets' Physical Features," *The American Journal of Sociology*, 90 (1): 125–50.

Mazzucato, Mariana. 2011. "The Entrepreneurial State: Overlooking the Key Role of the State in Promoting Innovation is One of the Biggest Mistakes of Market Fundamentalism," *Soundings*, 49: 131–42.

Mazzucato, Mariana. 2013. *The Entrepreneurial State: Debunking Public vs. Private Sector Myths*. London: Anthem Press.

McKenzie, Brian, and Melanie Rapino. 2011. "Commuting in the United States: 2009," American Community Survey Reports, ACS-15. U.S. Census Bureau, Washington, D.C.

McKibben, Bill. 2006. "The Hope of the Web," *The New York Review of Books*, 53 (7): 4–6.

McLaren, John and Shushanik Hakobyan. 2010. "Looking for Local Labor Market Effects of NAFTA," Working Paper 16535, November. Cambridge: National Bureau of Economic Research.

McNeill, William H. 1982. *The Pursuit of Power*. New York: Oxford University Press.

McQuail, Denis and Karen Siune. 1998. *Media Policy: Convergence, Concentration, and Commerce*. Thousand Oaks: Sage.

Mehta, Suketu. 2004. *Maximum City: Bombay Lost and Found*. New York: Vintage Books.

Meyer, Christopher. 2010. "A New American Revolution? Anti-establishment Tea Party is on the Brink of Election Victories that Could Leave Obama a Lame Duck," *Daily Mail*, October 25, 2010; http://www.dailymail.co.uk/news/article-1323047/Anti-establishment-Tea-Party-leave-Obama-lame-duck.html (accessed March 8, 2012).

Michels, Robert. 1998 [1916]. *Political Parties: A Sociological Study of the Oligarchical Tendencies in Modern Democracy*. New York: Free Press.

Micklethwait, John and Adrian Wooldridge. 2000. *A Future Perfect: The Challenge and Hidden Promise of Globalization*. New York: Crown Publishers.

Mikalson, Jon D. 2010. *Ancient Greek Religion*, 2nd edn. Oxford: Wiley-Blackwell.

Miliband, Ralph. 1969. *The State in Capitalist Societies*. New York: Basic Books.

Miller, Walter B. 2001. *The Growth of Youth Gang Problems in the United States: 1970–98, Report*. Washington, D.C.: Office of Juvenile Justice and Delinquency Prevention, U.S. Department of Justice.

Mills, C. Wright. 1956. *The Power Elite*. New York: Oxford University Press.

Milner, Murray, Jr. 1972. *The Illusion of Equality: The Effects of Educational Opportunity on Inequality and Conflict*. San Francisco: Jossey-Bass.

Milner, Murray, Jr. 1980. *Unequal Care: A Case Study of Interorganizational Relations in Health Care*. New York: Columbia University Press.

Milner, Murray, Jr. 1993. "Hindu Eschatology and the Indian Caste System: An Example of Structural Reversal," *The Journal of Asian Studies*, 52 (2): 298–319.

Milner, Murray, Jr. 1994. *Status and Sacredness: A General Theory of Status Relations and an Analysis of Indian Culture*. New York: Oxford University Press.

Milner, Murray, Jr. 2004. *Freaks, Geeks, and Cool Kids: American Teenagers, Schools, and the Culture of Consumption*. New York: Routledge.

Milner, Murray, Jr. 2005. "Celebrity Culture as a Status System," *The Hedgehog Review*, Spring, 66–77.

Milner, Murray, Jr. 2010. "Is Celebrity a New Kind of Status System?" *Society*, 47: 379–87.

Milner, Murray, Jr. 2014. "Postmodernism and Sociology: Can Solidarity Be a Substitute for Objectivity?" in *Postmodernism in Global Perspective*, chapter 8, eds. Samir Dasgupta and Peter Kivisto. Thousand Oaks: Sage Publications.

Mincer, Jacob. 1958. "Investment in Human Capital and Personal Income Distribution," *Journal of Political Economy*, 66 (4): 281–302.

Minsky, Hyman. 1986. *Stabilizing and Unstable Economy*. New York: McGraw-Hill.

Mintz, S. 2011. Moneywatch, CBS News, April 14; http://www.cbsnews.com/news/how-the-senate-financial-crisis-report-puts-the-less-in-toothless/ (accessed December 2, 2013).

Mizruchi, Mark. 2010. "The American Corporate Elite and the Historical Roots of the Financial Crisis of 2008," *Research in the Sociology of Organizations*, 30B: 103–39.

Mo, Yan. 2012. *POW!* London: Seagull Books.

Moretti, Enrico. 2011. "Real Wage Inequality," http://emlab.berkeley.edu/~moretti/inequality.pdf (accessed March 7, 2012).

Morris, Lydia. 1994. *Dangerous Classes: The Underclass and Social Citizenship*. London: Routledge.

Mosca, Gaetano. 1939 [1896]. *The Ruling Class: Elementi di Scienza Politica*, edited and revised by Arthur Livingston, translated by Hannah D. Kahn. New York: McGraw-Hill.

Mulcahy, Michael John. 2004. "Regulating Labor: The Formation and Effects of a World Labor Regime in the Twentieth Century," dissertation, University of Arizona.

Mullen, Faith. 1996. "Questions and Answers on Medicaid Estate Recovery for Long-Term Care under OBRA '93." Washington, D.C.: AARP Public Policy

Institute; http://www.aarp.org/research/assistance/medicaid/aresearch-import-629-D16443.html (accessed November 13, 2010).

Munro, Lyle. 2005. "Strategies, Action Repertoires and DIY Activism in the Animal Rights Movement," *Social Movement Studies*, 4 (1): 75–94.

Nafissi, Mohammad. 2004. "Class, Embeddedness, and the Modernity of Ancient Athens," *Comparative Studies in Society and History*, 46 (2), 378–410.

Nagourney, Adam. 2006. "Internet Injects Sweeping Change into U.S. Politics," *The New York Times*, April 2, A1.

Naím, Moisés. 2013. *The End of Power*. New York: Basic Books.

National Coalition for the Homeless. 2002. "How Many People Experience Homelessness?" NCH Fact Sheet #2, September. Washington, D.C.: NCH.

National Law Center on Homelessness and Poverty. 2004. "Homelessness in the United States and the Human Right to Housing," January. Washington, D.C.: National Law Center on Homelessness and Poverty.

Nevitte, Neil. 1996. *The Decline of Deference: Canadian Value Change in Comparative Perspective 1981–1990*. Toronto: Broadview Press.

Nevitte, Neil, with M. Kanji. 2001. "The Decline of Deference Revisited: Some Preliminary Findings from the 2000 WVS." Paper presented at World Values Survey Conference, Stellenbosch, South Africa, November.

Nightingale, Demetra Smith and Michael Fix. 2004. "Economic and Labor Market Trends," *The Future of Children*, 14 (2): 49–59.

Ober, Josiah. 1989. *Mass and Elite in Democratic Athens*. Princeton: Princeton University Press.

Osborne, Robin. 2010. *Athens and Athenian Democracy*. Cambridge: Cambridge University Press.

Ostwald, M. 1992. "Athens as a Cultural Centre," in *The Cambridge Ancient History*, ed. David M. Lewis, John Boardman, J. K. Davies, and M. Ostwald, vol. V, chap. 86, esp. 338–51. Cambridge: Cambridge University Press.

Pareto, Vilfredo. 1935. *The Mind and Society*. New York: Harcourt Brace.

Pareto, Vilfredo. 1968 [1901]. *The Rise and Fall of Elites: An Application of Theoretical Sociology*. Totowa: Bedminster Press.

Pareto, Vilfredo. 1976. *Vilfredo Pareto: Sociological Writings*. Selected and edited by S. E. Finer, translated by Derick Mirfin. Totowa: Rowman & Littlefield.

Parry, Jonathan. 1986. "The Gift, the Indian Gift and the 'Indian Gift,'" *Man*, 21 (3): 453–73.

Patterson, Cynthia. 1992. "Review of *Mass and Elite in Democratic Athens: Rhetoric, Ideology, and the Power of the People*, by Josiah Ober," *The American Journal of Philology*, 113 (1): 110–15.

Patterson, Cynthia. 2007. "Other Sorts: Slaves, Foreigners, and Women in Periclean Athens," in *The Age of Pericles*, ed. Loren J. Samons II. Cambridge: Cambridge University Press.

Patterson, Orlando. 1982. *Slavery and Social Death: A Comparative Study*. Cambridge: Harvard University Press.

Patterson, Orlando. 1991. *Freedom*. New York: Basic Books.

Pattillo, Mary E. 1999. *Black Picket Fences: Privilege and Peril among the Black Middle Class*. Chicago: University of Chicago Press.

Pear, Robert. 2002. "9 of 10 Nursing Homes in U.S. Lack Adequate Staff, a Government Study Finds," *The New York Times*, February 18, A11.

Pellegrin, Roland J. and Charles H. Coates. 1956. "Absentee-Owned Corporations and Community Power Structure," *American Journal of Sociology*, 61 (5): 413–19.

Perea, Juan F., ed. 1997. *Immigrants Out! The New Nativism and the Anti-Immigrant Impulse in the United States*. New York: New York University Press.

Perlez, Jane. 2012. "China Accuses Japan of Stealing after Purchase of Group of Disputed Islands," *New York Times*, September 11; http://www.nytimes.com/2012/09/12/world/asia/china-accuses-japan-of-stealing-disputed-islands.html (accessed July 25, 2013).

Perrucci, Robert and Earl Wysong. 2003. *The New Class Society: Goodbye American Dream?* Lanham: Rowman & Littlefield.

Pew Research Center for the People and the Press. 2004. "News Audiences Increasingly Politicized," *Pew Research Center Biennial News Consumption Survey*. Washington, D.C.: The Pew Research Center, June 8.

Phillips, J. A. 1989. "The Social Calculus: Deference and Defiance in Later Georgian England," *Albion*, 21 (3): 426–49.

Phillips, K. 2008. *Bad Money: Reckless Finance, Failed Politics, and the Global Crisis of American Capitalism*. New York: Viking.

Piketty, Thomas. 2014. *Capital in the Twenty-First Century*, trans. Arthur Goldhammer. Cambridge: Harvard University Press.

Pocock, J. A. 1976. "The Classical Theory of Deference," *American Historical Review*, 81 (3): 516–23.

Poggi, Gianfranco. 1978. *The Development of the Modern State*. Stanford: Stanford University Press.

Poggi, Gianfranco. 2001. *Forms of Power*. Cambridge: Polity Press.

Poggi, Gianfranco. 2006. "Political Power Un-Manned," in *The Anatomy of Power: the Social Theory of Michael Man*, eds. John A. Hall and Ralph Schoeder. Cambridge: Cambridge University Press.

Polanyi, Karl. 1957 [1944]. *The Great Transformation: the Political and Economic Origins of Our Time*. Boston: Beacon Press.

Portes, Alejandro and Rubén G. Rumbaut. 2005. "The Second Generation and the Children of Immigrants Longitudinal Study," *Ethnic and Racial Studies*, 28: 983–99.

President's Advisory Committee on Government Housing Policies and Programs. 1953. *A Report to the President of the United States*. Washington, D.C.: Superintendent of Documents, Government Printing Office; http://www.michaelcarliner.com/files/Eisenhower53_Pres_Advis_Commitee.pdf (accessed May 23, 2014).

Presser, Harriet B. n.d. "Working in a 24/7 Economy: Challenges for American Families." Washington, D.C.: Center for Disease Control, National Institute for Occupational Safety and Health; http://www.cdc.gov/niosh/topics/workschedules/abstracts/presser.html (accessed June 21, 2011).

Putnam, Robert D. 2000. *Bowling Alone: The Collapse and Revival of American Community*. New York: Simon & Schuster.

Quillian, Lincoln. 2003. "How Long Are Exposures to Poor Neighborhoods? The Long-Term Dynamics of Entry and Exit from Poor Neighborhoods," *Population Research and Policy Review*, 22 (3): 221–49.

Raaflaub, Kurt A. 2007. "Warfare and Athenian Society," in *The Age of Pericles*, ed. Loren J. Samons II. Cambridge: Cambridge University Press.

Rakoff, Jed S. 2014. "The Financial Crisis: Why Have No High-Level Executives Been Prosecuted?" *The New York Review of Books*, January 9, 61 (1): 4–8.

Ratz, Rhiman A. 1983. "Class Structure, Western 1300–1500," in *Dictionary of the Middle Ages*, gen. ed. Joseph R. Strayer. New York: Charles Scribner's Sons, pp. 419–29.

Read, D. D. (1981). " 'Deference' in the Nineteenth-Century North," *Northern History*, 17: 279–83.

Reardon, Sean F. and Kendra Bischoff. 2011. "Income Inequality and Income Segregation," *American Journal of Sociology*, 116 (4): 1092–153.

Redmond, William H. 2007. "Home Equity, Fungibility, and Consumption: The Increasing Rationalization of Society," *Review of Radical Political Economics*, 39: 201–13.

Reich, Robert B. 1989. "Consequences of the Global Economy for American Inequality," *The New Republic*, 200 (18): 23–8.

Reichl, Alexander. 2005. "Rescaling Urban Politics: Structure and Agency in the Global Era," *Polity*, 37: 149–66.

Rhodes, J. K. 1992. "The Polis and the Alternatives," in *The Cambridge Ancient History*, ed. David M. Lewis, John Boardman, Simon Hornblower, and M. Ostwald, vol. VI, chap. 11, pp. 565–91. Cambridge: Cambridge University Press.

Rhodes, P. J. 2007. "Democracy and Empire," in *The Age of Pericles*, ed. Loren Samons II. Cambridge: Cambridge University Press.

Ricks, Thomas E. 2006. "Rumsfeld Rebuked by Retired Generals," *The Washington Post*, April 13, A01.

Ritzer, George. 2008. *The McDonaldization of Society*. Los Angeles: Pine Forge Press.

Robinson, Matthew B. and Renee G. Scherlen. 2007. *Lies, Damn Lies, and Drug War Statistics: A Critical Analysis of Claims Made by the Office of National Drug Control Policy*. Albany: State University of New York Press.

Rohe, William and Michael Stegman. 1994. "Effects of Homeownership on the Self-Esteem, Perceived Control and Life Satisfaction of Low-Income People," *Journal of the American Planning Association*, 60 (2): 173–84.

Rojek, Chris. 2005. "P2P Leisure Exchange: Net Banditry and the Policing of Intellectual Property," *Leisure Studies*, 24 (4): 357–69.

Roksa, Josipa and Daniel Potter. 2011. "Parenting and Academic Achievement: Intergenerational Transmission of Educational Advantage," *Sociology of Education*, 84 (4): 299–321.

Roksa, Josipa and Daniel Potter. 2013. "Accumulating Advantages over Time: Family Experiences and Social Class Inequality in Academic Achievement," *Social Science Research*, 42 (4): 1018–32.

Rose, Arnold. 1967. *The Power Structure: Political Process in American Society*. New York: Oxford University Press.

Rosser, Barkley. 2012. "Robert Samuelson Playing Anti-Robin Hood Again," http://econospeak.blogspot.com/2012/04/robert-samuelson-playing-anti-robin.html (accessed July 18, 2013).

Roth, Guenther. 1968. "Introduction," to Max Weber, *Economy and Society*, eds. Guenther Roth and Claus Wittich. New York: Bedminster Press.

Runciman, W. G. 1966. *Relative Deprivation and Social Justice*. Berkeley: University of California Press.

Russell, A. 1987. "Local Elites and the Working-Class Response in the North-West, 1870–1895: Paternalism and Deference Reconsidered," *Northern History*, 23: 153–73.

Saguy, Abigail C. 2013. *What's Wrong with Fat?* New York: Oxford University Press.

Samons II, Loren J., ed. 2007. *The Cambridge Companion to The Age of Pericles*. Cambridge: Cambridge University Press.

Samuelson, Robert J. 2012. "Here Is What Washington Really Does," *Washington Post*, April 29; http://articles.washingtonpost.com/2012-04-29/opinions/35450636_1_food-stamps-security-and-medicare-supplemental-nutrition-assistance-program (accessed January 22, 2014).

Sankarn, Lavana. 2013. "Caste Is Not Past," *The New York Times*, June 16.

Sassen, Saskia. 2001. *The Global City: New York, London, Tokyo*. Princeton: Princeton University Press.

Sawhill, Isabel V. 2003. "The Behavioral Aspects of Poverty," *The Public Interest*, 153 (Fall): 79–93.

Scheuer, Jeffrey. 1999. *The Sound Bite Society: Television and the American Mind*. New York: Four Walls Eight Windows.

Schmitt, Mark. 2005. "The Legend of the Powell Memo," *The American Prospect*, April 27.

Schultz, Theodore. 1963. *The Economic Value of Education*. New York: Columbia University Press.

Schumpeter, Joseph. 1987 [1942]. *Capitalism, Socialism, and Democracy*, 6th edn. London: Unwin.

Schwartz, Alex F. 2006. *Housing Policy in the United States: An Introduction*. New York: Routledge, Taylor and Francis Group.

Scott, John. 2001. *Power*. Cambridge: Polity Press.

Senechal de la Roche, Roberta. 2004. "Theories of Terrorism," *Sociological Theory*, 22 (1): 1–105.

Sengupta, Somini. 2013. "Tech Industry Pushes to Amend Immigration Bill," *The New York Times*, May 19, Technology Section.

Serpe, Nick. 2013. "Reality Pawns: The New Money TV," *Dissent*, 30 (3): 13–18; http://search.proquest.com/docview/1438553942?accountid=14678 (accessed January 4, 2014).

Sharma, Ram Sharan. 1980. *Sudras in Ancient India*. Delhi: Motilal Banarsidass.

Shils, Edward. 1972. *The Intellectuals and the Powers, and Other Essays*. Chicago: University of Chicago Press.

Shirky, Clay. 2012. "Failing Geometry," *Columbia Journalism Review*, 51 (3): 29–30.

Sinclair, R. K. 1988. *Democracy and Participation in Athens*. Cambridge: Cambridge University Press.

Skocpol, Theda and Morris P. Fiorina. 1999. "Making Sense of the Civic Engagement Debate," in *Civic Engagement in American Democracy*, eds. Theda Skocpol and Morris P. Fiorina. Washington, D.C.: Brookings Institution Press.

Skrentny, John D. 2002. *The Minority Rights Revolution*. Cambridge: The Belknap Press of Harvard University.

Slaughter, Matthew J. and Phillip Swagel. 1997. "Does Globalization Lower Wages and Export Jobs?" *Economic Issues*, No. 11. Washington, D.C.: International Monetary Fund.

Smeeding, Timothy M., Robert Erikson, and Markus Jäntti, eds. 2011. *Persistence, Privilege, and Parenting: the Comparative Study of Intergenerational Mobility*. New York: Russell Sage Foundation.

Smelser, Neil and Paul B. Balfas, eds. 2001. *International Encyclopedia of the Social and Behavioral Sciences*. Amsterdam: Elsevier.

Smith, Brian K. 1994. *Classifying the Universe: The Ancient Indian Varna System and the Origins of the Caste System*. New York: Oxford University Press.

Smith, Kristin. 2002. *Who's Minding the Kids? Child Care Arrangements: Spring 1997*. Current Population Reports, P70-86. Washington, D.C.: U.S. Census Bureau.

Spitz, David and Starling D. Hunter. 2005. "Contested Codes: The Social Construction of Napster," *The Information Society*, 21: 169–80.

Stockton, David. 1990. *The Classical Athenian Democracy*. Oxford: Oxford University Press.

Strauss, Barry S. 1986. *Athens after the Peloponnesian War*. Ithaca: Cornell University Press.

Stryker, R. 2001. "Legitimacy," in *International Encyclopedia of the Social and Behavioral Sciences*, eds. Neil Smelser and Paul B. Balfas. Amsterdam: Elsevier, pp. 8700–4.

Stuckler, David and Sanjay Basu. 2009. "The International Monetary Fund's Effect on Global Health: Before and After the Financial Crisis," *International Journal of Health Services*, 39 (4): 771–81.

Susen, Simon and Bryan S. Turner, eds. 2011. *The Legacy of Pierre Bourdieu: Critical Essays*. New York: Anthem Press.

Swidler, Ann. 2008. "Comment on Stephen Vaisey's 'Socrates, Skinner, and Aristotle: Three Ways of Thinking about Culture in Action,'" *Sociological Forum*, 23 (3): 614–18.

Tawney, R. H. 1962 [1926]. *Religion and the Rise of Capitalism*. Gloucester: P. Smith.

Thapar, Romilla. 1966. *A History of India*. Baltimore: Penguin.

Tilly, Charles. 1984. *Big Structures, Large Processes, and Huge Comparisons*. New York: Russell Sage Foundation.

Tilly, Charles. 1985. "War Making and State Making as Organized Crime," in eds. Peter Evans, Dietrich Rueschemeyer, and Theda Skocpol, *Bringing the State Back In*. Cambridge: Cambridge University Press.

Timmons, Heather. 2006. "Dubai Port Company Sells Its U.S. Holdings to A.I.G.," *The New York Times*, December 12.

Tomaskovic-Devey, Donald and Ken-Hou Lin. 2011. "Income Dynamics, Economic Rents, and the Financialization of the U.S. Economy," *American Sociological Review*, 76: 538–59.

Torpey, John. 2009. "The Problem of 'American Exceptionalism' Revisited," *Journal of Classical Sociology*, 9 (1): 143–68.

Tucker, Steve. 1992. "A Push for Gang Peace; Jim Brown Convenes 50 Leaders in Bid to Settle Differences," *Chicago Sun-Times*, August 31, p. 5.

Turner, Graeme. 2006. "The Mass Production of Celebrity: 'Celetoids', Reality TV and the 'Demotic Turn,'" *International Journal of Cultural Studies*, 9 (2): 153–65.

U.S. Census Bureau. 1975. *Statistical Abstract of the United States, 1974*. Washington, D.C.: Superintendent of Documents, Government Printing Office, Table 589.

U.S. Census Bureau. 2005. "Income Inequality (Middle Class) – Narrative." Washington, D.C.: U.S. Census Bureau, Housing and Household Economic Statistics Division; http://www.census.gov/hhes/www/income/midclass/midclsan. html (accessed March 6, 2006).

U.S. Census Bureau. 2008a. "Historical Income Tables – Households. Table H-2. Share of Aggregate Income Received by Each Fifth and Top 5 Percent of Households (All Races): 1967 to 2006." Washington, D.C.: U.S. Census Bureau; http://www.census.gov/hhes/www/income/histinc/h02ar.html (accessed April 16, 2008).

U.S. Census Bureau. 2008b. "Historical Income Tables – Households. Table H-3. Mean Income Received by Each Fifth and Top 5 Percent of Households (All Races): 1967 to 2006." Washington, D.C.: U.S. Census Bureau; http://www. census.gov/hhes/www/income/histinc/h03ar.html (accessed April 16, 2008).

U.S. Census Bureau. 2010a. "Table 1177 – FDIC-Insured Financial Institutions – Number, Assets, and Liabilities: 1990 to 2010," Washington, D.C.: U.S. Census Bureau; http://www.census.gov/compendia/statab/2012/tables/ 12s1177.pdf (accessed April 11, 2012).

U.S. Census Bureau. 2010b. "Married Couples by Race and Hispanic Origin of Spouses: 1980 to 2009, as of March. Persons 15 years old and over: http://www.census.gov/compendia/statab/2010/tables/10s0060.pdf (accessed May 23, 2014).

U.S. Census Bureau. 2011. "Historical Census of Housing Tables"; http://www. census.gov/hhes/www/housing/census/historic/owner.html (accessed December 11, 2013).

U.S. Census Bureau. 2012a. *Statistical Abstract of the United States*, Table 539. Government Transfer Payments to Individuals – Summary: 1990 to 2009; http://www.census.gov/compendia/statab/2012/tables/12s0540.pdf (accessed January 2, 2014).

U.S. Census Bureau. 2012b. *Statistical Abstract of the United States*, Table 667. Gross Domestic Product in Current and Chained (2005) Dollars: 1970 to 2010; http://www.census.gov/prod/2011pubs/12statab/income.pdf (accessed January 3, 2014).

U.S. Bureau of Labor Statistics. 2010. Washington, D.C.: U.S. Department of Labor, January 21; http://www.bls.gov/news.release/union2.nr0.htm (accessed October 13, 2011).

U.S. Bureau of Labor Statistics. 2014a. "Economic News Release, Union Members Summary," http://www.bls.gov/news.release/union2.nr0.htm (accessed May 27, 2014).

U.S. Bureau of Labor Statistics. 2014b. "Databases, Tables & Calculators by Subject," Washington, D.C.: U.S. Department of Labor; http://data.bls.gov/pdq/SurveyOutputServlet (accessed May 22, 2014).

U.S. Department of Commerce. 2010. "International Investment Position of the United States at Yearend, 1976–2010." Washington, D.C.: Bureau of Economic Analysis; http://www.bea.gov/international/index.htm#iip (accessed February 28, 2012).

U.S. Financial Crisis Inquiry Commission. 2011. The Financial Crisis Inquiry Report. Pursuant to Public Law 111-21, January. Washington, D.C.: Government Printing Office.

U.S. Government Accountability Office. 2006. Military Recruiting: DOD and Services Need Better Data to Enhance Visibility over Recruiter Irregularities, GAO-06-846. Published: August 8, 2006; publicly released: August 14, 2006; http://www.gao.gov/products/GAO-06-846 (accessed May 23, 2014).

U.S. Senate. 2011. Wall Street and the Financial Crisis: Anatomy of a Financial Collapse, Permanent Subcommittee on Investigations, Carl Levin, Chairman, Tom Colbern, Ranking Minority Member, Washington, D.C., April 13; http://www.hsgac.senate.gov/subcommittees/investigations/reports?c=112 (accessed December 1, 2013).

USA Today/CNN/Gallop Poll. 2005. USA Today, May 22. http://www.usatoday.com/news/polls/tables/live/2005-05-23-poll.htm (accessed July 10, 2005).

Vaisey, Stephen. 2008a. "Socrates, Skinner, and Aristotle: Three Ways of Thinking About Culture in Action," Sociological Forum, 23 (3): 603–13.

Vaisey, Stephen. 2008b. "Reply to Swidler," Sociological Forum, 23 (3): 619–22.

Verba, Sidney. 1987. Elites and the Idea of Equality: A Comparison of Japan, Sweden, and the United States. Cambridge: Harvard University Press.

Verser, Rebecca and Robert H. Wicks. 2006. "Managing Voter Impressions: The Use of Images on Presidential Candidate Web Sites During 2000 Campaign," Journal of Communication, 56 (1): 178–97.

Wacquant, Loïc J. D. 1992. "Toward a Social Praxeology: The Structure and Logic of Bourdieu's Sociology," in An Invitation to Reflexive Sociology, by Pierre Bourdieu and Löic J. D. Wacquant. Chicago: Chicago University Press, pp. 2–59.

Walks, R. Alan. 2001. "The Social Ecology of the Post-Fordist/Global City? Economic Restructuring and Socio-spatial Polarisation in the Toronto Urban Region," Urban Studies, 38 (3): 407–47.

Wallace, Robert W. 2007. "Plato's Sophists, Intellectual History after 450, and Sokrates," in The Age of Pericles, ed. Loren J. Samons II. Cambridge: Cambridge University Press.

Wang, W. "Public Says a Secure Job Is the Ticket to the Middle Class," http://www.pewsocialtrends.org/files/2012/08/Job-report-final.pdf (accessed December 12, 2013).

Watson, Tara. 2009. "Inequality and the Measurement of Residential Segregation by Income in American Neighborhoods," *Review of Income and Wealth*, 55 (3): 820–44.

Wayne, Mike. 2004. "Mode of Production: New Media Technology and the Napster File," *Rethinking Marxism*, 16 (2): 137–53.

Weber, Max. 1968. *Economy and Society*, ed. Guenther Roth and Claus Wittich. New York: Bedminster Press.

Weber, Max. 1976a [1909]. *The Agrarian Sociology of Ancient Civilizations*, trans. R. I. Franks. London: New Left Books/Verso.

Weber, Max. 1976b [1905]. *The Protestant Ethic and the Spirit of Capitalism*, trans. Talcott Parsons; introduction by Anthony Giddens. New York: Charles Scribner's Sons.

Weber, Max. 2009. *The Protestant Ethic and the Spirit of Capitalism*, trans. Stephen Kalberg. New York: Oxford University Press.

Whitmeyer, Joseph M. 2002. "Elites and Popular Nationalism," *British Journal of Sociology*, 53: 321–41.

Williams, Ray. 2011. "Good Looks Will Get You That Job, Promotion and Raise: Beautiful People Have the Advantage in the Workplace," *Psychology Today*, September 3.

Wilson, Reid. 2013. "Missouri Gov. Jay Nixon Calls Special Session for Boeing Tax Breaks," *The Washington Post*, November 30.

Winters, Jeffrey A. 2011. *Oligarchy*. Cambridge: Cambridge University Press.

Wong, Edward and Jonathan Ansfield. 2013. "Fallen Leader Is Indicted in China," *New York Times*, July 24; http://www.nytimes.com/2013/07/25/world/asia/bo-xilai.html?ref=world (accessed July 25, 2013).

Woodburn, James. 1982. "Egalitarian Societies," *Man*, New Series, 17 (3): 431–51.

Wright, Erik Olin and Joachim Singelmann. 1982. "Proletarianization in the Changing American Class Structure," *American Journal of Sociology*, 88 (Supplement): 176–209.

Wulfhorst, Ellen. 2006. "Americans Commute Longer, Farther Than Ever," *The New York Times*, April 20; http://www.nytimes.com/reuters/world/international-life-work.html (accessed April 20, 2006).

Yang, Anand A. 1985. "Dangerous Castes and Tribes," in *Crime and Criminality in British India*, ed. Anand Yang. Tucson: University of Arizona Press, 1985.

Yang, Jia Lynn. 2013. "Companies Turn to Stock Buybacks to Lift Shareholders," *Washington Post*, December 16.

Young, Russell Lee. 2005. "A Time Series Analysis of Eco-Terrorist Violence in the United States: 1993–2003," Ph.D. dissertation, The Humanities and Social Sciences, Sam Houston State University, Huntsville, TX.

Zeleny, Jeff and Megan Thee-Brenan. 2011. "New Poll Finds a Deep Distrust of Government," *New York Times*, October 25, New York Times/CBS Poll;

http://www.nytimes.com/2011/10/26/us/politics/poll-finds-anxiety-on-the-economy-fuels-volatility-in-the-2012-race.html?_r=1 (accessed April 11, 2012).

Zickuhr, Kathryn and Aaron Smith. 2012. "Digital Differences," Pew Internet and American Life Project, Pew Research Center, April 12; http://pewinternet.org/Reports/2012/Digital-differences.aspx (accessed September 19, 2012).

Index